Multiscreen UX Design

Multiscreen UX Design
Developing for
a Multitude of Devices

Wolfram Nagel

AMSTERDAM • BOSTON • HEIDELBERG • LONDON
NEW YORK • OXFORD • PARIS • SAN DIEGO
SAN FRANCISCO • SINGAPORE • SYDNEY • TOKYO

Morgan Kaufmann is an imprint of Elsevier

Acquiring Editor: Todd Green
Editorial Project Manager: Charlotte Kent
Project Manager: Punithavathy Govindaradjane
Designer: Maria Inês Cruz

Morgan Kaufmann is an imprint of Elsevier
225 Wyman Street, Waltham, MA 02451, USA

ISBN: 978-0-12-802729-5

British Library Cataloguing-in-Publication Data
A catalogue record for this book is available from the British Library.

Library of Congress Cataloging-in-Publication Data
A catalog record for this book is available from the Library of Congress.

For Information on all Morgan Kaufmann publications
visit our website at www.mkp.com

ELSEVIER   Book Aid International   Working together
to grow libraries in
developing countries

www.elsevier.com • www.bookaid.org

Contents

Foreword

Back in the 1970s, Alvin Toffler wrote *Future Shock*, a book about the pace of technological change. It may seem surprising to us now, but the technology changes of the 1960s provoked a type of intellectual paralysis.

So many things were changing so quickly that it was difficult to understand what to do. During the past 40 years, that pace has only increased. Even in the short years that define my career, the shift to the desktop computer was a huge leap. Then, just a decade later was the subsequent jump to mobile phones. This was a disorienting shift as we had to throw away many of the lessons we had just learned a few short years earlier.

It is difficult to let go of models that work well! But eventually, we do let them go, and we are better for it.

I am not, however, convinced that the rate of change is actually a problem. Change is just a crucible that helps us grow and understand the world better. It is not learning the new thing that is difficult; it is learning to let go of the old that trips most of us up. As Toffler said, "Change is not merely necessary to life—it is life."

The computer was a great leap forward, and the mobile phone was yet another. Just as we get one paradigm figured out, another one comes along. However, we can start to see a pattern here. It is not really the devices that are interesting but, rather, the fact that we have so many: Numerous devices are stitched together by "the cloud" so the data you change on one device can be experienced on all of them. This is a real, more fundamental shift. We are collecting a menagerie of devices that now not only share data but also spread that entire experience across them all.

I remember that early "Aha!" moment when I first used web-based e-mail. "You mean, I can get my email *anywhere*?" It was a mind-boggling concept. It was not the device that was important but, rather, its ability to reach through the screen to all of my stuff. The device became a vessel, a temporary container that I could discard if necessary. ChromeBooks, a web-based laptop, took this to an extreme in 2010 with a series of ads that showed you working on one device, the device getting destroyed in a gruesome manner, and you picking up your work again effortlessly on another one.

Now, of course, the technology world is still growing and in addition to mobile phones, we have TVs and watches joining the mix. However, instead of being completely separate devices, they join this connected party. I can "favorite" a YouTube video on Twitter from my phone, share it through e-mail on my laptop, and watch it at home on my TV. Screens are becoming our digital portals. They allow us to not only view all of our digital stuff from multiple vantage points but also to push content to other screens.

We are just beginning to understand the depth of this screen revolution.

It is not really about the screens themselves but, rather, the experiences (and the underlying data) that are shared between them. That is why I like this book. It is a thorough analysis of the many screens that are shaping our digital lives and, more important, how these screens affect and connect the people that use them. It builds up a way of understanding and thinking about screens, creating a model for content design and a UI architecture for multiscreen projects. This is one of the key topics that we need to discuss in the coming years, and I am glad this book has started the conversation.

—Scott Jenson

Guest Commentary from the Publisher of the German book

The first version of this book has been published in 2013 in German by digiparden Verlag, the publishing unit of SETU GmbH, a German software engineering company, developing content management solutions for major brands since 2001.

Dear readers,

When Wolfram started the German book project in 2011, we didn't expect it to become a standard for multiscreen development in the German market. So seeing this book being published internationally is really a great pleasure for us.

We at SETU develop content management solutions. Our company name derives from Sanskrit and in figurative sense means *bridge*. Our aim is to bridge the gap between technical demands and the most important factor in any process—the people involved.

Yesterday, when discussing software the focus always was on a technical process to be optimized. Still today it is common to create solutions that superficially improve a process, but results in increased complexity for the user. Increased complexity often results in overloaded UIs with overwhelmed users who can theoretically do anything at any time, but in reality never have the information required at that very moment. This is an expensive and unsuccessful approach and produces frustrated users. Developing solutions with a user-centered multiscreen approach seems to be a natural way on focusing on information that really matters.

When regarding today's successful digital service companies it becomes obvious what is critical to success. The examples are well-known: eBay supplants the classified advertisement; travel portals supplant travel agencies; PayPal oppresses the banks; Google supplants the Yellow Pages, the telephone book, and the street map; and Amazon supplants booksellers and also even publishing houses.

So what do all these companies have in common? They have successfully supplanted traditional offerings with their systems. They regard their offerings as a service and work on the user experience of their customers. They improve their offerings successively. By means of a desktop website, tablet, smartphone, and so on, they succeed in making the use of their offerings into daily-use articles because today's user does not search for a long time: He utilizes the suitable offerings in which he trusts—regardless of whether he is at the office, at home, or in the movie theater. He uses digital services just like other trusted daily-use articles. Multiscreen has become a requirement for successful digitalization of business.

For our new software release we have set ourselves a goal: to offer a technical platform that allows to focus on contents derived from the need for information and subsequently to model the resulting business process for an exceptional user experience in a multiscreen environment. Therefore we focus on two key issues: What information does it need—at a particular time—to support the user optimally to fulfill his job? And what are the most appropriate actions to start from the given situation?

With our SETU Platform 3 Release an information architect has the ability to define a data structure that covers real life complexity, define an appropriate work-flow from which the user interface gets its action elements, and finally generate a high fidelity multiscreen user interface that can be used generic out-of-the-box or modified to implement a UI for special user requirements.

We are glad you seem to share our vision of developing next generation user experience solutions. Presumably it is also your assignment to make a service into a daily-use article! We hope that this book will help you to quickly and successfully reach your goal.

Michael Dengler
CEO, SETU SOFTWARE

Preface

People are increasingly using various digital devices: whether in the subway, in the office, in the street café, or also at home. Everything is cross-linked. One can be online constantly. You yourself are possibly working on a *multiscreen* project right now. The users expect that, in the future and even now, information and services will, insofar as this is possible, be available on all (relevant) screens, touchpoints, and output channels and function across all devices.

Over the short- and medium-term, the focus will be on four to five established widespread device classes: Smartphones, tablets, laptops or desktop PCs, and smart TVs. Probably smartwatches will be a fifth one that should be taken into account in the near future. We describe approaches based on these core device classes, and beyond that also introduce methods and thoughts how you could achieve a future-ready (and thus multiscreen-ready) concept by focusing on content and user. The presented methods and patterns can be applied to other screens as well.

I have been dealing with and thinking about the topic of Multiscreen since I worked on my first university degree in 2006. One year later, the "mobile revolution" began with the release of the first *Apple iPhone*. Since then I worked extensively with this thematic field which has become a stand-alone project in the meantime.

In 2013 I published the German book "Multiscreen Experience Design" together with the publisher digiparden (an imprint of SETU GmbH). It was the first book at all about that topic. It got very good feedback and we recognized that there is a huge demand for an English version. That is why we decided to republish it together with Morgan Kaufmann. And that is why you hold this book in your hands now—translated, completely revised, updated, and with new ideas and two additional chapters.

Through the book, we are supplying a research-based and nonetheless practically oriented and holistic approach with examples, references, and sources from practical experience. We have collected, selected, and compactly summarized many ideas and pieces of knowledge regarding the themes of multiscreen, service design, and user experience design, combined these with our own experiences and supplied them in readable tidbits. The book, which is to be understood as a compendium, will be complemented by a supporting online platform.

The book is supposed to serve as an inspiration and to offer assistance during the development of strategy and conception work for digital services (website, apps, data, database, contents, and information). We show what is important, offer suggestions, and make recommendations that you should take into consideration when conceiving multiscreen projects. It is shown how the various screens can be sensibly combined with each other and how you take the various users and the respective context of use into consideration. Thoughts and insights about the future of content (management), content design, and UI architecture complement this topic.

The technical implementation of applications and web layouts is not the focus of this publication.

The ideas and recommendations in this book are a current stock-taking. We summarize the approaches that, from our perspective, are relevant and sensible. Some ideas are relatively new and still being discussed. The theme is still active, and the technical development will likewise continue. On a regular basis, there will be supplements to and comments on the contents and current information provided on the online platform at http://www.msxbook.com/en.

I look forward to a lively discussion, constructive suggestions, and feedback. Enjoy the book!

Wolfram Nagel
SchwäbischGmünd, December 2015

Acknowledgments

Writing a book is a big challenge. Thankfully I got a lot of help during this project. Many thanks to my employer Michael Dengler at SETU for supporting the Multiscreen project and the book(s) since a long time. Thank you to Jens Franke, Kevin Albrecht, Andreas Croonenbroeck, and Pascal Raabe for their very helpful feedback. Thanks also to my professors Steffen Süpple and Ulrich Schendzielorz at the University of Design in Schwäbisch Gmünd. Thank you Christian Solmecke for your advices and straightforward support concerning legal issues. And of course thank you to Morgan Kaufmann for being our publisher, especially Charlie Kent, Todd Green, and Punithavathy Govindaradjane. Thank you very much to Scott Jenson for the preface. I'm absolutely honored that he contributed some thoughts to this book. Thank you to my former fellow student Valentin Fischer for the smartly drawn illustrations, the contribution as co-author to the German book and our constructive and critical discussions. It has been inspiring to work with you on the project!

Thanks also to Cennydd Bowles, Josh Clark, Rod Farmer, Brad Frost, Bertram Gugel, Marc Hassenzahl, Stephen Hay, Karen McGrane, Stephanie Rieger, Johannes Schardt, Rasmus Skjoldan, Christoph Stoll, Gabriel White, and other colleagues for inspiring personal conversations, feedback, their talks, presentations, articles, reports, commentaries, or books. There is a more detailed compilation of important sources of ideas and frequently cited authors on a separate page in the Appendix (see Chapter 9, Section 9.1).

I would also like to thank all the other persons who supported me with their constructive criticism, their comments and ideas during the writing of the book and furthermore contributed to the *Multiscreen Experience Project*. Your support and inspiration helped me to write this book in this form.

Finally, special and deep thanks goes to my family. Thank you to my wife Amelie and my son Lasse for your understanding. Your loving patience and endless support made this book possible!

Introduction

Users and information offerings are cross-linked ever more strongly. Information is retrieved all day long via a wide array of touchpoints. In this chapter, the influential factors and important terms are discussed in detail.

1.1 MULTISCREEN

Two of the most important assets of the digital society are information and content. The easier they can be retrieved, the more successful the provider will be.

The term *multiscreen* or *multi-screen* is composed of the words "multi" (multiple) and "screen." I prefer the notation without the hyphen because of the hashtag capability and because typographically it looks better. In general, multiscreen means that (multiple) various screens and/or devices are used for or during one activity. In this case, "screen" serves representatively for a device with a firmly built-in screen. With regard to the devices, the term "multidevice" is popular.

> *Multiscreen is about developing a single application for multiple interfaces—one for each screen type: smartphone, tablet, desktop, and television.*
>
> Radley Marx (cofounder of cloud.tv)

Information in the (digital) information age

We live in a time in which there is a flood of information (Evsan, 2013c). Due to the Internet, today potentially all users are simultaneously senders and recipients of information that is available at all times. Thus, it has become even more important that information arrives to the recipient(s) as easily as possible. The higher the quality of information, the higher the probability that it is relevant for someone. Offering maximally user-centered, relevant, and exciting information is a challenge that is increasingly gaining in importance in conjunction with cloud-based multiscreen scenarios.

> *Online time is screen time.*
>
> Luke Wroblewski

In his article "The UX of Data," Scott Jenson (2011) explains why data must be processed in a user-friendly and sensible manner and, in this context, he uses the description "(user) experience of data."

The relevant information should be provided at all times in a context-relevant manner. It is all about enabling people to have the easiest access possible to digital services via as many channels and devices as desired. Thus, think about how to enhance the information experience at all levels.

The next step in the digital information age in which everything and all information will be completely connected is the Internet of Things. Screens and nearly all imaginable other objects will be controlled remotely. They will also exchange data with other devices, objects, or data sources independently without any human or user involvement.

Challenges

Due to the increasing dissemination of mobile devices and increasing connectivity, the use of devices and services (e.g., websites, apps, and information) is becoming increasingly more fragmented. Thus, the user behavior and the attitude toward and access to information have changed.

RECOMMENDED READING

Interesting articles that also discuss the theme in detail and describe current and future challenges are collected on the website and can be found at www.msxbook.com/en/mschllgs.

According to a Microsoft study, in 2010, there were approximately 20 million multiscreeners living in Europe (Microsoft Advertising, 2010b). Those are *users who are constantly online with some type of device and alternate between multiple screens during the course of a day*. The numbers have rapidly grown since then, and it is now quite common for a large number of people to behave like multiscreeners. In a Google study from 2012, approximately 90% of participants responded that they use more than one device for getting a task done (Google et al., 2012). This user group and similarly categorized users demand multiscreen-compatible offerings. Ultimately, it is a matter of offering a service that is more or less available without any restrictions on all screens and touchpoints.

> *When we talk about apps for devices these days, we are talking about a multitude of devices and device platforms.*
> **Serge Jespers (Adobe Evangelist)**

A multiscreen world

We live in a multiscreen world. People behave in a multidevice way. Thus, it is misleading if one measures the use of only single devices (which is still often the case). When people do anything with a device, they use the most convenient device available at that moment (which can potentially be more than one). Thus, it is not relevant what percentage of action is done on and with a specific device. Your service has to be available in the best possible way for all relevant screens. Thus, you should measure the number of users, not the number of devices (which is quite challenging or not accurate). Users behave increasingly more like multiscreeners.

If you do not have a multiscreen strategy and a multiscreen-ready service, people will not (want to) use your service on different screens. Therefore, a statistic that is used to decide whether a specific strategy is necessary or not will provide false information if it is based on misleading measurements. If you give people a bad experience on any screen, it reflects on all the other channels as well and thus impacts the experience with your service at large.

You can't choose not to support one device. They all have to be good because you don't control when, where or how people might need you. It's like having hot running water in both your kitchen and your bathroom. Sure, you probably use more hot water in your bathroom, but that doesn't mean that it's any less important in your kitchen.

Thomas Baekdal (author and strategic consultant)

I agree with Thomas Baekdal that being multiscreen-ready is not a decision: It is the absence of a decision (Baekdal, 2014). Single-device design does not suffice anymore. Even if "mobile" seems to be statistically not yet relevant for your projects, it is important, especially for this very reason, to "think multiscreen."

1.2 IMPORTANT TERMS

Here, we explain the most important terms and how we use them. More detailed definitions are provided in the credited sources.

Device and **screen** are used synonymously for an operatable, digital device with a screen. Such a device can output and display contents, it is in principle cloud compatible (i.e., cloud computing), and it is individualizable through the installation of software. With it, data and information can be depicted, retrieved, and processed (see Chapter 2). The terms *screen* and *device* are largely used in this book with the identical meaning.

Device Touchpoint describes the contact and/or touchpoint with a digital device. The following are decisive: Frequency, intensity, and the variance of the media and/or device usage (see Chapter 3, Section 3.2.1). In order to understand the *multiscreen* user, it is important (in addition to his daily routine) to know his potential *device* touchpoints, i.e., to know with which devices he comes into contact when, why, how and in what scope. For the service itself, naturally all other *service* touchpoints are relevant (e.g., contact with employees, the print communication, or analog letter post).

User Experience (abbreviated as UX) encompasses all aspects of the experiences (perception, reaction, behavior) of a user during the interaction with a product, system, service, environment or institution. This also includes the software and IT systems. The term encompasses the full spectrum of interactive possibilities (source: Wikipedia [de]: user experience, n.d.). The term experience or *user experience* is concerned less with technology, product design, or an interface and more with the aid of a digital device, creating a sensible and meaningful experience for the user. An experience is subjective, comprehensive, situation- and location-related, and thus context-related, dynamic, and valuable (Hassenzahl, 2010, 2011) (see Chapter 3, Section 3.3). "An experience is a story, emerging from the dialogue of a person with her or his world through action" (Hassenzahl, 2010, p. 8). The field of user experience is very complex and comprises many intersecting topics and disciplines, such as user research, usability (engineering), information architecture, user interface design, visual design, interaction design, and content strategy. A more detailed definition of "(user) experience (design)" and additional sources can be found at http://www.msxbook.com/en/uxdef.

Design means not just visual design and the presentation and styling of information but also creativity, innovation, improvement, development, and management. In graphic design, the focus is on the organization of information. Experience design focuses on the user's behavior and/or the user experience.

Interface: In this book we sometimes use the abbreviated term "interface" in two different meanings. Mostly we mean the (Graphical) User Interface/(G)UI that allows users to interact with physical devices that display the information (that is, what the user can see or touch on the "screen"). A secondary usage of interface is the application programming interface (API). It is a set of routines, protocols, and tools used by software developers. With an API you can combine, integrate and exchange functionality, data and information of and between different services (see Chapter 5, Section 5.11). Normally the API is not visible but used by the (G)UI.

Information generally equates to significance (meaning) or conveyed knowledge. Through the digitalization of any information, data are created.

Information experience describes the user experience for and while receiving and consuming information and data. Such information and data must be provided in a context-relevant form in every situation and optimized for the respective device. The definition is based on the article from Scott Jenson (2011) in *UX Magazine* regarding the "user experience of data." (See also http://www.msxbook.com/en/ix and Chapter 6.)

A **service** generally describes an intangible business activity or service. With an offering of information, certain contents are supplied to a certain target group in such a manner that they can be assumed, understood, and used by them. A service constitutes contents in a digital ecosystem. In conjunction with this project, the term refers mainly to applications, websites, data, and information. The terms *service* and *information offering* are used synonymously here.

Service design is an interdisciplinary approach that focuses on people's requirements and customers' requests, and it means a comprehensive and holistic design of service systems. It is a matter of making services useful, usable, and desirable for the users. For the providers, it is a matter of making the service efficient and effective (Knecht, 2011).

Service experience describes the user experience during the use or availment of a service.

Touchpoints are all contact points that one encounters with a service. In this book, the (device) touchpoints refer mainly to all situations and contact points with the service in which information is retrieved and depicted on a digital device with a screen. Touchpoints of a bank, for example, are the website, online banking portal, smartphone banking app, customer magazine, mailings, newsletters, communication by e-mail, greeting cards, cash point, International Savings Day, or a date with the customer consultant.

The **usage context** (or context of use) consists mainly of the three parameters of usage mode, situation, and environment. In addition, this also includes respectively the user or users and the device or devices being used. These parameters influence each other reciprocally and ultimately define the individual context of use (see Chapter 4).

Multiscreen means "multiple screens." We focus on the digital devices that currently (2015) are being most widely disseminated and generally used: smartphone, tablet, laptop or desktop PC, and Internet-compatible TV device (smart TV) (see Chapter 2, Section 2.3). We also discuss smartwatches as a potentially fifth relevant device class. The term and its meaning can be differentiated between applications and scenarios.

A **multiscreen application** is usable with various devices (and often on various platforms) and is thus cross-device compatible. Examples of multiscreen applications are the offerings or apps of YouTube, iTunes, Google, Evernote, Wunderlist, Instapaper, Twitter, or Facebook. In this regard, the data are often synchronized in the cloud or at least regularly by the device's storage (medium) with a server and are thus made available between devices. Cloud computing enables users and enterprises to store, use, and process data in third-party data centers and to run applications that need not be installed on the local device.

In a **multiscreen scenario**, multiple devices or screens (and thus also information offerings) are used at the same time. For example, when you watch TV, you can, on a parallel basis, use Twitter and Facebook on a tablet, write a short message with your cell phone or smartphone, or process e-mails on your laptop. The screens do not necessarily have to originate from one manufacturer and/or one platform. For example, a private multiscreen setting can consist of a Sony TV with a plugged-in Apple TV, a Windows PC, a Samsung cellphone with an Android operating system, and an Apple iPad. In this regard, see the discussion of the user prototype Larry Newton (beginning in Chapter 3, Section 3.5.9) or user type multiscreener (Chapter 3, Section 3.5.14).

Multiscreen experience refers to the (subjective) user experience during the use of a digital service and various screens in order to retrieve, receive, manage, or publish information and contents.

Multiscreen experience design is the strategic development, conception, and design of products, and services (applications, websites, and data) for various devices and screens. It involves the use and outputting of services on the relevant screens or generally the consideration of the fact that people will use various digital devices in their daily lives in the future in order to perform a wide array of tasks.

1.3 THE BOOK AND ITS USAGE

Principles, patterns, and factors for the strategic development and conception of multiscreen projects

During the past few years, there has been much new knowledge and many new recommendations from the areas of usability, user experience design, interface design, interaction design, website conception, content strategy, and user research. We have compiled them as well as aggregated and continued to develop them for use in the multiscreen context.

Book sections

The book is divided into three main sections. Chapters 2–4 present the most important influential factors: device and/or screen, user, and context of use. Chapter 5 describes and recommends various patterns, principles, approaches, and examples of handling, strategic development, and the conception of multiscreen projects. Chapters 6 and 7 discuss what multiscreen especially means for content flows, processes, workflows, and tools now and in the future.

All methods, sources, prototypes, work materials, and aids serve as recommendations. In this regard, technologies are not in the forefront. The supplemental online platform, http://www.msxbook.com/en, is similarly structured like the book.

Compendium principle

You can read only individual chapters, subchapters or sections—for example, Chapter 4, Section 4.4 titled The Mobile Context of Use or, if you are focusing on the users, Chapter 3 Users and Their Typification. The compendium is supplemented by a comprehensive collection of source materials.

> **NOTE**
>
> At http://www.msxbook.com/en, we provide supplemental content, information, examples, and work materials. All examples and screenshots (in this book) serve as examples. They serve to explain the respective principle or pattern. The applications may also be available on other platforms in addition to the depicted platforms.

The goal of our approach is to help the reader understand users, devices, and other framework conditions and to more quickly be able to begin concrete problem solving and/or task formulation in order to develop sustainable solutions and concepts for constantly changing digital ecosystems. The user is always the main focus. Our recommendations are not patented formulas or ready-to-use cure-alls. It must constantly be weighed which recommendations are best for completing a task. Empathy, creativity, and a detailed requirements analysis are the foundation for a successful project.

Four Main Sections:
FOUR SCREENS
USERS AND THEIR TYPIFICATION
CONTEXT OF USE
STRATEGIES AND EXAMPLES

Principles, patterns and methods

With the multiscreen experience design approach, we describe principles that we find very helpful. We also mention other approaches that are subjectively not our first choice, but perhaps are relevant for your project requirements. You should consider all of them and weigh up what matters most to your project. It is possible that some of the described principles may not function together or are contrary in certain circumstances. You should and will not apply all of them at the same time. It always depends on what you need. It is up to you to choose the appropriate methods and approaches.

Supplemental methods

We recommend examining and developing ideas, concepts, and drafts with suitable design methods. You can find a collection of helpful methods, for example, in the Design Methoden Finder (a German collection of various design methods) at http://www.designmethodenfinder.de.

Content and legibility

The contents in this book have been essentially created through aggregation, interpretation, and the reformulation of a wide array of ideas and approaches. If anything in this book turns out to be unclear or incorrect, then it is our sole responsibility alone.

We have carefully selected the credited literature sources. If we have overlooked important works or proven knowledge or if an idea has not been sufficiently and appropriately cited, we ask for your understanding and ask you to please notify us of this.

For reasons of better legibility, we have refrained from simultaneously using male and female forms. All references to persons apply equally to both genders.

Images, illustrations, and examples

The device illustrations as well as all examples, in which devices are depicted, are exemplary and serve to be representative of a certain approach or a principle. The similarity of the device drawings and other illustrations to Apple devices has been chosen only for standardization purposes. Alternatively, devices and platforms from other manufacturers could be used in order to discuss and explain a principle in detail.

Images and screenshots serve for illustration purposes and have sometimes been revised. In this case as well, the model character is in the forefront (not the 100% correct depiction of the initial materials). It is possible that screenshots, devices, and illustrations originate from older versions. It is also possible that some services and examples changed their business case or have been closed but still serve as good examples to show the underlying principle.

1.3.1 CORRELATIONS

In this book, we use many technical terms. In order to more easily classify the terms, we show them in a diagram. Such a depiction is naturally subjective and never absolutely correct (Wilson, 2013). Based on the respective perspective, you can group the terms in a different manner. We think that the diagram is a sensible supplement for orientation purposes.

The diagram is supposed to help depict the most important terms used in this book in their contentual context. It contains multiple focuses. On the left, everything is arranged around the users (see Chapter 3). In the lower right, the focus is on the information and content, and in the upper right, everything is grouped in such a manner that its focus is on the screens. The blue terms indicate the patterns and principles (see Chapter 5). A PDF of the diagram is available via www.msxbook.com/en/msxdgr. We look forward to receiving your comments about and opinions of the depiction.

1.4 ORIENTATION AIDS AND CENTRAL THEMES

1. **Think multiscreen.**
   Multiscreen is no longer just a "nice supplement" but, rather, obligatory. Convince customers or project participants with good examples, even if "mobile" is statistically not relevant yet. See Chapter 5.

2. **Know your Screens.**
   It is helpful and important to be familiar with all relevant device (classes), its features, typical use, and combination possibilities. Note that the smartphone is the most important device in daily media consumption. It is used most frequently and serves mostly as the starting point when multiple devices are being used. See Chapter 2 and specifically Section 2.5.1.

3. **Put the focus on the user.**
   Research the target group(s): Who are the most important users, what devices are they using, and what are their motives and requirements? See Chapter 3, Section 3.5.

4. **Analyze the daily process.**
   What does a typical day look like in the life of the typical user? How does his workflow look? What are the typical touchpoints—that is, what device is being used, when, by whom, and for what purpose? See Chapter 3, Section 3.2.1.

5. **Context is king.**
   Know, understand, and define the relevant contexts of use and the parameters of the user, device, usage mode, situation, and the environment. Do not forget: The context of use is everywhere. See Chapter 4.

6. **Content is king (as well, of course).**
   Multiscreen-capable data are of critical importance. Make sure that there are flexible and dynamic layouts and contents. In order to do this, it is necessary to have suitable content management workflows and a strategy for how contents are supposed to be handled. Naturally, you can never regard the contents as being isolated from the potential user and the context of use. See Chapter 5, Sections 5.8.1 and 5.10, and Chapter 6.

7. **Is everything in order legally?**
   The legal aspect plays an important role. You should responsibly follow the valid legal directives regarding copyright law, competition law, data protection law, and others. See Chapter 5, Section 5.19.

8. **Without the Internet, (almost) nothing at all works.**
   Internet, synchronization, and cloud computing are fundamental requirements for a functioning multiscreen concept. Think about fallback solutions if the data connection is bad—for example, in a "dead zone." See Chapter 5, Section 5.6.

9. **Tackle the future of content (management).**
   Consider content flows and how information is created, managed, published, and received. Optimize the back end UX for authors and content curators, and use a centralized content hub for channeling and aggregation. See Chapter 6.

10. **Apply and establish the building block principle.**
    Build content and user interfaces in a modular and structured manner based on the smallest possible units. Consider the correlation between these elements, larger components, types, and concrete objects. See Chapter 7.

11. **Challenges are opportunities.**
    Focus as early as possible on the project-related challenges and opportunities for cross-device and cross-platform concepts with regard to information, interaction, communication, and collaboration.

12. **Live like a multiscreener and have fun at work.**
    Those who like to work and focus on the theme, at work and also privately, will find it easier to design suitable services and future-oriented concepts.

Additional information and tips are provided on the project website at http://www.msxbook.com/en.

Four Screens

2

In this book, multiscreen *refers primarily to the four screens of smartphone, tablet, laptop or PC, and smart TV, but also considers the smartwatch as a fifth potential relevant screen.* Screen *in this context is synonymous with a digital device. The various device classes as well as their specific features and differences are presented in this chapter.*

2.1 OVERVIEW

With regard to usability, layout and contents cannot simply be upscaled or downscaled for the various screens. The adjustments must be carefully thought through. When in doubt or at least at the beginning, you can first concentrate on the most important points.

Before you take up a multiscreen project, all participants must be aware of the important differences between the various platforms and devices. In this regard, you should always bear in mind how the service ultimately is perceived by the target group and/or by each individual user.

In our *multiscreen experience design* approach, we focus on the four device classes that are currently most important and that can be called the "core devices" or "core screens." We also mention smartwatches as a probable fifth important and popular device in the near future. The devices (and/or screens) are determined and categorized based on various criteria. Sometimes, the transitions are fluid. Commonalities, differences, and special features are presented here.

Smartphone

With a smartphone, you are potentially always online. It is almost always handy. Most online actions are started on it.

Laptop or desktop PC

A mouse, a keyboard, and the comparatively strong computer power make the laptop or desktop PC the most efficient and most effective work device.

Tablet

With a tablet, you can read and surf very well. Although it is a mobile device, it is used frequently in a stationary situation.

Smart TV

The smart TV, which tends to have the largest screen of all the devices, is well-suited for visual information and, due to the screen size, also for groups of persons.

Smartwatch

With a smartwatch, you can get instant and glanceable information. They have the smallest screens and are always on (your wrist).

Whether the smartwatch will become a relevant and coequal device depends on its potential integration and combination capabilities with other screens and whether it supports inter alia consistency, complementarity, and a fluid experience (see Section 2.6 and Chapter 5).

Despite the sometimes huge variations between and even within (these) device classes their classification will still be relevant, because there are similarities concerning typical usage context, usage and interaction patterns, and combination possibilities. A completely device agnostic approach cannot include these details.

2.2 CATEGORIZATION OF DEVICES

There are numerous devices with a wide array of screen sizes and resolutions. In order to gain a better understanding of this diversity, it can help to define device and layout groups or *device prototypes*. For classification purposes, device characteristics, input capabilities, tasks typically handled with the respective devices, typical user posture with a specific device, and other factors should be taken into consideration, in addition to screen size.

When you categorize devices by screen size (which is not the only characteristic you should take into account), you should—in practice—pay attention to the actual screen size and not to the pure screen resolution. The resolution has (except for the sharpness and display quality) little influence on interaction and usability. The required button size is dependent more on the screen size and the type of operation (navigation or control) than on the resolution and should thus be measured in centimeters rather than pixels.

Relying just on screen size could lead to wrong assumptions and decisions because there is still no relationship between screen size and bandwidth or input methods—for example, if the device is controlled by touch gestures or mouse and keyboard (Wroblewski, 2014a, 2014c).

Each device is different, has special advantages in certain situations, and can be less beneficial in other situations. Thus, each feature does not necessarily need to be available on each device. How a device is used and how a task is completed with it are more or less typical and frequently executed based on a uniform pattern.

In order to be able to assess devices, you should be familiar with and analyze the various contexts of use and their special features (see Chapter 4). Individual devices can often be allocated to one or more typical (probable, suitable, and expected) contexts of use.

> **HINT**
>
> In "Framework for Designing for Multiple Devices," Sachendra Yadav (2011) provides practical tips about the approach.

From the categorization, device classes that are better manageable can be derived.

2.3 DEVICE CLASSES

A device class describes a group of similar digital devices with comparable features. Device classes are defined based on distinct user requirements, the context of use, and the technical possibilities or restrictions.

For example, a user who is in a city he does not know well would like to retrieve the nearest bus stop, the related bus schedule, and a map of the surrounding area as quickly and easily as possible with a smartphone. In most cases, an Internet connection is required. Is there network coverage? How good is the connection quality? With a smartphone, position-finding is often very easy. However, does the position-finding function? How is the weather? Is it possibly cold and the operation of the smartphone display is made more difficult because the user is wearing gloves or has numb fingers?

The manner in which one interacts and/or navigates with the device is important. The physical conditions, the average display size of the screen, and the typical distance between the user (eyes) and the screen are likewise relevant for the design.

The viewing distance on small screens and therefore mainly mobile devices can vary significantly. There is a difference between viewing content from a 10-cm distance (e.g., when reading in bed) and viewing it during breakfast at an average distance of approximately 30 cm (Mod, 2011). Viewing distance also can impact the way in which the user interacts with the content on the device and how the content should be presented.

Four screens

In conjunction with the development and design of web applications, according to a former post from Luke Wroblewski, there are five device classes (Wroblewski, 2011a, 2011d). His classification also included so-called feature phones.

Our focus is on the four devices that are currently and in the short-term most relevant: Internet-compatible TV devices (smart TVs), desktop PCs and/or laptops, tablets, and smartphones. We exclude normal cell phones and/or so-called feature phones due to the lack of flexibility and relevance in the multiscreen context. They play only a minor role in the *multiscreen experience project*, but they must likewise be taken into consideration in principle in the sense of a comprehensive service experience just like nondigital touchpoints (e.g., print or employee contact). This depends on the target group and its typical media usage and device affinity. In the medium term and near future, you should also consider smartwatches as a fifth important device class (Wroblewski, 2015e). They will likely become more relevant and popular in the near future. That's why they are considered and described here as well.

There are also alternative output forms for the exemplary screens. For example, in many cases, the consideration of a large video screen (used with a projector or in cinemas) makes sense that would, based on the type, be classified in the category of the largest screen (smart TV).

Of course, there are other device classes, most notably the just mentioned smartwatches. However, most of these devices are not yet as popular as the four screens on which we concentrate. Our classification is currently accurate, but must be kept in mind that additional device classes and screens will be established in the future and must accordingly be taken into consideration in a multiscreen concept (e.g., data eyeglasses; Evsan, 2013a). Multitouch tables, which are used, for example, in restaurants and museums, automotive displays (see Chapter 4, Section 4.4), and similar devices, are, from our perspective, (still) disseminated too little and are not sufficiently combinable with the discussed screens in order to take them into consideration here in a similar form.

No matter if this classification is complete or difficult in some cases, you will still talk about specific device classes in your projects. Of course, if smartwatches or data glasses are a main consideration in your service or product, these should be integrated into your strategy.

If you want to design and develop for an uncertain future, you should plan ahead and produce smart and future-friendly content and flexible user interfaces (see Chapter 5, Sections 5.8.1 and 5.10, and Chapter 7). Regarding this idea, Trent Walton (2014) discusses a "device-agnostic" approach. Nonetheless, when you design interfaces and interactions, you will still have to consider different device classes and their specific characteristics.

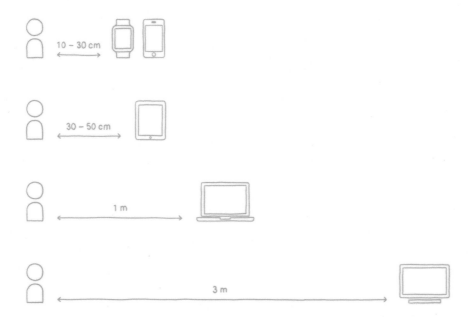

Typical device features

Each of the aforementioned device classes is definable with regard to the following:

- Average display size—that is, not just the resolution ("wall-to-wall," large screen, display for desks, laptop display, hand-sized, thumb-sized, etc.)
- Main input method (mouse, physical buttons, keys, keyboard, keypad, numeric keypad, remote operation in a wide array of variants, [multi]touch, gestures, sensors, Bluetooth, fingerprint, audio and voice recognition, language, camera, NFC [near field radio communication between two proximate devices], accelerometer, digital crown, etc.)
- Typical average distance between the user (eyes) and the screen (based on the device being between 10 cm and 3 m from the user; distances with smartphones and smartwatches are quite similar)
- Typical posture of the user (lean back or lean forward)

- Context of use (e.g., lean back situation on the sofa with 3 m of distance to the device, more extensive usage at the desk, and brief and frequent usage activities in short intervals throughout the day at various locations) (more details in Chapter 4)

Luke Wroblewski (2015a) published an interesting matrix that shows the correlation of input methods and device types. The devices and their characteristics, special features, and differences have a decisive influence on the user experience, which can be delimited and influenced by the aforementioned parameters. The platform used, the manufacturer, and the product and its haptics often also play a role. In many cases, different or at least adjusted and optimized user interfaces make sense.

The interface and interaction concept is dependent on the context of use (see Chapter 4), typical and learned interaction patterns, as well as various screens and resolutions of the respective devices. For cross-device applications, a certain visual and interactive consistency should be guaranteed so as not to confuse the user and to preserve the visual appearance of an application and/or a provider (see Chapter 5, Sections 5.8.1 and 5.9). However, you must ensure that, despite compromises that may have been made, you can still exploit the advantages of a device.

In many cases, limitations can also have a positive effect—for example, if you design a website initially for a small display (e.g., a smartphone) and, by so doing, the complexity of the contents and/or the interface must be mandatorily reduced and designed to be more clearly arranged (see Chapter 5, Section 5.1). You must always decide whether a corresponding device makes sense in the application and context of use (see Chapter 4). In many cases, and based on the target group and service, not every application and every piece of information must be made available on the TV and the smartphone.

Delimitation of the device classes

The four device classes (smartphone, tablet, laptop, and TV) are prime examples of many detailed characteristics of devices. The categorization dissolves somewhat and/or the transitions and delimitations are fluid. Many (mini)tablets are somewhat smaller than large smartphones. For laptops with a touchscreen or tablets to which a keyboard can be connected, the boundaries are likewise fluid. The prototypes introduced in Section 2.5 are a recommendation. You must decide to which category a target device belongs or work with intermediate categories and conform the breakdown to the respective project requirements.

You should also take into account whether your potential users already are using or are likely to use and consider smartwatches (or any other device class) as a serious and useful device in the context and purpose of the service you are designing and developing (see Section 2.5.5).

Class-specific differences

After the relevant device classes have been identified, you will encounter a similar challenge. Within the device classes, there are major differences regarding display size and screen resolution (e.g., desktop PC in comparison with a 13-inch notebook or the great variation between an iPad mini with an 8-inch screen and the iPad Pro from 2015 with a 13-inch screen). In addition to the screen-relevant parameters, you must also focus on the performance, interaction, and navigation of the devices. A modern offering of information should be displayable on each device. If the device (and media) characteristics change, often you must also adjust the layout.

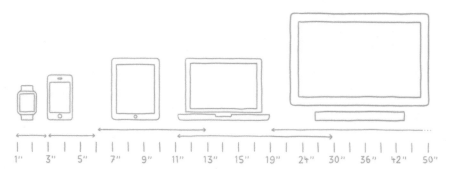

| 1" | 3" | 5" | 7" | 9" | 11" | 13" | 15" | 19" | 24" | 30" | 36" | 42" | 50" |

Different device classes and their customary screen sizes in relation: Smartwatch, smartphone, tablet, laptop and/or desktop PC and Internet-compatible TV device (smart TV).

Adjustable layouts

In order to help deal with this challenge, *responsive* or *adaptive web design* can be used. This design uses flexible, scalable, and adjustable layouts that respond to the respective devices and/or screens and their features (Marcotte, 2010; Tran, 2011).

Although responsive design is indeed a good approach, the contents do not always automatically also conform to the various contexts of use but, rather, are merely arranged differently on the screen. Responsive design in discussed further in Chapter 5, Section 5.8.1.

Various device parameters

Luke Wroblewski (2009) describes various parameters that are also applicable to the devices that we have selected and defines *networked consumer device platforms* as follows:

- Networked: Cross-linked devices can independently create an online connection and, by so doing, can read or process Internet contents and start cloud services.
- Consumer device: Standard devices for consumers that are designed for daily usage and not just for professional and special tasks.
- Platform: You can build (develop) something on this. Software developers can program software for this. Product developers can build hardware in order to integrate the platform. Editors can publish on a platform.

Additional examples of devices in this context are game consoles (e.g. Xbox, PlayStation, and Wii) and TV devices with an Internet connection (e.g., Samsung

SmartTV or Sony Bravia HDTV). We do not separately analyze game consoles because, as a rule, they are part of the TV screen and/or the TV screen serves as the output device for them.

2.3.1 MOBILE DEVICE

Differentiation and classification

What exactly is a mobile device anyway? How do you classify devices that are more or less mobile? Markus Tschersich (2010) recommends three criteria for the assessment: localizability, location independence, and availability. These parameters are indeed somewhat subjective, but the approach for the classification of mobile devices is nonetheless beneficial because you can better differentiate and classify the various types of devices.

The primary starting point for this is not typical device features such as display, frame size, or amenities and hardware. The most important basic function is the communication—"whether it be the classical voice communication or the data communication which is becoming more and more important" (Tschersich, 2010).

The question of whether a device is mobile can unfortunately seldom be clearly answered "yes" or "no." Basically, almost every device is mobile to some extent. There are many intermediate forms. The individual device classes accordingly have a different level of mobile quality. Smartphone, tablet, and laptop are respectively mobile devices that, however, differentiate themselves from each other with regard to localizability, location independence, and availability. Additional typical features of mobile devices are the independence of the electrical power network and their handiness (small and/or no stationary setup required). Exceptions that are definitively not mobile are the TV device and the desktop PC.

Mobile (e.gs., mobile phone) no longer has the original meaning (mobile telephone, "on the go," in a hurry—thus, a typical *mobile situation*) (see Chapter 4). "Mobile" today is used more to mean when a mobile device is used. Thus, this can almost always be the case. Therefore, the term is increasingly also being used to describe situations in which you are neither on the go nor using a mobile telephone.

In order to differentiate mobile devices from desktop PCs, Josh Clark recommends the term "desknots" for all non-desktop screens. This ultimately means more or less "non-desktop" (not stationary). In principle, it is a good approach for summarizing all mobile devices with one term: "Desknots are connected devices that present alternative contexts and form factors for non-desktop computing" (Clark, 2012a).

Mobile applications

Mobile applications are those that have been developed for installation and use on mobile devices and can accordingly be used on the go, in a mobile situation, and in a mobile context of use (see Chapter 4, Section 4.4).

Potential of mobile devices

Novel digital mobile products and platforms offer many possibilities and can clearly transcend the limitations of the Internet with customary web browsers. They distinguish themselves through additional input methods such as multitouch, gestures, fingerprint, sensors, GPS, accelerometer, gyrometer, audio and/or voice input recognition, camera, photo, or video, and many others.

ING DiBa (a direct bank operating inter alia in Germany) offers a service called "photo transfer." You can take a picture of an invoice, the app recognizes the relevant information, and the money can be transferred without typing (ING-DiBa, 2015).

Mobile devices can be very precisely localized (GPS and WiFi), exploit the motion and orientation of the device (accelerometer), measure the surrounding light (ambient light), or identify objects nearby (RFID). Biometric recognition (face or fingerprint) is already possible. The initial solutions are already on the market. Mobile devices can also serve as complementary devices to control services and other devices by text input (see Chapter 8, Section 8.3).

What is a mobile device?

The individual device classes have different levels of mobile quality. At least one criterion must be fulfilled to some extent. The classification is only a point of reference because the features can vary within the device classes (GPS, Internet option, etc.). Desktop PCs and TV devices are not mobile at all.

Device	location-independent	power supply system independent	available*	handy	localizable
Smartwatch	●	●	○**	●	○
Smartphone	●	●	●	●	●
Feature phone	●	●	●	●	○
E-Book-Reader	●	●		●	
Tablet	●	●	○	○	○
Netbook	●	●		○	
Laptop	●	○	○	○	○
Desktop-PC					
Television					

*Means contactable by telecommunication or cellphone service.
**Unfilled circle means partially fulfilled criterion.

Do not just think mobile

Users indeed have different needs and use different devices. However, insofar as this is possible, the contents should remain the same. When conceiving purely mobile offerings (regardless of whether it makes sense), you must take all potential and relevant devices as well as use cases into consideration. Therefore, you should not develop just for mobile devices (Cho, 2011).

2.4 DEVICE DIFFERENCES

Using the approach introduced here or other methods and process models and by integrating the design guidelines (corporate style guide, visual guidelines, communication goals, content strategy, etc.), you can conceive a flexible and device-independent service and, at the same time, create a fluid and consistent multiscreen experience.

2.4.1 CONCEPTUAL CONSIDERATIONS

It is important to be familiar with the differences, commonalities, special features, and definitions of the various screens and device types. With this knowledge, you can utilize a device prototype in order to forecast the various and potential contexts of use of a service and the respective device usage of the users being addressed and also to model usage scenarios (see also the discussion of user prototypes and context prototypes in Chapters 3 and 4). You should not just take the screen resolution into consideration but, rather, start with the device itself and utilize its possibilities in a targeted manner.

Holistic user experience

Depending on the situation, the same or similar information is obtained from various screens—in a time-delayed or parallel manner. The reception and consumption of information is fluid (see Section 2.6.2). In order to create and ensure a holistic user experience, all relevant screens and devices as well as service and device touchpoints must be considered. There must be no interruption when you change devices.

Interface, layout, interaction, information offerings, and contents must be harmonious across the devices and logically compatible with each other. They must both be suitable for the native experience and interaction of a platform and/or a device and take into consideration the context of use (see Chapter 4) and the respective potential users and their needs (see user types, beginning with Chapter 3, Section 3.1).

In the article "Shrink to Fit: Designing Scalable User Interfaces," the Punchcut agency provides tips and suggestions about how scalable user interfaces can help to master demanding challenges (Punchcut, 2012a). In the following, we mention and discuss some ideas, questions, and approaches for the use and implementation of scalable interfaces.

Device type and service

What role does a device type play in the respective context of use in a multiscreen ecosystem? Primarily, it is sensible to initially focus on the conception and design of a service and ensure that it contains the essential functionalities (a type of basic version). You can then ponder what additional benefits or additional function the respective device can still contribute or provide on an individual basis. Punchcut calls this method *device personas* (White, 2011). It is important to strategically conceive the service so that it can be upgraded through individual devices with the goal of creating a holistic user experience with individual optimizations.

The basic philosophy should always remain the same, regardless of the device or touchpoint. There is indeed no patented formula for a successful service, particularly because the requirements can change quickly; however, the basic idea and the approach during conception retain their validity.

Overall package more important than details

At the beginning, it is important to not get lost in details during the conception and design work. During this phase, you cannot consider 100% of all platform features, aspect ratios of the screens, screen sizes, and screen resolutions. It is more important to keep the "overall whole" in sight as well as the most important user groups, requirements, and the superordinated service experience. Of course, this can initially be at the expense of quality. However, the details can be optimized later (see Chapter 5, Section 5.16).

When you design interfaces for various screens, you should concentrate on the most important resolutions and screen sizes; use scalable design elements (especially when the layout must be very flexible); take flexible distances into consideration; and, insofar as this is possible, use content and layout elements that, as required, can adjust themselves instead of just scaling endlessly or possibly also senselessly.

Lastly, it is important to examine the interface on the target devices and target platforms for readability, operability, color display, contrast, layout, distances, button size, and interaction. Interactive prototypes and animated transitions are recommendable methods—ideally tested on the relevant devices. It makes a major difference whether you can test and evaluate an interface on the target device or not.

Intention and interaction

Users use various devices in various contexts with various individual requirements. However, often, the same services are used to repeatedly access the same contents. This means that the same task can theoretically be completed with different devices if the same or similar services (e.g., apps) can be used in different ways on the devices. In this regard, the following is important: Depending on the device, its benefit (value) can also change, as can the manner in which how it or the service is used (White, 2011). Various device types are used differently.

2.4.2 DEVICE EXPERIENCE

Other important factors for an appealing cross-device service experience are the user experience with the device itself—the *device experience*—and the relationship between the various devices.

On the one hand, a smartphone or a laptop is just a device. On the other hand it is the (material) thing that provides and uncovers information to a user and evokes emotions and therefore generates an experience with that specific device. "The difference between an experience and a thing is not straightforward. The material and the experiential are two sides of the same coin. The material is the tangible arrangement of technology; the experiences are the meaningful, positive moments created through interacting with this arrangement" (Hassenzahl et al., 2013).

According to Hassenzahl et al. (2013) it is not primarily about, for example, a movie or TV show in high definition, with stereo surround, but about watching it in a meaningful, satisfying way. That means, that it is not just about technical characteristics and device features, but also about the whole situation, attendant persons, the atmosphere—in short—the situation in which an action or an event takes place.

The device in focus

The following are relevant questions: Does the target group fit the devices and vice versa? Which users use which devices? To whom does the device belong? Who else uses it? When and for what is the device used and in what context of use? The device experience must be conformed to the context of use.

Usage purpose of the device

Is the device (e.g., tablet) used only at home? In what environment is the device used? Are alternative or supplemental devices used? Is the device still being used by other persons besides the owner (roommates, partners, children, etc.)? Is the device used for productivity or primarily for entertainment? For what is the device optimally suitable, and for what is it less suitable? All these questions are important to answer in order to correctly assess the respective device in conjunction with the service to be conceived (White, 2011).

Useful methods for examining this include user journey maps and device touchpoints (see Chapter 3, Sections 3.2 and 3.3), examination of the context of use (see Chapter 4), and the use of user prototypes (see Chapter 3, Section 3.5). Moreover, the following question is important: How can the various devices be used and combined? This can also be examined through, among other methods, corresponding design methods such as simulation or role play (see http://www.msxbook.com/en/dmfsim and http://www.msxbook.com/en/dmfrol).

Relationship between the device and the user

The better you can clarify the previous questions, the better the relationship between the user and the device can be assessed—and indeed in both directions: How does the user use his devices? And how can he use the devices? Gabriel White (2011) recommends creating and/or using device personas in order to examine the following questions about the planned service.

How do the various service and device touchpoints look? What happens when the user comes into contact with the device? Do the devices have a certain "personality"? Which one? How is the perspective "from the view of the device"? If you take car models as an example and compare a sports car with a luxury limousine, a classic car, and a family car, it quickly becomes clear what is meant with this approach. You can undertake a similar comparison with smartphones. The manufacturers (e.g., Apple, HTC, and Microsoft), models (e.g., iPhone, Desire, and Lumia), and operating systems (e.g., iOS, Android, and Windows Phone) give each smartphone its own character and allow conclusions to once again be drawn about the owner's/user's personality.

If you correspondingly characterize each device and/or each screen and the potential touchpoints, the relationship between the device and the user can be clarified and its role can be depicted and communicated in a more comprehensible and more understandable manner.

It is very important to define the role of each device type in conjunction with a service. You must know how and when the devices can be used in a different way, when they can be used in a similar way, and when they can be used together—that is, when their combination makes sense. What is the added value for the product or the service if you can use multiple different devices? We describe the fundamental role of the devices and the prototypical users here. For the concrete project, you should be familiar with the features of the relevant device types and device models and the respective users as well as their motives and habits.

Device awareness

Consumers who use various devices expect that the applications and services can be used as seamlessly as possible. They want to be able to complete their tasks on all devices as easily and efficiently as possible. The user experience on the respective device must meet the user's expectations. The better the individual devices can be integrated into the fragmented device environment, the better.

> *Understanding your users, their devices, and how they use them should be every designer's first step.*
>
> Andy Gilliland and Nate Cox (Punchcut)

2.5 DEVICE PROTOTYPES

The device type influences what and how contents and services are used by the users and also accordingly prescribes when which information or which features are sensible and useful.

The various devices and/or screens are used during the day at different times, for various time frames, in various frequencies, and with various intentions.

The same or comparable contents are accordingly used and consumed in various ways on various device types at various times of the day and with various durations. Whereas a usage sequence on a smartphone may last only a few seconds or minutes, a TV may be used for substantially longer periods of time (e.g., multiple hours at a time). This behavior will continue to change due to the continued technical developments (Wroblewski, 2011e). It is a fundamental requirement to know the most important screens as well as to correctly assess and utilize them.

SUPPLEMENTAL INFORMATION AND CURRENT DATA

On the website, we collect current information (e.g., study results, analyses, descriptions, and examples) about the individual device classes (see http://www.msxbook.com/en/devptyp).

In the following sections, the most important and most common device classes are introduced, described, and summarized: smartphone, tablet, laptop (and/or the desktop PC), and Internet-compatible TV (smart TV).[1] The text and information are based on our own knowledge and have been inspired by Cohrs and Rützel (2012), Google et al. (2012), Gugel (2012), Hannemann (2012), Itzkovitch (2012), Menzl (2012), Wroblewski (2015b,c), and Schätzle (2015c). Note that additional devices (classes) and screens are potentially relevant and will be or may become relevant in the future (see Section 2.3).

---

[1] Because smartwatches could possibly play a larger role in multiscreen experience design in the near future, we added a section on this device class.

2.5.1 SMARTPHONE

Strengths: Communication, networking, and availability

With a smartphone, the user can constantly remain in contact. It is the basis of uninterrupted networking and connection and can be used both at home and on the go, including also often in short, successive time frames and when the user must quickly and urgently obtain information. It is more quickly at the ready than any other device (except a smartwatch). The most important tasks, motives, and needs for smartphone usage are communication, networking with other people, and entertainment.

My phone…. I consider it my personal device, my go-to device. It's close to me, if I need that quick, precise feedback.

Typical smartphone user (Google et al., 2012)

Smartphone usage

A large portion of daily media usage is conducted via the smartphone. Smartphones are very personal devices with which you have a stronger connection, so to speak, than with other devices. They are often used to obtain place-related information, to entertain, to communicate, or for smaller tasks—obtaining information quickly, examining status updates, killing time, or social networking (see Chapter 4, Section 4.4.1). The smartphone is quasi-permanently at the ready. The owners of smartphones are potentially always online ("always on") (see Chapter 3, Section 3.5.14 "Smart Natives"). The devices are optimally suited for mobile usage, but they are not just used in-transit ("on the go"). Sometimes, they even serve as a substitute for the desktop computer (see Chapter 4, Section 4.4).

Smartphones are indeed the devices with the shortest usage duration and the shortest usage sessions. Thus, they are used most frequently to start a digital action. This means that the majority of all online activities, such as surfing, searching for information, online shopping, watching online videos, or social networking, are begun on a smartphone and then continued on other devices—presumably because the device with the larger screen is easier to use (Google et al., 2012). Google calls this "sequential device usage." Moreover, smartphones are used most frequently on a parallel basis with other screens (see Chapter 5, Section 5.2).

The context of use depends strongly on the sense and purpose of the application being used. A smartphone can be used both in *lean forward* and in *lean back* mode and naturally also in a stationary situation. It is not well-suited for intensive use.

Optimally, the application addresses the assumed context of use and, in addition to the features that are general and available on all devices, also supplies special customized features. The memo application Evernote, which is used across all platforms and devices, does this quite well and, in the smartphone app, offers the possibility of quickly and simply collecting text memos, photos, or voice memos by intentionally resorting to the device-specific features (e.g., camera and microphone).

Typical features

Smartphones are very small, portable, and can be used everywhere and at any time. Their advantages compared to conventional cell phones or feature phones are as follows:

- They are operated mainly with a touch-based user interface. Hardware buttons and a physical keyboard are not required.
- The average screen size is approximately 3–6 inches. Screens smaller than 3 inches make touch-based interaction more difficult, whereas screens larger than 6 inches make the device more difficult to transport.
- Smartphones contain a web browser with useful CSS and JavaScript support, optimally CSS3 and HTML5.
- Smartphones are used at a data or volume rate price (not just a rate price for voice telephony).

RESOURCE AND INFORMATION

The website Our Mobile Planet (http://think.withgoogle.com/mobileplanet/en) provides much information and knowledge about the theme "mobile" (smartphone, device usage, user, and context of use). The global smartphone study was conducted by Google in cooperation with Ipsos and the Mobile Marketing Association in order to learn more about the dissemination and use of smartphones in more than 40 countries. Additional information is available via http://msxbook.com/en/smartphone and in Chapter 4 (Section 4.4) and Chapter 5 (Section 5.1).

2.5.2 TABLET

Strengths: entertainment and relaxation
The tablet is used primarily as an entertainment device. Although it is a mobile device, it is primarily used at home in rather loose time frames in a relaxed and comfortable atmosphere. The most important motives and needs for tablet usage are entertainment and communication.

When I need to be more in depth, that's when I start using my tablet. The other part of it is where I disconnect from my work life and kind of go into where I want to be at the moment.... I'm totally removed from today's reality. I can't get a phone call, I don't check my e-mail—it's my dream world.
Typical tablet user (Google et al., 2012)

Tablet usage

The daily media usage is less frequent than with a smartphone. A tablet is often used in a targeted manner and as a pastime—primarily for entertainment, general media consumption (films, videos, photos, etc.), reading books, surfing the web, or to retrieve e-mails. Additional typical activities that are begun on a tablet are online shopping, watching online videos, and planning holidays and trips. Naturally, articles are also searched for or read on the smartphone, but as soon as a tablet becomes available or it makes sense in a situation (e.g., on a longer train trip or at home on the sofa), the tablet is most often used.

Tablets are used in situations, environments, and locations in which a keyboard or a mouse is either disruptive or not required (e.g., in addition to the previously mentioned activities, also watching TV in bed or while standing). They are lighter and more transportable than laptops and are preferred at home (in a stationary situation) and may be used for relatively long periods throughout the day. The tablet is used primarily in the lean back rather than the lean forward mode. In contrast to smartphones, tablets are "shared devices" that are frequently used by multiple persons and, based on the usage purpose, represent an alternative to the desktop computer or laptop.

Because the screen on a tablet is larger than that on a smartphone, the device is better suited for reading, watching films and viewing photos, and writing texts. The tablet is still not regarded as a work device or replacement for the desktop computer. The tablet device class has its justification and constitutes the best option for certain usage purposes. The devices are optimal for media consumption. In a non-desk environment, they can be used substantially more comfortably and conveniently than, for example, a PC on the desktop. With increasing technical developments, corresponding operating systems, interface concepts, and in combination with an external physical keyboard, tablets could perhaps someday supplant desktop computers in some situations. Additional information is available via http://msxbook.com/en/tablet and in Chapter 4 (Section 4.4) and Chapter 5 (Section 5.1).

2.5.3 LAPTOP OR DESKTOP PC

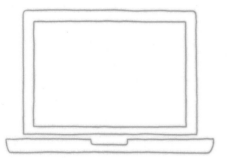

Strengths: Working and obtaining information

Desktop PCs and laptops are used both for work and for recreational purposes. As previously discussed, the classical "computer" is the best device for productivity, completing targeted tasks, and obtaining information in a targeted manner.

And then moving to the laptop, well, for me that's business. That's work. I feel like I've got to be crunching numbers or doing something.

Typical PC user (Google et al., 2012)

PC usage

The percentage of daily media usage on the PC is relatively high. Many people spend much time working on computers, and their work requires a high degree of concentration. The mouse, the keyboard, and the comparatively strong computing power make the desktop computer or the laptop the most efficient and most effective work device—optimal for serious and time-consuming research work. More complex tasks are best executed and completed on PCs.

A PC is primarily used in a stationary environment—this also applies in principle for laptops—and is almost always available at home and at the workstation. A laptop is also suited for mobile situations. The most important motives and needs for PC usage are the thorough search for information, to work productively, and to keep up-to-date. Thus, it is used primarily in the lean forward mode.

Users surf the Internet, obtain information about applications or themes, and (continue to) obtain additional information or interact with the service on another device. In the private sphere, watching online videos and doing complex activities such as vacation planning or monetary transactions are frequently begun on the PC.

When designing cross-device applications and services, the other device classes can be sensibly supplemented, integrated, and combined with the desktop PC (see Section 2.6). Additional information is available via http://msxbook.com/en/laptop and in Chapter 5 (Section 5.7).

2.5.4 SMART TV

This device prototype is an example of all "large screens" (thus also video screens, screen/projector combinations, or other large stationary displays).

Strengths: Entertainment and parallel usage
A TV is well suited for visual information with or without a small amount of text (moving-image contents or photo galleries) and, due to the screen size, also for groups of people. Frequently, another device is used on a parallel basis.

I'm sometimes shopping, sometimes looking for recipes, sometimes typing them up, you know. Sending e-mails, reading, I could do anything on there. It's not often that I just sit and watch TV and do just that.

Typical TV user (Google et al., 2012)

TV usage

Smart TV is a popular and general term for Internet-compatible TVs. The devices are connected to the Internet either through a direct connection or with the aid of a supplemental device (e.g., Apple TV). With them, you can play videos, play games, access the cloud (in the case in which data are saved and available via the Internet), install various apps based on the platform and provider, obtain general information, and surf the Internet.

A TV is used exclusively in stationary situations. As long as there are no sensible lean forward interaction options, the TV will be used predominantly in the lean back mode (for media consumption).

When you design interfaces for TV screens, you must keep in mind that due to the relatively large distance, the elements on the screen appear to be smaller than on the computer screen (see Section 2.3). Based on the concept and requirements and because contents on TV are the most complicated to control, it can make sense to focus on TV and proceed according to the TV-first approach (see Chapter 5, Section 5.1). You can assume that most users in the TV context of use will be in a stationary situation—for example, in the living room—in a comfortable mode (lean back) with the need to relax or entertain themselves (see Chapter 4, Sections 4.2.2 and 4.2.3). The typical use is generally of longer duration (TV series, videos, entertainment shows, movies).

The main input device is often a remote control (the functions of the remote can sometimes be performed by smartphones). A mouse or a keyboard is seldom used or only reluctantly. The interface must be correspondingly easy and understandable. Users must be able to operate the device with their fingers (mainly thumbs) and without looking at the remote control.

On some platforms, smart TVs can be operated and combined with other devices, especially mobile devices (tablet and smartphone). A tablet or a smartphone can be used to provide a program overview in order to obtain additional, supplemental information or as a remote control. The interfaces on the supplemental device should be kept as simple as possible for usage that occurs on a regular basis or for short intervals. In order to use it for a longer broadcast, more complex interfaces are less disruptive (Itzkovitch, 2012; Mischel, 2011). The simultaneous use of a TV and a second device (second screen) has become common. In some cases, the TV is the second screen and a smartphone or tablet is the first screen (see Chapter 5, Sections 5.2 and 5.3).

The TV can serve as a supplement to other devices by using the large screen to display streamed photos, videos, or music from a tablet or smartphone. It is conceivable that the TV and/or generally the large screen will, in the future, serve as the projection area for contents that are retrieved via other (mobile) devices and transferred to the large screen (see Chapter 5, Section 5.4). A web interface and a program guide will be displayed directly on these additional screens. The secondary screen will become the primary screen (Gutjahr, 2013). In this case, the large screen will receive a signal from the mobile device. This will be able to be used simultaneously in order to control the display on the large screen (remote control) (see Chapter 5, Section 5.5).

In the future, TVs and other devices will perhaps be operated only with gestures—that is, by natural user interface (NUI). NUIs enable users to interact with an interface in a natural and direct way by wiping, tapping, pushing, moving, swiping, flipping, touching, or voice control. The input methods are very similar to natural usage. Users can directly interact with content and the interface.

The possibilities with Microsoft Kinect are certainly only a beginning. With technologies and devices that can respond to gestures and movements, the TV experience and the interaction quality of TV will improve. In combination with facial and voice recognition, innovative interface concepts can be realized. Additional information is available via http://msxbook.com/en/smarttv and in Chapter 5 (Sections 5.2–5.4).

2.5.5 SMARTWATCH

It is highly likely that smartwatches will play a major role in multiscreen experience design in the near future. As such, they are included here.

Strengths: Instant and glanceable information
Screens of smartwatches are always visible and always on (because they do not have to be pulled out of a pocket). They are good devices for just-in-time and distraction-free notifications.

I control the TV from the sofa, at the airport I check in, and in the shop I check my bank balance and pay with it. Notifications on the wrist, notes on the smartphone, and elaboration on the PC feels quite convincing to me.
Representative fictitious early adopter of a smartwatch

Smartwatch usage

A smartwatch requires less attention than other devices and enables instant access to software and information. With a smartwatch, people are more connected to other people—no matter if they are physically or just virtually present. People are less distracted by the device. Experiences with wearables are much more compact and as short and fast as possible (Wroblewski, 2015b). Smartwatches (wearables) are always on (preconditioned that they are worn on the wrist) compared to other devices that are not always at one's fingertips (even smartphones do not fulfill this requirement).

Smartwatches serve quite well to display short information, messages, and instant notifications. Therefore, microjoyment plays an important role for this device class. They also serve as a complementary screen to the smartphone. If you want to obtain further information, you can switch to the phone and get more detailed information on that device.

> *On the wrist glanceable, contextually relevant updates and information and lightweight actions in response work well. Initiating tasks happens a lot less often and usually requires more time focusing on the watch than necessary. In other words, actions, not apps seem to make for better wrist-based experiences.*
>
> Wroblewski (2015c)

A smartwatch is not with you, but on you. It is on your wrist, not in your pocket. It is part of your life (as are other potential wearables). Widgets are the interface of the future: small applications, fast and easily accessible, and reduced to the minimum for frequent usage (Schätzle, 2015c).

There are two possible conceptual approaches to design and display information and user interfaces on smartwatches. You can use a visual and hierarchically consistent order that will always remain the same (see Chapter 5, Section 5.8 "Consistency"), or you can offer context-relevant information depending on meta-information about the context of use (see Chapter 4, Section 4.2.4).

It is quite challenging for users to understand user interface, gesture, and interaction patterns on smartwatches because they can differ on diverse operating systems. Many features are available that require knowledge of touch gestures, voice commands, or hardware controls (Wroblewski, 2015c). Gestures are sometimes hidden in these user interfaces and not instantly obvious. Therefore, it is more important than ever to offer coherent interfaces and fluid interaction paradigms across various device classes (see Chapter 5, Sections 5.8, 5.8.1, and 5.9). Additional information is available via http://msxbook.com/en/smartwatch and in Chapter 4 (Section 4.4) and Chapter 5 (Section 5.1).

Designing and developing for wearables on the wrist

An interesting study by Jan Pohlmann (2015) offers helpful tips that you should consider when designing smartwatch applications. It has to be discovered in which scenarios and use cases smartwatches can really offer added value, in which contexts they can be sensibly used, and which functionalities on a watch are useful. Notifications won't be a sufficient use case over the long-term. There are particular characteristics that offer real benefit. A smartwatch can react very well to particular situations and usage contexts in the real world to show relevant information (context relevance). Sensors can be used, for example, for geo-location and heartbeat-measuring.

In contrast to the smartphone, smartwatches can be used hands-free. You can have a look onto the watch screen while both hands are already being used. Sensible use cases can be sporting activities (fitness tracker), traveling (hands-free and context relevant travel information), or cooking (hands-free showing recipe step-by-step).

Some helpful aspects: Focus on just a few things. A typical usage should not take longer than 5 seconds and should require as less interaction as possible. Use large push areas and gestures. Be aware of hardware- and platform-specific guidelines and characteristics (not all devices have the same hardware buttons and gestures available, such as the Digital Crown or Force Touch on the Apple Watch).

Screen size and interaction options on smartwatches are limited. But there are also new options, thanks to novel sensors and output options. There should only be one or two actions available on a screen at once. They have to be easily distinguishable from each other and must have enough spacing in between. You can only apply short and concise texts. Use icons and consider established conventions and usage patterns of the particular platforms. Avoid complex inputs and utilize voice recognition whenever possible. Too many notifications can be annoying. Test usage in a typical usage context, and consider environmental conditions, and when a user needs what kind of information (see Chapter 4, Section 4.2 "Context Relevance"). Does the user have to do other things simultaneously? Consider the actual screen size and device usage by the user.

User experience design for smartwatches and multiscreen ecosystems that incorporate these small wearables are a challenge and chance at the same time.

2.6 MULTISCREEN ECOSYSTEMS

There are various options for combining multiple screens and thus also interfaces, information offerings, and services with each other. You can use various screens at the same time. The information on the main screen and the second screen can supplement each other. Information or contents can be shifted back and forth between the screens or displayed across multiple screens. Moreover, devices can reciprocally control each other. For example, a mobile device can serve as a remote control for another screen.

2.6.1 ECOSYSTEMS

Multiscreen ecosystems consist of certain requirements and environments or a combination of various devices of a single manufacturer or multiple providers and partners in which the different screens are used for the acquisition, creation, or dissemination of information and services.

Ecosystems comprise not only hardware and software—that is, the device and the installed operating system and/or the respective platform. They generally also include information services and digital services. Stephen Elop (CEO of Nokia) believes that they also include, among others, developers, applications and/or apps, e-commerce, advertising, search, social applications, the integration of social networks and community as well as location-based services, and uniform communications and data transmission standards (Stickdorn, 2012).

> *The battle of devices has now become a war of ecosystems.*
>
> **Stephen Elop (CEO, Nokia)**

With the Internet and TV media centers, users can, for example, watch any content on any screen whenever they want. They become independent from the TV schedule and from the TV device, and the content can be watched on each device that is connected to the Internet. Despite this fact, people still watch TV at set times and simultaneously communicate with friends in real time. Thus, the ability to view particular content, on a specific device, and in a certain social context is now part of the TV viewing experience. Depending on the other available devices and other parameters of the specific context of use, each device plays a different role (nurun, 2013).

> *The more we understand that any screen can be the first, second, or even the third screen, the better we will become at enhancing the user experience across that ecosystem.*
>
> **nurun (design and technology consultancy)**

It is important to understand whether and how the different screens interact. This mostly depends on and evolves with the (technological) opportunities and the gradually changing and emerging behavior of the users. How users consume and interact with digital content depends on the devices themselves. There are typical user behavior patterns depending on the capabilities, interaction, and input modes of each device class (see Sections 2.3 and 2.5 and Chapter 4, Section 4.2.3).

2.6.2 ECOSYSTEM AND EXPERIENCE CATEGORIES

Whenever one speaks of multiscreen, it often entails multiple devices being integrated into a product or a service. Michal Levin describes "multiscreen ecosystems" with the aid of three main categories (inspired by Itzkovitch (2012) and Freimark (2015)).

Consistent experience

The user and/or service experience is similar and consistent on all screens. The same content and features are available on multiple screens. Consistent does not mean identical. For example, the Google search offers a comparable "search experience" across all devices and applications. The individual devices do not mandatorily have something to do with each other. Consistent experience is affected by visual consistency and supports service equality. It does not consider context, device relationships, and preferences and connected information. The main features should be available as much as possible on all devices. Content and information architecture should be coherent and look consistently on all relevant screens to facilitate orientation for the user (see Chapter 5, Sections 5.8, 5.8.1, 5.9, and 5.10).

Despite this fact, you should try to offer a consistent experience across all channels. The following online shopping example explains why (Google et al., 2012):

Consumers shop differently across devices, so businesses should tailor the experience to each channel. It's also important to optimize the shopping experience across all devices. For example, consumers need to find what they are looking for quickly and need a streamlined path to conversion.

Complementary experience

Screens are combined, work together, can communicate with each other, and can reciprocally influence each other. They complement each other, can reciprocally control each other (e.g., when you use the smartphone as the remote control for the TV), or exchange information by shifting contents back and forth between two or more screens. Different devices either collaborate as a connected group or control each other.

With Apple TV and AirPlay, videos can, for example, be shifted from the small screen of the iPhone or the iPad to the large TV screen. The devices need each other reciprocally, which means that multiple devices are required for the total experience. Google Chromecast and Airtame are similar features that even work on and across different operating systems and ecosystems (see Chapter 5, Sections 5.2, 5.3, 5.4, 5.5, and 5.7).

Continuous/fluid experience

The creation of a fluid experience can be considered as the supreme discipline in the multiscreen experience design because it represents the most complex challenge and requires very well-founded research and analysis. For a fluid, continuous, and cross-device user experience, a wide array of patterns and approaches as well as all relevant parameters and factors of influence (device, user, and context of use) must be taken into consideration. On a parallel basis, the screens can be used or information can be exchanged between the devices. With a *watch later* or *read later* function, films or articles must, for example, be available or synchronized across devices (compare example "Continuity" in Chapter 5, Section 5.4). Data can be stored via a collective data service (database).

The goal is to always be able to supply the user with context-relevant information—that is, to offer the best possible service at the respective point in time. It is important to know when, where, by whom, and why a service is being used (see Chapter 4, Section 4.3).

The principles of and/or patterns for coherence, fluidity, and adaptability (discussed in Chapter 5) together formulate a type of meta-principle of fluid experience. *Coherence* refers mainly to the interface and the design. Regarding *adaptability*, we recommend approaches that mainly focus on the layout and the content. *Fluidity* focuses on the service and the interaction with the service. These three principles sometimes overlap (see Chapter 5, Sections 5.8 and 5.9).

Single activity flows (e.g., reading a book or watching a movie) can last over a longer period of time and happen in different contexts, but they do not change. The longer such an activity lasts, the more likely it is that it will not be completed in a single engagement. Therefore, the context of use or the device on which the activity will be continued or completed can change. To support such a *sequenced activity*, you need to aim for an appropriate fluid experience and consider user flows and user behavior (see Chapter 3 Section 3.2 and Chapter 4, Section 4.3).

> ## SUGGESTION
>
> Understand your users (see Chapter 3). Analyze the users' daily routine and check when and how they use the service and/or survey the customer journey and how the users interact with the service over a longer period (e.g., holiday planning, flight booking, holiday start, departure, flight, and arrival). Develop use cases or typical activity flows. Based on these findings, focus on the core devices with their capabilities, limitations, and typical usage in mind.

2.7 CONCLUSION AND TIPS

1. **Know your screens.**

   It is helpful and important to know the relevant devices (classes) and their features, differences, and typical use. Find out if there are more devices relevant for your project than the principally discussed in this book.

2. **With the smartphone, you are "always on."**

   The smartphone is the most important device in daily media consumption. It is used most frequently and often serves as an entrance when multiple devices are being used.

3. **Mobile device = mobile context of use.**

   Whenever you use a mobile device, you are in a mobile context of use.

4. **The device must suit the user.**

   The device experience has a decisive influence on the user's user experience with a service. How is the respective device touchpoint defined? Does the device suit the user? Is it even available when he needs it and is it the right option for a task?

5. **Each device model has a personality.**
   The devices can be characterized. What type of device is it? And what type of device and platform will appeal to what users? Device models, platforms (operating systems) and accessories can allow you to draw inferences about the users.

6. **A device is seldom alone.**
   These days, each device is potentially always connected to or with another device. In a multiscreen ecosystem, devices are used sequentially or simultaneously and can be combined and, for example, reciprocally control each other. It is important to be familiar with the combination possibilities.

7. **There are still more screens and devices.**
   The commitment to and focus on the smartphone, tablet, laptop, and TV are certainly correct in the short and medium term. Other "screens," such as large displays, screens used together with projectors, smartwatches, auto-interfaces, and data glasses, will become relevant sooner or later for a multiscreen scenario. On the Internet of things, potentially each object will be connected to the Internet.

8. **Think about the user first!**
   The question is not how an application, a service or website works on any device. Instead you should first ask: Who are your users? Which user goals should the application serve? And then you can ask, which devices are appropriate for these goals and which devices will be used by your users in which context? Focus on the user, then think about relevant devices.

Users and Their Typification

3

The digital society consists of a wide array of people. All have various needs, live and spend their day differently, and frequently use digital devices differently. These persons can be roughly classified into eight typical and representative user types— from predominantly analog media users to totally networked multiscreeners.

3.1 UNDERSTANDING USERS

So that information and applications support the (multiscreen) daily process instead of dominate it, you should take the behavioral patterns of the users into consideration during the design process. Whoever is designing concepts and interfaces for multiple screens should always keep in mind that he or she is designing a service for humans.

By taking into account the fact that a user interacts with multiple devices in different ways for different purposes depending on the context, we can get a better understanding of engagement styles and design optimal user experiences that can adapt to each screen.

nurun (2013)

It is important to know your target group(s) as well as possible. Moreover, it is helpful to understand the users and their environment as well as their motives and needs. Who are the most important users and what devices are they using? What does a typical day in the life of the user look like? How does his or her workflow look? What are the relevant device touchpoints? That is, which device is used when, where, by whom, why, how, how frequently, and for what?

In order to answer these questions, in addition to the prototypical users, we introduce three tools in this chapter:

- The touchpoint matrix supplies comprehensive information about the daily routine of the (potential) users.
- The multiscreen day flow offers a compact overview of the daily routine of a user and his device usage.
- With the emotion maps, the (implicit) motives and needs of the users can be depicted and synchronized with the brand values and/or features of a service. The approach is based on findings from psychology.

3.1.1 DEVICE USAGE

Speaking in a general and sweeping manner, people use (depending on the device availability as well as the goal and purpose of an action) more or less all devices in order to more or less do everything. In the 2012 Google study, a differentiation is made between two multiscreening modes: sequential use and simultaneous use.

Sequential usage

A large number of users use various devices at various times during the day and alternate between them in order to complete a task. Sequential screening is not typical behavior. The activity is often completed within 1 day.

Typical *sequential screening* activities (when the user begins on one screen and continues his activity on another screen) are surfing the Internet, social networking, online shopping, obtaining information/searching, monetary transactions, vacation planning, and watching online videos (see Chapter 5, Sections 5.4 and 5.6).

A shopping activity (and many other activities) is frequently started on the smartphone and is then continued and completed on the laptop or tablet.

People use any platform to do anything.

Giles Colborne (2012)

Simultaneous usage

Comparable with the previously described multiscreen scenario (See Chapter 1, Section 1.2), at least two devices are frequently used. The various activities can be directly related to each other (complementary usage) or not (multitasking) (see Chapter 5, Sections 5.2 and 5.3).

3.1.2 PROTOTYPICAL USERS

In order to simplify the (initial) process of target group definition, it is helpful to work with prototypical users. In Section 3.5, we describe the corresponding user prototypes—representative for the entire population in Germany. The digital society includes all persons from totally networked multiscreeners (see Section 3.5.14) to the digital outsider.

Based on the research findings, you should identify the relevant users, their motives, and especially their media usage in order to gauge the device priority and ultimately to be able to conceive, design, and develop for the relevant devices. Moreover, with the aid of user prototypes, the recruitment of test persons can be limited.

Digital society

The term goes back to the study of Initiative D21 (2010). The study is particularly well-suited for our thematic area due to the focuses on media usage, media affinity, and competence in working with digital devices. Among others, it was sponsored by the German Ministry of Economics and Technology, by Wolters Kluwer, TNS Infratest, and DIE ZEIT. Initiative D21 e.V. is a nonprofit association located in Berlin.

In the study, the digital infrastructure and the digital user behavior of the Germans are analyzed. Despite the naturally existing differences, we assume that the study can be considered to be representative for the majority of digital users in other countries and regions as well with regards to the content-related focus. The identified groups are comparable, but can be clearly delimited with regards to the digital potential as well as their attitudes and usage.

Over the course of the years, the six same digital society types have emerged. This shows that the described user types—from the digital outsider to the digital Avantgarde—are stable and can be replicated well. Thus, we have used them as the basis and for the definition and classification of the User Prototypes (see Section 3.5).

3.2 DAILY ROUTINE

There are various options for data collection for depicting and communicating the typical daily routine of a potential user.

3.2.1 TOUCHPOINT MATRIX

The *touchpoint matrix* is a very detailed variant of a user journey map (also called a customer journey map) that depicts a user's daily routine with the focus on device usage, user needs and context of use. In it, the daily interaction or the user experience with a service (service experience) and the media usage are visualized and described. A touchpoint is any kind of contact with a service in which information is retrieved and displayed (on a screen) (see Chapter 1, Section 1.2). The touchpoint matrix helps to design a holistic service experience, and therefore encompasses and touches on a service design approach. User journey maps do not necessarily describe a daily routine and refer to exact 24 hours of a day. They often represent a user's journey and different touchpoints throughout a user activity or task. Such a journey can last longer than a day.

In a tabular overview, the map shows typical activities, places and environments, the most likely needs, the media and devices (and screens) used, and the device touchpoints during the course of a day. The matrix is offered in order to conduct a comprehensive survey and analysis of users and to become familiar with the daily routines of the user prototypes. A complete matrix is depicted in an exemplary manner for the user prototype Larry Newton (digital avant-garde) beginning in Section 3.5.9. Additional information can be obtained from the formulated, compact daily routine in text form. The creation is more time-consuming and the information is more comprehensive than with the *multiscreen day flow* (see Section 3.2.2).

Blank forms and examples of the touchpoint matrix can be downloaded from the website at http://www.msxbook.com/en/tpmtrx.

Obtaining knowledge

The examination of the daily routine supplies important knowledge about the user. Often, it depends on the context of use and which device you will have during a certain time frame. What type of task or activity do you have to or want to do? What goal do you want to realize? What is your motivation for doing something? How much time do you have or need for it? How is your mental mood and how do you feel? Where are you located? Are other persons present? What is the technical environment like?

Eight time frames

We have broken down the daily routine into eight time frames from "waking up" to "going to sleep." These time frames are used in the *touchpoint* matrix and in the *multiscreen day flow*:

- Waking up
- Early in the morning
- Mid-morning
- Mid-day
- Afternoon
- Early evening
- Late evening
- Going to sleep

Note that there are tasks that are not completed in one time frame. Activities can overlap time frames and be continued in another one and potentially with another or an additional device (see Chapter 2, Section 2.6.2).

	Time frame (8 per day)
Activity	What does the user concretely do in that time frame?
Location	E.g., living room, kitchen, garden, park, office, bus, pub
Environment	Private, semipublic environment, public environment, on the go (see Chapter 4)
Needs	See motives, wishes/desires and values in the Emotion Map
Channel	Internet, radio, print, television
Device Touchpoint	☐ ☐ ▭ ▭

Touchpoint matrix
In the matrix, for each of the eight time frames, the relevant information has been broken down in tabular form—for example, the activity, place, and environment and the devices used. For more in this regard, see user prototype Larry Newton (Sections 3.5.9 and/or 3.5.11).

TIP

Similar methods for analyzing and depicting user's daily routines or other flows within a product or service are storyboards, use cases, experience maps, flow diagrams, alignment diagrams (Kalbach, 2011), mental models (Young, 2008), and the customer journey canvas from "This Is Service Design Thinking" (Schneider and Stickdorn, 2011). To analyze a distinct user flow with a specific service that lasts longer than a day and concentrates just on the touchpoints with that service, a user journey map, or any of these methods are helpful tools. Various methods are purposeful (e.g., camera journal, observation, or interviews) for collecting the required (preliminary) information. A collection of the useful methods can be found at http://www.designmethodenfinder.de.

Context drives device choice: Today consumers own multiple devices and move seamlessly between them throughout the day.

Google (2012)

3.2.2 MULTISCREEN DAY FLOW

The *multiscreen day flow* is a very compact, simplified depiction of a user journey map and constitutes only the essential information. The circular illustration in the form of an infinite loop flow diagram can be combined with the touchpoint matrix (see Section 3.2.1). It visualizes the daily routine based on the most important information: user, time frame, and device usage (see the discussion of user prototype Larry Newton in Section 3.5.9).

The day flow chart provides a compact overview of a user's daily routine and the device usage in the individual time frames, and it is offered when you primarily would like to find out which device a user will use and when. When there is little time, things must happen quickly, or easy-to-collect information is requested, the day flow is a useful tool.

People are nearly always online; they switch between different screens, but a smartwatch is always on the wrist and information is reachable at a glance (Wroblewski, 2015d). Please consider that if potential users wear and use smartwatches, those screens will almost always on and with the users during the entire day.

A blank form of the multiscreen day flow can be downloaded as a spreadsheet on the website. The day flows for the individual user prototypes are also available there (see http://www.msxbook.com/en/msxdfw).

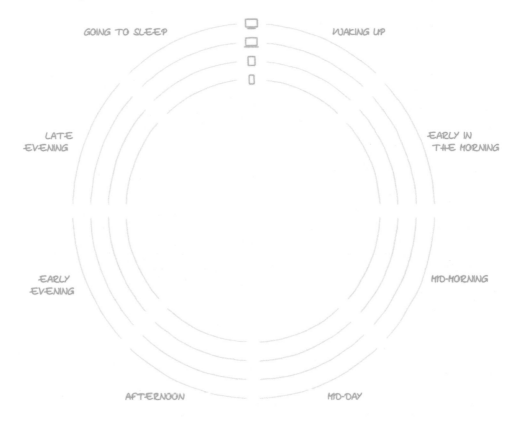

Multiscreen day flow (blank)

On the blank form, you can enter information regarding the eight time frames (e.g., the precise time of day), regarding the device usage and the user. In the time frames in which the respective device is being used, the line will be drawn thicker. See a filled-out multiscreen dayflow in the example of Larry Newton (Section 3.5.12).

HINT

Print the blank forms on transparent paper, mark the relevant lines on the day flow for each user or persona, and lay all the papers on top of each other to relatively easily determine which time frames and devices are most important to the different personas or user types.

3.3 MOTIVES AND NEEDS

In the *user-centered design* the user is in the forefront. It is a matter of finding out the motives, goals, and needs of the potential users, and the limitations of a product or service and taking them into consideration during the conception and design work. Focus on the users. Only when you know them you should think about devices they use.

While taking the relevant devices and the context of use into consideration, you should anticipate the motives as best as possible in order to be able to adapt and adjust the interface and the application to them. It is important to ponder when, how, where, and why a service could be used with a device. Then the service experience can be designed as best as possible and, as required, influenced.

»*What we are creating is less a product than a context for experience.*«

Bill Buxton (Microsoft Research)

Psychology and user experience design

When it concerns the users' motives and needs, the user experience plays a central role. *User experience design* also always has something to do with psychology and emotion. It concerns not only the functionality and the usability of a product—thus to attain certain goals effectively, efficiently, and satisfactorily (see definition in accordance with DIN ISO 9241-11), but rather also the experience and discovery as well as the fulfillment of human needs during the usage.

Building blocks of a good user experience

Functionality and usability are the prerequisites for pleasure. In order to experience pleasure, however, functionality and usability are still not enough. Thus, the goal of the methods subsequently introduced is to attain a positive user experience with a user-centered and comprehensive approach (Fischbein, 2010). Pleasure, emotion, psychology, and the user experience are closely related to each other (see Chapter 5, Sections 5.15, 5.12, 5.14, and 5.13).

Marc Hassenzahl and colleagues put the question if it is not possible "to 'design for happiness' by enriching people's everyday lives with positive experiences through artifact-mediated activities." They argue that it is actually the fulfillment (or frustration) of psychological needs that renders an experience positive (or negative) and personally significant, that is, meaningful (Hassenzahl et al., 2013).

An experience (e.g., an event, concretely attending a concert with friends) can be described and understood as a pattern with a general structure that "suggests three phases (i.e., anticipation, event, cooling-off), important time points (i.e., the appointment, the beginning of the event), and some general rules or norms (i.e., don't interact too much during the event, talk about the event in the cooling-off phase, don't miss a part). [...] When a really close relationship was felt, the related experiences may have featured most of the elements mentioned in this pattern (i.e., phases, time points, norms)" (Hassenzahl et al., 2013).

3.3.1 EMOTION MAP

The life motives and needs of people are very different. Accordingly, different are also the motives and needs of the user prototypes (see Section 3.5) which are representative for the entire digital society. We show this based upon emotion maps which are, in turn, based upon different psychological approaches and motives and personality models, such as, the Limbic Map (Häusel, 2011), Be-Goals (Hassenzahl, 2010 and Sheldon et al., 2001, via Fischbein, 2010), 16 basic desires according to Steven Reiss (Reiss Profile Europe B.V., n.d.), 25 Positive Emotions in Human-Product Interactions (Desmet, 2012), the Emotion Grid from Mareike Roth and Oliver Saiz (Roth/Saiz, 2014), or the model of the reward profile mentioned and explained in the German book "Was Marken erfolgreich macht" (Scheier/Held, 2007). These link current findings from brain research and psychology. The emotion maps are based upon the information regarding needs in the tabular daily routines (see Sections 3.2.1 and 3.5.11) of the respective user prototypes which are described in the Sections 3.4 and 3.5.

The **Emotion Map** is a self-interpretation and adaption of different scientific sources. I am not a neuroscientist and I do not pretend to be so. That map might not be exact under scientific considerations. It shall help to think about motives and needs of human factors of your users, help to understand, to evaluate, and to visualize them under an emotional point of view. You can and shall also try to concern other psychological approaches and have a look at, for example, the Limbic Map (Häusel, 2007), Be-Goals (Hassenzahl, 2010 and Sheldon et al., 2001, via Fischbein, 2010), Reiss profiles (Reiss Profile Europe B.V., n.d.), the Emotion Grid (Roth/Saiz, 2014), the model of Scheier/Held (Scheier/Held, 2007), or other neuroscientific and neuropsychological findings.

I combined the mentioned scientific approaches, arranged the different motives and emotions (Limbic and Emotion Grid), psychological needs (Be-Goals), 16 basic desires (Reiss), and basic rewards (Scheier/Held, see also Section 5.13) in a circle (based on Roth/Saiz and Scheier/Held, see Section 5.15, "Motives and Needs (or Rewards and Values)"), and added relevant motives that are—in my point of view and based on my estimation—important concerning information consumption and interaction on and with different screens.

These models are all similar in a way. In the end it's just about the question which of the main rewards, motives, and need-drivers (based on the "Zürcher Model of Social Motivation") are important to a human being or to a specific user or persona prototype (in the context of interaction and user experience design to user). Other terms could be applied as well. You could even only use the Be-Goals or the "Positive Emotional Granularity Cards" to classify users. The example with the beer commercials in Chapter 5.15 explains basic human reward profiles that are differently addressed with different core messages of different brands. Or just contact the award-winning design office hochE from Mareike Roth and Oliver Saiz and evaluate how to apply their Emotion Grid.

If you are able to classify and describe your users or target group on an emotional level by knowing their main motives and goals, you probably already know how you have to promote and communicate your product accordingly. You know what motives and values your product and your UI have to deliver and stand for to meet your users' needs. And you can also anticipate how to tell the story of your service (Storytelling, see Section 5.14).

I'd be happy to start a discussion on that idea that brings that aspect of user experience forward and generates methods and tools to work on that topic.

Neuropsychology: different scientific approaches and findings

1. Dr. Christian Scheier and Dirk Held explain implicit rewards for the brain in their book "Was Marken erfolgreich macht" (Scheier/Held, 2007) based on the "Zürcher Model of Social Motivation," with three fundamental basic rewards: Security, Autonomy, and Excitement. These three reward areas are often called motives. They recommend using these three basic rewards together with their hybrid types for marketing practices (I mean that they are also relevant and interesting when you have to think about and design for humans). These six basic rewards and different motives (in brackets) are explained by Phil Barden (2013) as follows: Adventure (Adventure, Courage, Thrill), Autonomy (Success, Recognition, Status), Discipline (Discipline, Control, Orderliness), Security (Security, Warmth, Protection), Enjoyment (Pleasure, Relief, Carefree), and Excitement (Zest for life, Inspiration, Vitality).

2. The model *Limbic*® was developed by the Gruppe Nymphenburg under the supervision of Dr Hans-Georg Häusel (Häusel, 2011). It provides a well-founded basis for the better understanding of the motives and needs of humans. The emotion, motive, and personality model links current findings from brain research and psychology. The term goes back to the limbic system, a functional unit of the brain, which handles emotions and creates instinctive behaviors. The findings from (neuro-)psychology have already been frequently utilized in (neuro-)marketing and are also helpful in user experience design.

   The success of a product depends largely on whether it fits the users' needs. On the "Limbic Map", brands, products, and people are shown (with their motives and needs) and examined for congruency. Thus, it can examine whether the values, the aura, or the image of a product, an application or a service will fit the motives and wishes of the potential users or target group.

3. Mareike Roth and Oliver Saiz developed together with other experts in the fields of psychology, neuromarketing, and behavior research the Emotion Grid that shows various emotions and motives in a comb chart around the three axes fascination, urge, and harmony and the areas sensuousness, activity, and countenance (Roth/Saiz, 2014). It's a similar underlying approach and comparable to the Limbic Map and the orientation of the motives in the chart of Scheier and Held.

4. With the "Be-Goals" from Hassenzahl and Burmester, the users and the user types can be assessed upon the psychological level based upon needs and motives. They address why it is that people do something and accordingly also refer to their motivation (more in this regard in Fischbein, 2010). In his definition, Marc Hassenzahl uses similar terms such as Hans-Georg Häusel. Important psychological needs are accordingly, among others, autonomy and independence, competence, connectedness, self-worth, security, order, money and luxury, influence and popularity, health and physical fitness, self-actualization as well as joy, pleasure, and stimulation (according to Hassenzahl, 2010 and Sheldon et al., 2001, via Fischbein, 2010).

   In his interesting paper "Designing Moments of Meaning and Pleasure," Hassenzahl and his colleagues outline the application of Experience Design, an approach which places pleasurable and meaningful moments at the center of all design efforts. They suggest psychological needs as a way to understand and categorize experiences, and "experience patterns" as a tool to distill the "essence" of an experience for inscribing it into artifacts (Hassenzahl et al., 2013) and narrowed the set of various needs to a relevant set of six: autonomy, competence, relatedness, popularity, stimulation, and security. Hassenzahl and his team of researchers also developed seven need cards (Hassenzahl, 2013) based on these findings with an additional need (meaning) that describe these (now seven) psychological needs. The card-set is comparable to the tool developed by Yoon/Jeong (2013, see below). The cards provide both orientation and inspiration for the design of interactive products.

5. Dr Steven Reiss presented his theory of the 16 basic desires in the mid-90s. These fundamental psychological impulses define an adult's personality; these aspects of motivation capture what any individual is striving for. The 16 basic needs according to Steven Reiss (Reiss Profile Europe B.V., n.d.) are: Power, Independence, Curiosity, Acceptance, Order, Saving, Honor, Idealism, Social Contact, Family, Status, Vengeance, Romance, Eating, Physical Activity, and Tranquility.

6. According to Pieter Desmets findings people can experience at least 25 different positive emotions in response to a product or a service (Desmet, 2012). With the "Positive Emotional Granularity Cards," Jay Yoon and Nuri Jeong developed a tool to facilitate an understanding of nuances in these 25 different positive emotions. The tool is also based on the findings of Yoon/Desmet/Pohlmeyer (2013) and consists of 25 cards that incorporate definitions of emotion labels, eliciting conditions, and visuals of expressive behavioral manifestations.

   The card-set can be used in design research and design practice as a tool for communication and as a source of inspiration. For instance, designers are enabled to communicate their design intentions in terms of emotional impact, and end-users are enabled to report the distinctiveness of emotional experiences. Furthermore, divergent thinking in design conceptualization can be facilitated by exploring the relationship between varied eliciting conditions of positive emotions and product features (via Yoon/Jeong, 2013). The 25 emotion types are categorized into generic terms, for example, inter alia empathy, affection, enjoyment, assurance, interest, and gratification. References: Yoon/Desmet/Pohlmeyer (2013), Desmet (2012), and Yoon/Pohlmeyer/Desmet (2014). For more information visit http://www.diopd.org.

I combined these scientific approaches, arranged the different motives in a circle (based on Scheier/Held, 2007) and added relevant motives that are—in my point of view—important concerning information consumption and interaction on and with different screens.

MSX EMOTION MAP v2.0

Emotion Map with motives and human needs

The Emotion Map classifies basic human needs (or values) to the six most important need-drivers. The six need-drivers are shown in the circle around the map. The motives and needs are arranged within the circle depending on to which need-driver each one is associated with. The Emotion Map is an own illustration based upon and inspired by the illustration "reward profiles of beer brands" Scheier/Held (2007) and the Emotion Grid (Roth/Saiz, 2014). The terms are inspired by and based upon the sources of the different scientific approaches and findings mentioned in this section and the blue box, with some added own terms. (See also Section 5.15, "Motives and Needs (or Rewards and Values)".) You can see an applied specific Emotion Map in the example of Larry Newton (Section 3.5.9).

Need-driver

The various need-drivers are defined by means of the users' motives, values, and wishes. The needs and motives in the descriptions of the user prototypes (that are also used and shown in the Touchpoint Matrix) are based on the Emotion Map. A need generally refers to the wish or the demand for something. Motives and needs (as well as rewards) motivate people to do something and/or are the fundamental motivation for an action or a behavior. (See also Chapter 5, Section 5.13, where "Motivating Game Mechanics" are explained.)

3.3.2 APPLICATION OF THE EMOTION MAP

The Emotion Map in combination with the Touchpoint Matrix (see Section 3.2) shall help to discover, identify, and focus on important basic needs and motives of your users to conceptualize and design a meaningful and user-focused experience of your service, application, etc.

How to apply the emotion map?

Combine the Touchpoint Matrix (see Section 3.2.1) with the Emotion Map and the motives used in the Emotion Map. Evaluate if a motive (of the Emotion Map) is relevant in a time frame. The more often a motive appears in one of the eight time frames of a day the more relevant it likely is for the user prototype. Therefore these terms are emphasized in the Emotion Map.

I used three levels of typographic differentiation for one appearance, two to four appearances, and more than four appearances of the Emotion Map motives in the Touchpoint Matrix. All of them are highlighted in blue; the unused terms are kept in gray with small font size. You can see how it is executed in the Emotion Map of Larry Newton (see Section 3.5.13). Compare it with the motives in the Touchpoint Matrix of Larry Newton (see Section 3.5.11). *You can also just mark each motive with strokes in the map and use different colors to emphasize the importance and relevance.*

After having applied the motives of the Touchpoint Matrix with and emphasized in the Emotion Map you get a tendency of the most relevant needs of a user and thus how he can be motivated. It is about fulfilling individual needs. Security, for example, relies on rituals. Therefore, you should probably try to consider that when designing an application for that kind of user, with a user interface concept that changes as seldom as possible. If excitement is an important basic need for a user, he probably values new things and change and therefore can be motivated with a more explorative user interface approach. You get it.

Understanding, determining, and facilitating

With the "Positive Emotional Granularity Cards," Yoon/Jeong (2013) explains different techniques and parts in which the card-set can be applied. That is also valid for the Emotion Maps. You can either use it to understand nuances in emotions and motives, determine emotional intention of a product, or facilitate creativity in design conceptualization.

Understanding: First get an overview of nuances. Reflect on how different motives and emotions are related with one another and also reflect on the moments in which you had experienced these emotions in relation to products. Repeat that with all relevant needs, motives, and emotions. Then identify (expected and focused) user emotions in relation to a product and discuss how they can be addressed and fulfilled.

Determining: Identify potential activities and user goals in a specific design and context of use that might be relevant before, while, and after using a product and select key activities that can be supported through designs. Specify the key motives and emotions that you want to design for in relation to the chosen key activities and user goals (see Section 3.2.1). Try to evoke these emotions and fulfill their needs while taking a specific action.

Facilitating: Clarify the product, service, use case, or context to design for. Identify the kind of (eliciting) conditions that need to be addressed to fulfill (the most relevant) user needs and to evoke specific emotions. Start generating ideas. Repeat that for all relevant users' needs and motives and finally try to find out synergies and overlaps that could be focused on.

These techniques are based on the description of Yoon/Jeong (2013), which also offers a detailed explanation.

As you see there are different approaches that are quite similar in a way. They are combinable. Depending on project and goal they are differentially helpful to solve various challenges. All methods can also be combined with and adapted to other design methods (see www.desginmethodenfinder.de, a German web-based collection of various design methods).

3.4 TYPIFICATION AND SEGMENTATION

Because it can be difficult to analyze each individual potential user in detail, it is beneficial to group people together with similar needs, features, and life circumstances. The data collection for this is time-consuming. The allocation or definition of representative user types can simplify the user-centered design process because you can work in this case without any preliminary work directly with these representative categorizations.

As the basis for the typification and the creation of user prototypes (see Section 3.5), we have used the user groups from the study "D21–The Digital Society" (D21–Die Digitale Gesellschaft) (Initiative D21, 2010a). The annual study is a comprehensive empirical stock-taking of the state of the German society in the information age. Despite this regional evaluation, the classification is also usable for international purposes. The approach and focus of the study fit very well with the theme of multiscreen and therefore is representative for the whole digital society.

In the segmentation, the society is broken down into clearly delimitable user groups. The identified groups have manifested themselves over several years and are comparable but nonetheless relatively well-delimitable with regard to their digital potential as well as their attitude and usage. The groups are as follows:

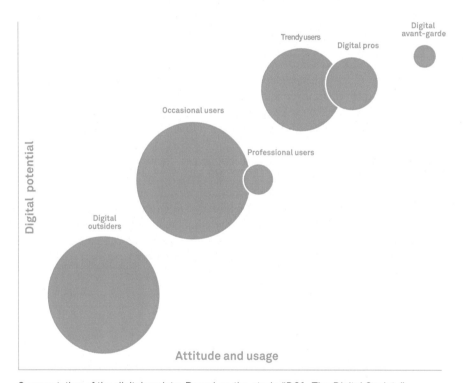

Segmentation of the digital society: Based on the study "D21–The Digital Society" (D21–Die Digitale Gesellschaft) (Initiative D21, 2010a) the digital society can be segmented into six clearly delimitable user groups. Its percentage distribution is varying.

Type 1: Digital outsiders
Average age of 65 years
Primarily female
Primarily not gainfully employed
Primarily minimal formal education levels
Below average income

Type 2: Occasional users
Average age of 45 years
Slightly more females than males
Minimal percentage of gainfully employed persons (approximately half)
Primarily simple/medium formal education levels
Average income

Type 3: Professional users
Average age of 45 years
Higher percentage of women (more than half)
Higher percentage of gainfully employed persons (75%)
Mainly simple/medium formal education levels
Above average income

Type 4: Trend users
Average age of 37 years
Higher percentage of men
More job-related activities
Medium formal education levels
Slightly above average income

Type 5: Digital pros
Average age of 38 years
Primarily male
Highest percentage of gainfully employed persons
High formal education levels
Highest average income

Type 6: Digital avant-garde
Average age of 34 years
Higher percentage of men
Primarily gainfully employed persons
High formal education levels
Tend to have above average income

The user prototypes that we describe next are based on the user groups of the digital society that are mentioned here.

3.5 USER PROTOTYPES

Because people form the focus of digital ecosystems, successful information offerings and services must address their behaviors and needs.

Personas

With the persona method, you model various representative users in the form of prototypical fictitious personalities. The method is helpful for developing a joint understanding of potential users, for obtaining insight into the user group, and for taking the users' perspective into consideration when making design-related decisions. By so doing, misunderstandings can be avoided and requirements can be more easily prioritized.

Personas are prototypical descriptions of users. They convey the essential characteristics of the target group—such as demographic and biographical information, needs, preferences, and requirements—and help to assess how the described person would use a service (app, application, website, product, etc.). You can place yourself in the user's shoes better and, by so doing, develop user-centered, requirements-appropriate products and applications (Design Methods Finder, n.d.-a; see also Cooper et al., 2007).

Real and realistic personas

Personas are essentially a communications resource during the analytical and conception phase. When creating personas, you can differentiate between two approaches: *real personas* (according to Cooper, 2004) and *realistic personas* (according to Norman, 2004). Real personas are based on representative market research data and attempt to convey an image of the target group that is as precise as possible. Realistic personas are usually based on empirical values and assumptions and the idea that sufficient knowledge of the respective target group is available. As a rule, they are created through workshops in which the knowledge about the users is compiled from the perspective of sales, marketing, development, and service (Schubert, 2012).

The descriptions of the "realistic personas" are created in joint cooperation between the project participants. In so doing, the existing knowledge about the actual users can be utilized. Costs and time expenditures are normally lower than those of the data-oriented approach. Regardless of this, with many projects, there is often not sufficient time or budget available for modeling personas. Particularly in these cases, the prefabricated representative personas are helpful.

User prototypes (of the digital society)

In order to facilitate the project start, we describe and illustrate the potential users in the digital society. These *user prototypes* are representative (for the entire population in Germany) and based on the user types in the study "D21–The Digitale Society" (Initiative D21, 2011). Admittedly, the segmentation and description is slightly western European oriented, but it comprises all users from digital outsiders to completely connected digital pro users. There are so many different types of people throughout the world that it is almost impossible to have representative user types from all regions of the world. If necessary, create your own prototypical users (based on the provided user prototypes in this book) and use the correct and appropriate methods. We offer work material such as user prototypes and a blank form to build personas on our website (see http://www.msxbook.com/en/usptyp and http://www.msxbook.com/en/persbl).

Regarding the user prototypes, the focus is generally on the technology, the media affinity, the device usage, the context of use, and the user's needs. Based on the project, various or all aspects are relevant. For each user type, there is a description in text form. The types are as follows:

- Digital outsiders
- Occasional users (two subgroups)
- Professional users
- Trend users (two subgroups)
- Digital pros
- Digital avant-garde

In the groups *occasional users* and *trend users*, there are respectively two significant groups that we have separately created. With the occasional users, there are the best agers (retirees, more than 60 years old, silver surfers) and the less tech-savvy. Trend users comprise young persons between age 15 years and the early 20s and gainfully employed, usually male adults who are age 30 years or older.

We have concentrated on the core points of the study (see Section 3.4). Naturally, there are, for example, also occasional users who are male, have a high formal education level, and have an above average income. Each person will find that he is in multiple user groups. The depictions and descriptions are exemplary and should not be regarded as being absolute.

Our user prototypes contain text descriptions in various categories—for example, technology, media usage, profession, income, family, friends, free time, housing, lifestyle, and standard of living. On a supplemental basis, the exemplary and tabular daily routines (broken down into eight time frames) and motive and need maps (emotion map) serve to visually summarize the general needs and motives of the respective type from the touchpoint matrix.

The user prototypes are briefly introduced next. A complete depiction of the most progressive user representatives in the digital society follows directly thereafter. The persona *digital avant-garde* describes a typical multiscreener (see Section 3.5.14) who is almost always online and uses all devices very frequently. You can find detailed and complete descriptions of all prototypes on the online platform (http://www.msxbook.com/en).

Use of the user prototypes

The user prototypes serve as a communications resource with the project participants and facilitate the project start. With the prototypes, fundamental decisions can be made.

The potential users of the service that is to be created (website, app, software, etc.) can be classified into the user prototypes. In most cases, there is overlap. Tendentially, two or three prototype descriptions fit the respective target user groups.

Personas are no cure-all. Project managers and the project team must accept the methods, recognize their added value, and in principle think and act in a user-oriented manner. If the method has been well integrated into the work process, design-related decisions are made jointly and not just at the upper hierarchical levels, and the personas are described practically and clearly, use of the method is in any case worthwhile. In the multiscreen experience design and the approach described in this book, the user prototypes take on a central role.

The prototypes are just a start and not patented formulas. Optimally, they should be adapted to your own target group, the conditions, and the respective project requirements, and they should be used in combination with the device prototypes (see Chapter 2, Section 2.5) and the context of use and/or the context prototypes (see Chapter 4, Section 4.5).

In principle, there are three options for acting in a user-oriented manner:

- Information about the (potential) users is already available.
- No information is available. Personas are created on your own.
- You use (at least initially) the user prototypes presented here.

ALTERNATIVES AND SUPPLEMENTAL SOURCES

As supplemental sources for a typification, the Sinus milieus (for details, see Design Methods Finder, n.d.-b) or "Medien Nutzer Typologie" (media user typology) 2.0 (Oehmichen, 2008) are used. A similar approach for creating user prototypes is the use of "meta-personas" (Krökel et al., 2012). The classification is based on the Sinus milieus (DIVSI, 2012).

We recommend examining the life motives and the user needs with motive and need maps (see Section 3.3.1), using user journey maps and questionnaires, and applying other research methods. The better you know the potential users, the better you can adapt a service to their needs and requirements.

On the website, we provide different models and work materials, including touch-point matrix, multiscreen day flow, emotion map, (user) prototypes, and a blank form to build personas (see http://www.msxbook.com/en).

3.5.1 OVERVIEW OF USER PROTOTYPES

As an overview, here we show all of the user prototypes. Additional details can be found on the website at http://www.msxbook.com/en/usptyp.

Margaret Brown
Digital Outsider
Housewife, Retiree (Age 69 Years)

Barbara Stewart
Occasional User (Best Ager)
Housewife, Retiree (Age 61 Years)

Kelly Adams
Occasional User
Teacher/Temp (Age 47 Years)

Melissa Anderson
Professional User
Assistant to the Executive Management
(Age 43 Years)

Andrew Collins
Trend User (Young)
Pupil/High School Graduate (Age 20 Years)

Mark Hudson
Trend User (Gainfully Employed)
Event Manager/Event Agency (Age 35 Years)

Robert Sullivan
Digital Pros
IT Entrepreneur (Age 39 Years)

Larry Newton
Digital Avant-Garde
Screen Designer/Clerk (Age 32 Years)

3.5.2 MARGARET BROWN

Digital outsider

69 years old, widow
Four grown children and six grandchildren

Housewife, retiree (trained salesperson)

"I don't want to deal with computers anymore at my age. I do not understand them anyways. I am already happy if I can operate my cell phone."

A typical day begins at 6:30 a.m. and ends at approximately 10 p.m. Margaret stays at home a lot, attends to her garden, and is happy when her family comes to visit. She owns no smartphone (only a feature phone) and uses exclusively a TV that is not connected to the Internet. She maintains contact with like-minded persons nearby.

Margaret has only a few device touchpoints. Her life's motives and needs are mainly in the areas of excitement and harmony. Margaret is curious and places special value on family, entertainment, and tradition. She interacts almost exclusively in her private environment.

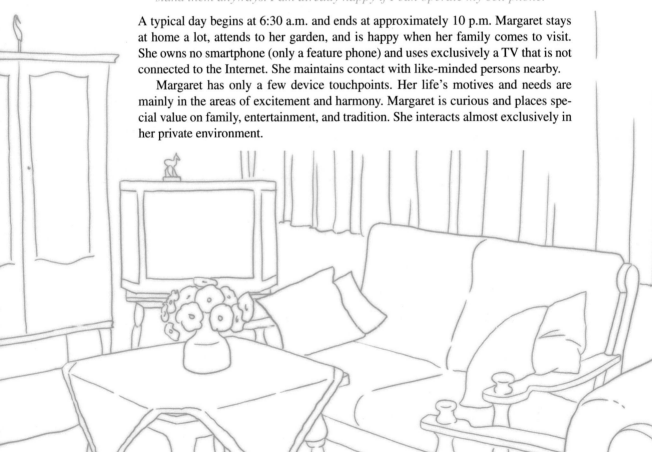

3.5.3 BARBARA STEWART

Occasional user (best ager)

61 years old, married
Two adult children and three grandchildren

Housewife, retiree (trained florist)

"Since I have a PC with an Internet connection, I can comfortably do many things from home. I use my cell phone only for talking on the telephone."

Barbara's typical day begins at 7:30 a.m. and ends before midnight. She and her husband stay at home the majority of the time and pursue their hobbies there. She attends to her housework, likes to watch TV, and occasionally surfs the Internet. Healthy nutrition and her physical appearance are important to her.

Barbara has no smartphone (only a feature phone). She uses a TV and a laptop, and overall she has rather few device touchpoints. Her life's motives are mainly enjoyment, harmony, and discipline. Barbara places value on family and varied types of relaxation. She interacts primarily in her private environment.

3.5.4 KELLY ADAMS

Occasional user (not very tech savvy)

47 years old, married, two children

Teacher/temp
Realschule (secondary school) diploma and
vocational training

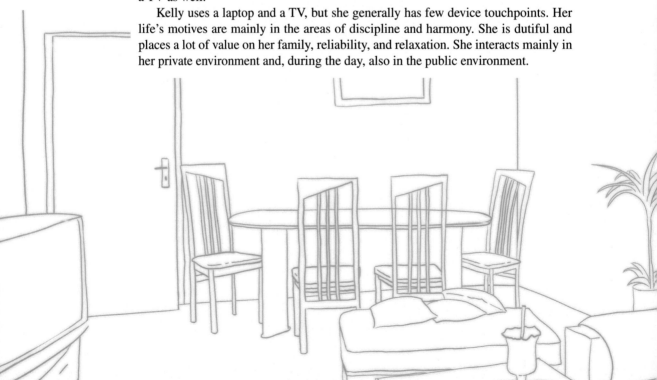

"For writing and printing out simple texts, a computer is sometimes quite useful. I don't need a smartphone. I can still talk on the telephone with my old cell phone."

A typical day begins promptly at 5:30 a.m. and ends at approximately 10 p.m. Kelly has a lot to do—she works half-days and also attends to her family and housework. In the afternoons, she has a little time for her hobbies. She seldom does work for her job with the PC but, rather, uses it at home in order to surf the Internet, and she owns a TV as well.

Kelly uses a laptop and a TV, but she generally has few device touchpoints. Her life's motives are mainly in the areas of discipline and harmony. She is dutiful and places a lot of value on her family, reliability, and relaxation. She interacts mainly in her private environment and, during the day, also in the public environment.

3.5.5 MELISSA ANDERSON

Professional user

43 years old, married, no children

Assistant to the executive management
Business management studies (earned
diploma in business management)

"Without a PC and a cell phone, my day-to-day life would be inconceivable—above all at work. But I am more of just a user. I leave the installation and maintenance to others."

Melissa's typical day begins at 6:00 a.m. and ends before midnight. Her entire daily routine entails work-related activities. She is career-oriented and works a lot and gladly. After work, she also maintains contact with colleagues. She rarely watches TV, regularly uses a smartphone, and, during work, uses a laptop or a PC.

Melissa has various device touchpoints allocated throughout her day on a regular basis. Her life's motives are concentrated very strongly on the areas of discipline, countenance, and autonomy. She is ambitious and diligent, but she also places value on relaxing pleasure. She travels a lot and interacts relatively equally in all four environments.

3.5.6 ANDREW COLLINS

Trend user (young)

20 years old, single

Pupil/high school graduate

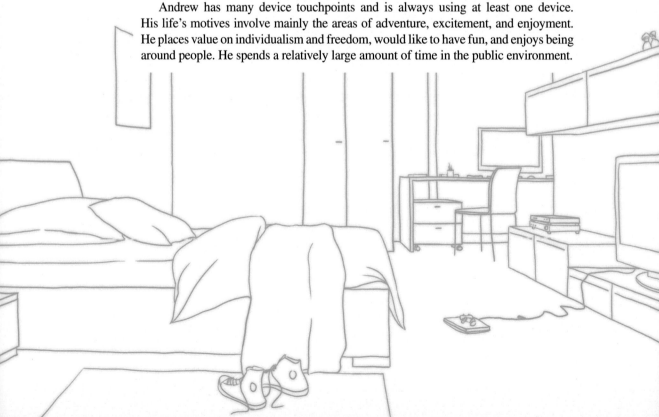

"My new smartphone is really cool. It can do almost everything and the many apps are top-class. After school, I often play with my friends on the PlayStation."

Andrew's typical school day begins at 6:30 a.m. and, depending on how the day goes, ends at approximately midnight. Actually, he does only typical activities at home. Otherwise, he is not home a lot, and he gets together with friends and acquaintances. He is constantly using his smartphone as well as relatively often his laptop and his TV.

Andrew has many device touchpoints and is always using at least one device. His life's motives involve mainly the areas of adventure, excitement, and enjoyment. He places value on individualism and freedom, would like to have fun, and enjoys being around people. He spends a relatively large amount of time in the public environment.

3.5.7 MARK HUDSON

Trend user (gainfully employed)

35 years old, single

Event manager/event agency
secondary school level I and training

"I am usually the first to buy new devices. I also already know what my next smartphone will be. A life without Facebook is unimaginable—all my friends are there."

Mark begins a typical day relatively late and also goes to bed late. He can flexibly allocate his working time. During his free time, he is often on the go, getting together with friends and enjoying life. He uses his smartphone around the clock, a PC at work, a tablet privately, and a TV in the evenings rather infrequently.

Mark uses mainly his smartphone and has many device touchpoints. His life's motives are above all characterized by adventure, excitement, and enjoyment. He enjoys his life and his freedoms; loves carefreeness, individualism, and special things; and likes to be with other people. He is active relatively equally in all four environments throughout the day and is on the go often.

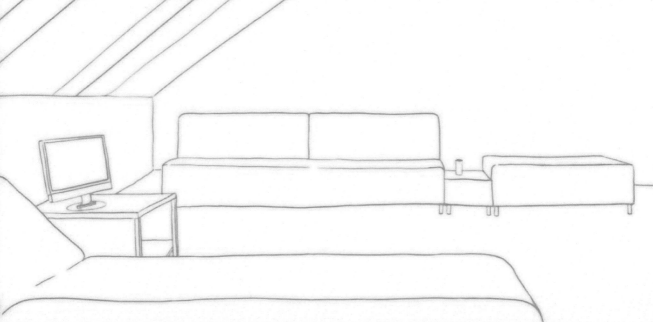

3.5.8 ROBERT SULLIVAN

Digital pros

39 years old, in a relationship

IT entrepreneur, studied at a university of applied sciences and did postgraduate studies (earned diploma in informatics and a master's of science)

"Quality has its price. Thus, I always buy the best devices. Then I know that everything will work right. In my home, everything is networked. Regardless of whether it is HDTV, a media hard disk, or my laptops."

Robert's typical day begins very early and ends relatively late. As an entrepreneur, he is in the office or on the go for his job almost the entire day. He carefully structures his minimal free time. He uses his smartphone and laptop for his job; in his private environment, he supplements them with his tablet and his TV.

Robert has very many device touchpoints. His life's motives are predominantly in the areas of discipline, enjoyment, and excitement. He is curious, diligent, ambitious, and distinguishes himself through his top-class work and conscientiousness. His environment alternates very strongly between the workplace (semipublic environment) and private (at home).

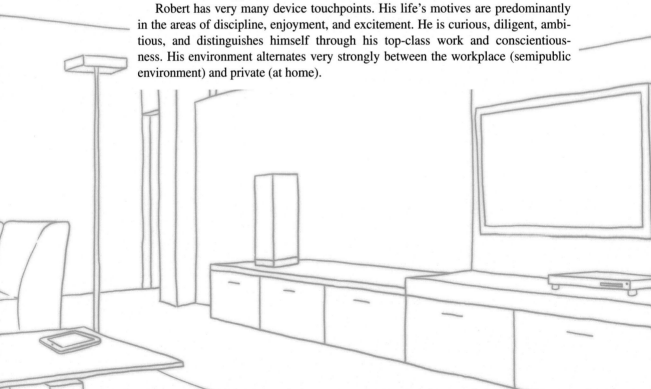

3.5.9 LARRY NEWTON

Digital avant-garde

32 years old, single

Screen designer/clerk
University studies (Bachelor of Arts)

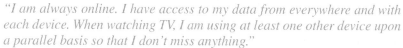

"I am always online. I have access to my data from everywhere and with each device. When watching TV, I am using at least one other device upon a parallel basis so that I don't miss anything."

The day begins for Larry at approximately 7:30 a.m. and ends at approximately 11:30 p.m. During the day, he works or gets together with friends. During a typical evening, he uses all devices on a parallel basis at home. He relaxes, surfs and communicates on the Internet or reads digital articles, watches TV on a parallel basis, or sometimes works at the same time on the laptop.

Larry is a multiscreener (see Section 3.5.14). He uses all devices very excessively and has an extremely large number of device touchpoints. His life's motives involve mainly the areas of excitement, enjoyment, and autonomy. He is curious; interested in many things; and places value on social contacts, individualism, and efficiency. He is active in the public environment often and for long periods; he is otherwise at home or at the workplace.

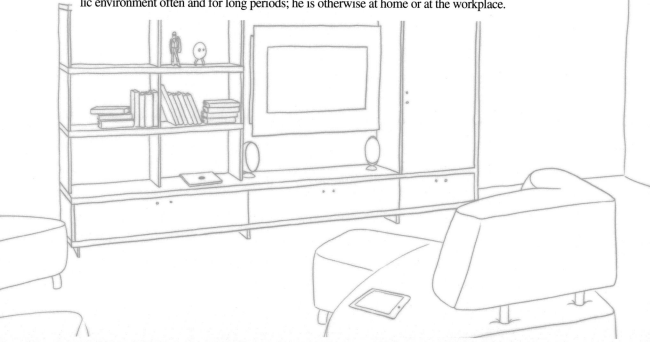

3.5.10 TYPICAL DAILY ROUTINE OF LARRY NEWTON

🕐
7:30
Waking up (private) Larry would like to gently become awake and immediately become updated. For this, he uses a smartphone because it is mobile and handy.

🕗
8:00
Early in the morning (private) At breakfast, he reads the digital version of a daily newspaper on the tablet or, rather rarely, a printed variant (primary wish: information and most up-to-date news). In the bathroom, he listens to the Internet radio or uses his smartphone as a music player.

🕘
9:00
Mid-morning (on the go, semipublic) On the way to work, the smartphone serves as his communication and information medium (appointments, to-dos, e-mails, and messages). At the office, the laptop is his main work device. On a parallel basis, a mobile device serves as a compact information source and as a news and/or social media ticker.

🕐
13:00
Mid-day (semipublic, public) During his lunch, he reads the current news feeds or the social media timeline on the smartphone or tablet. He uses another medium or at least an app that is not part of his customary workflow in order to relax a little.

3.5.11 TOUCHPOINT MATRIX OF LARRY NEWTON

	Waking up	Early in the Morning	Mid-Morning	Mid-Day
ACTIVITY	Getting up	Eating breakfast, surfing the Internet, obtaining information, showering	Commuting, working, obtaining information	Eating, communicating
LOCATION	Bedroom (bed)	Dining room (dining table), Bathroom	Commuting (local public transportation network), office (desk)	Office (desk, kitchen), bar (dining table)
ENVIRONMENT	Private	Private	On the go, semi-public environment	Semipublic environment, public environment
NEEDS	Curiosity, friendship, social contact, tranquility	Antagonism, curiosity, excellence, freedom, individualism, self-determination	Autonomy, curiosity, efficiency, friendship, individualism, order, social contact, status	Autonomy, Bon Vivant, curiosity, efficiency, entertainment, openness
CHANNEL	Internet	Internet	Internet	Internet
DEVICE TOUCHPOINT	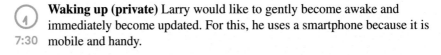	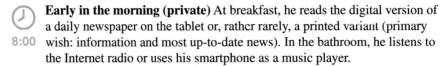	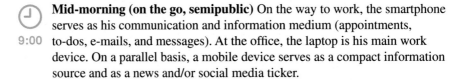	

Afternoon (semipublic) Larry works with the laptop or the desktop PC. The smartphone or the tablet is always at the ready as a ticker for

15:00 information of all kinds.

Early evening (public, private) He gets together after work with people or reads information on a mobile device that he had saved for this point in time

17:30 (read later). On the way home, the smartphone serves as an information source and for organizational purposes. During dinner, he allows himself to "absorb" information from the TV.

Late evening (private) After dinner, he watches TV or reads (read/watch later or print magazines). On a parallel basis, he uses social networks. In the

20:00 evening, Larry potentially uses all devices (generally for communication, zoning out, winding down, and private time). In exceptional cases, he may also be working or learning a program.

Going to sleep (private) As a typical multiscreener, he uses his tablet once again (surfing, e-book, read later) before falling asleep. He saves longer

23:30 articles as breakfast reading for the next day.

	Afternoon	Early Evening	Late Evening	Going to Sleep
ACTIVITY	Working, obtaining information	After work, friends, reading, task management, watching TV	Watching TV, reading	Going to bed
LOCATION	Office (desk)	Bar, living room (sofa, dining table)	Living room (sofa), home office (desk)	Bedroom (bed)
ENVIRONMENT	Semipublic environment	Public environment, private	Private	Private
NEEDS	Curiosity, efficiency, friendship, individualism, order, status	Amusement, efficiency, enjoyment, entertainment, friendship, fun, joy, social contact, zest for life	Coziness, curiosity, efficiency, entertainment, individualism, inspiration, relaxation, social contact	Curiosity, efficiency, individualism, relaxation, tranquility
CHANNEL	Internet	Internet, TV	Internet, print, TV	Internet
DEVICE TOUCHPOINT	▯ ▯ ⬒ ⬜	▯ ▯ ⬜ ⬒	▯ ▯ ⬜ ⬒	▯ ▯ ⬜ ⬜

3.5.12 MULTISCREEN DAY FLOW OF LARRY NEWTON

The following day flow illustration shows, compactly and in a simplified form, the daily routine of Larry Newton (digital avant-garde) and the usage intensity of the four screens allocated to the individual time periods of his day. As you can see in the illustration, he uses his smartphone in each time frame and normally all devices in the late evening.

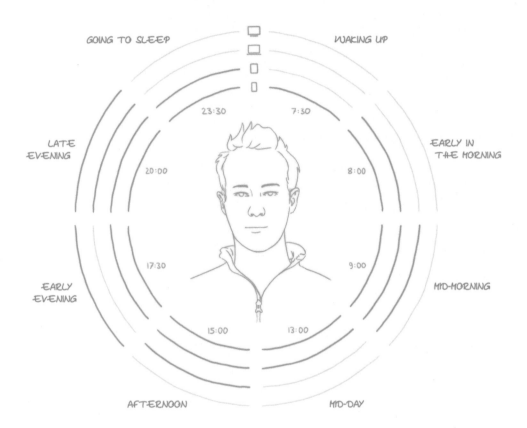

3.5.13 EMOTION MAP OF LARRY NEWTON

On the emotion map, the basic needs and life motives of Larry Newton are depicted. Harmony and discipline are less important to him than excitement, autonomy, or enjoyment. He is curious and places value on efficiency, individualism, and friendship.

3.5.14 PIONEERS OF THE DIGITAL SOCIETY ANALYZED IN DETAIL

In the digital society, there are various user types (analyzed in detail) who use the new media (inter alia all mentioned screens) and networked, digital information offerings and services earlier and more intensively than other people. Sooner or later, their pioneering behavior in using the digital media is adopted by other user types.

The characteristics of these pioneer types somewhat overlap. For example, a multiscreener is simultaneously a smart native and also covered by the definition of the digital avant-garde. A smart native is not necessarily a multiscreener. The user types are similar to each other. The terms have been used in various studies and serve as more in-depth information.

Pioneers as role models

Pioneer types are the trailblazers for using digital media. You can assume that the behavior of the average user will correspond to the behavior of the pioneers within 2 or 3 years. Thus, these user types are sometimes very well-suited as personas and as a starting basis for the conception of innovative interfaces and concepts that, based on experience, only become ready for the market sometime after the project start and then eventually become suitable for the masses and/or the average person. After a certain period of time, occasional users will use the media, technology, and the Internet similarly to how the trend users, digital pros, and multiscreeners did some years before them while the pioneers will once again be discovering new technologies and media for themselves.

EARLY ADOPTERS

Early adopters are (like the actual innovators) among the first who accept new ideas. They are trailblazers. They are followed by the early majority, the late majority, and the "stragglers" (*late adopters*). They are the first to buy a new product, use the newest variants of products, and own the latest technical devices and achievements.

SMART NATIVE

The smart native is characterized by his usage intensity as well as tech and web savviness. He uses primarily and mainly a smartphone. Almost daily, he obtains information on the go or occupies his free time with online entertainment. He constantly has his smartphone with him and is seemingly and potentially always online ("always on" and "always in touch").

DIGITAL AVANT-GARDE

The term originates from the study "The Digital Society" (Initiative D21, 2010). The user group digital avant-garde possesses an exceedingly good digital infrastructure. Mobile Internet access is practically a given. The Internet is also used intensively for business. A member of this user group is extremely knowledgeable in the areas of the Internet, technologies, and complex digital themes. A comparison of the digital avant-garde with the other user types in the digital society was provided in Section 3.4. The description of the user prototype Larry Newton is based on the definition of the digital avant-garde.

MULTISCREENERS

Multiscreeners use various devices (screens) several times per day and frequently another medium while they watch TV. They constantly alternate between the devices (inspired by Microsoft Advertising, 2010a). A multiscreener is a smart native. A smart native is not necessarily a multiscreener. The user prototype Larry Newton is a typical multiscreener.

3.6 CONCLUSION AND TIPS

1. **Place the focus on the users.**
   Research the target group(s) and get to know the potential users. Who are the most important users, which devices do they use, and what are their motives and needs?

2. **Analyze the daily routine.**
   How does a typical day in the life of the typical user look? How is his or her workflow? What are the relevant touchpoints? That is, which device is being used when, by whom, why, and for what?

3. **Consider the motives and needs.**
   The psychology is an important aspect in the user experience design. Findings from (neuro)psychology and neuromarketing can also be utilized here.

4. **Define the prototypical users.**
   Use existing information about the potential users, create personas, or work with the eight representative user prototypes.

5. **User-centered design only works collectively.**
   The process must also be accepted at the management level. All participants must be won over to the method. Decisions must be made collectively by the team and may not be decided only "down from above."

6. **Scrutinize and iterate.**
   The user prototypes are not patented formulas. Scrutinize whether they are suitable. The same applies for individually created personas. The user groups from the D21 study are a point of reference and represent significant features. In the individual case, there can and will be overlappings and deviations.

7. **Pioneers are the trailblazers of the mainstream.**
   Get to know the pioneers of the digital society. The early adopters and smart natives of today will be the average users in 2 or 3 years.

Context of Use

4

In order to design a digital service, in addition to the users and the devices, you must also pay attention to the context of use. The relevant parameters and special characteristics of and differences between the various contexts of use are discussed in this chapter. The special characteristics in the mobile context of use are likewise explained in detail.

The device we choose to use is often driven by our context: Where we are, what we want to accomplish, and the amount of time needed.

Google et al. (2012)

4.1 THE CONTEXT OF USE

Context describes the factors that influence a certain event or a situation. The context of use refers to the conditions in a certain environment or a situation during the use of a service (software, app, information offering, website, etc.) with a digital device (for example, smartwatch, smartphone, tablet, laptop/PC, or TV). A *mobile context* of use in the sense of this book always then exists whenever a mobile device is being used (see Chapter 2, Section 2.3.1).

In accordance with Norm EN ISO 9241-11, the context of use is defined by the following parameters: user, activity (goal or task), work equipment (hardware and software), and physical and social environment (Wikipedia, n.d., EN ISO 9241).

Mobile devices and the context problem

With mobile devices, the context of use can sometimes not so easily be defined or predicted. The boundaries between mobile usage and desktop usage melt away to form a whole, and the mobile aspect of the Internet has less importance. However, the lynchpin is the Web. In the respective usage situation, that device is used which is available and makes the most sense (Rieger, 2011; Schubert, 2011).

Constantly networked and online

Today's average mobile phone was considered a high-end device 2 years ago. Almost all new mobile phones have a Web browser. Three out of four or more people throughout the world own a mobile device. The constant availability of the Internet has had a profound influence on the behaviors and expectations of users. For many people, a mobile device is their sole interface to the Internet. Internet usage is no longer a deliberate activity: The Internet is simply there and accessible on every available device. Most people use mobile devices while they are waiting for something, while watching TV, for doing research while shopping in a store, for doing research in order to then later shop in a store, or to first surf a mobile website and then to go to the (desktop) PC (sources and related documentation in Rieger (2011) and Schubert (2011)).

4.1.1 CONTEXT COMPLEXITY

With the *context of use* method (according to Maguire, 2001), the circumstances of the context of use can be examined in detail (see Section 4.2.4). During the description of the methods, Martin Maguire addresses important questions and parameters for the analysis of the context of use. Who does what and/or carries out which action? When and why does he does this? How are the technical requirements and the external conditions? How is the general environmental situation?

The context of use has many facets and is complex. Essentially, it is determined by the user, the device(s) being used, and the environmental situation (physical and social environment). Because the transitions are fluid, a pure differentiation between a stationary situation and a mobile situation is not sufficient.

The various device classes are indeed respectively well-suited to varying degrees for various contexts of use and are in principle used in typical environments and for typical tasks (see Chapter 2, Section 2.5). However, you cannot always draw clear conclusions (see the examples in Section 4.4). Smartphones are naturally optimally suited for on the go, but they can also be used on the couch or in the kitchen. A TV on the go makes no sense at all and has been explicitly conceived for a stationary situation. Frequently, the user wants to be able to retrieve mobilely available or mobilely created information (e.g., on a smartphone and tablet) in a stationary manner as well (e.g., at the PC or the TV). Most important, it concerns how you can output the contents on the various devices and display them.

You must also ponder the various input options (e.g., voice input, camera, gestures) (see Chapter 2, Section 2.3) and the combination options for the various screens (see Chapter 2, Section 2.6). The respectively used device has a major influence on user behavior. Additional elementary factors of influence are the content and the context of use. In a certain environment, you are bound to certain conditions.

You must regard the context of use from a holistic perspective. There are numerous different factors and parameters. Their interplay (not only their sum) defines the respective context of use. These aspects and challenges are discussed here.

There is no Mobile Web. There is only The Web, which we view in different ways. There is also no Desktop Web. Or Tablet Web.

Stephen Hay (Zero Interface)

4.2 PARAMETERS OF THE CONTEXT OF USE

In practice, there is often not enough time or budget to very precisely examine all details. Often, not all details are relevant or known. You never have absolute certainty about the potential usage situation anyway. In these cases, it helps to forecast the context of use and the relevant parameters as best as possible.

The parameters of the context of use

The definition of the context of use can be reduced in simplified form to what is essential. In addition to the *user* (see Chapter 3) and the *device being used* (see Chapter 2), it is characterized by the parameters of the *usage mode* (lean back or lean forward), *situation* (stationary or mobile), and *environment* (private, semipublic sphere, public sphere, and on the go). These parameters influence each other and ultimately define the individual context of use that prescribes the framework conditions. The usage intention (intention, task, or goal) of the user is also co-determining.

In the lean back mode (usually more often in the private environment), the user is predominantly relaxed and passive. Conversely, the *public sphere* is accessible to everyone and not private. As such, based on the project and factors associated with it, you can conclude that users in this environment possibly want no audio output or do not want to use language as an input method because it can be unpleasant for them or even restricted.

An information offering or service must be adapted to the context of use in a maximally flexible manner. In the context, we recommend not differentiating between mobile and stationary. The publisher, provider, and creator of information cannot predict in what context, by whom, and with what device the information will be obtained. Thus, in principle, only one offering is retrieved in various contexts of use.

In addition to the user and the device being used, the context of use is influenced by the parameters of usage mode, situation, and environment.

Differentiation between the parameters of situation and environment

A *situation* comprises all the current circumstances that have a determining effect on our action (activity environment). The word "situation" refers to the framework conditions for an activity, the connection to circumstances, or psychologically to the effectiveness of a (clearly) defined circumstance such as an emergency situation, read situation, written situation, speaking situation, stressful situation, or traffic situation.

An *environment* generally describes the totality of the natural and social circumstances. Concretely, it involves a group of persons who surround the individual (social environment) or an area that surrounds a location (the physical environment). Synonyms are *milieu* and *surroundings*.

4.2.1 ENVIRONMENT

In the respective environment, you are bound to certain conditions. The individual circumstances can influence each other. The environment is relevant for the breakdown of the daily routine for the user prototypes (see Chapter 3, Section 3.5). For pupils, university students, and similar groups of persons, you must weigh whether you should define their environment (school) as a public or semipublic sphere.

Private

The private environment and generally all private spatial situations are in principle not accessible to third parties or outsiders.

Private refers to *one's own four walls* or to space to which you have exclusive access (e.g., a hotel room on vacation). At home, you are in a private atmosphere. There are no persons or, in exceptional cases, only a few persons who can influence your actions. For friends, acquaintances, or relatives, the environment has a similar private character. In your private environment, you have the greatest influence on the devices in your environment.

Semipublic space

A semipublic space is tendentially accessible only to a restricted group of persons. This often concerns a temporary stay at a location.

You are in a semipublic space in the workplace, in the conference room on the client's premises (generally during work), and in a hotel room. To some extent, the office environment has a private character. Your own workstation (regardless of whether it is at a desk or in a factory) can have a private atmosphere depending on individual design and the spatial situation. The device situation is somewhat predetermined, but it can be influenced by the user.

Public space

The public space is accessible to everyone. Each person can participate in the situation. It is not private.

In a public space, humans act differently than in a private environment. Regardless of whether it involves shopping, dealings with government agencies and public institutions (e.g., at city hall), sitting in the waiting room at a doctor's office, being in a (public) park, visiting museums, or attending events, you are in a more or less public situation. You have no direct influence over the persons and devices in your environment.

On the go

You are on the go, changing locations, and are on the way to another location. The current location changes until you have reached your destination.

On the go, you do not stop—you are constantly in motion in order to reach a designated geographical destination. Depending on the transportation method, an in-transit situation can either be more private (private passenger vehicle) or public (public location transportation, train, etc.). Depending on the transportation method, you can also be sitting and passively continue to move (train). In transit, exclusively mobile devices can be sensibly used.

4.2.2 SITUATION

Depending on the environment, location, and usage intention (knowingly or unknowingly), the user can find himself in a situation in which he carries out various tasks to reach his goals. A differentiation should be made between a mobile and a stationary situation. In a mobile situation, you can use only transportable (thus mobile) devices. Locally restricted movement by the user is possible both in a mobile and in a stationary situation. Modes and situations can overlap and cannot always be transparently differentiated.

Mobile

On the go and mobilely, primarily handy (movable) devices are used. The duration of mobile device usage is typically brief and intermittent. A mobile situation (e.g., going on foot or by bicycle) is the time frame between the starting point and the destination of a change of location.

Mobility or *being mobile* refers to the motion of the user in space and time. The user is bound to no permanent location. He retrieves rather compact, clear, and temporarily useful information. Long-term information consumption occurs rather rarely in a mobile situation. There are mobile situations in which you are indeed in transit but in one location for an extended period of time, such as riding on a train. In these situations, the information offerings are used or processed for a longer period of time.

The cell phone or smartphone is used throughout the entire day—often for short durations and in a wide array of locations (e.g., when waiting in a line, on a train station platform, and when shopping). A mobile situation is often rather hectic and not very relaxing.

> **NOTE**
>
> Do not mix up (mobile) situation and (mobile) context of use. A mobile device can also be used in a stationary situation (see Section 4.4 and Chapter 2, Section 2.3.1).

Stationary

The device usage and/or the situation is bound to a fixed location. The term is derived from the noun "station" and from the definition of fixed location.

In a stationary situation, you are not moving and the device with which you are working is not moving (or at least moving only in a locally restricted way, such as in the room). In contrast to a mobile situation in which you are constantly in motion or at least have the option of changing locations, you are stationarily in a tendentially calm, stagnant situation (persistently restricted to the location).

Typical devices for stationary utilization, such as a desktop PC or a TV, are large, immobile or difficult and uncomfortable to transport. In a stationary situation, naturally also mobile devices can be used.

4.2.3 USAGE MODE

Depending on the context, device, and usage intention, the user finds himself (knowingly or unknowingly) in a certain usage mode. If you would like to relax, you use a suitable device and opt for a mode that supports this need. There are two modes in which a person can find himself and in which a person can use corresponding devices. Modes and situations can overlap and cannot always be transparently differentiated. Almost any device can be used in both modes.

Lean back

In the *lean back* mode, the user is primarily relaxed and passive. The interaction with the device is sporadic, temporary, and not permanent. The user consumes information and allows information to be "sprinkled" on him.

Lean back situations occur more often during recreational times than during work. Of course, there are exceptions, but the situation is fundamentally casual, relaxing, and less or not strenuous. Typical situations in which you are in the lean back mode are watching TV on the sofa in a relaxed posture leaning back or comfortably using a tablet (reading an e-book) in bed.

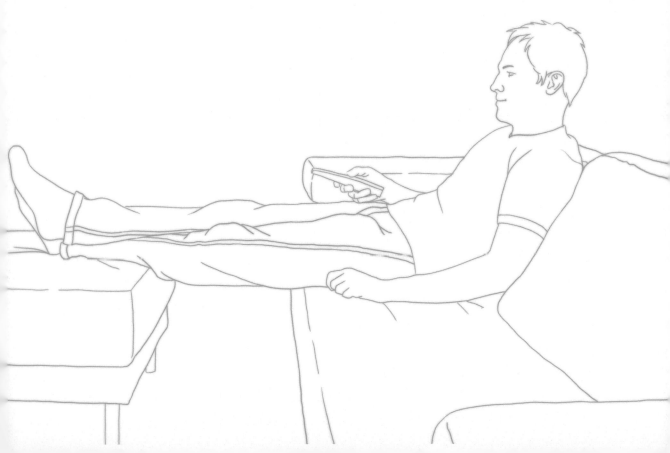

Lean forward

In the *lean forward* mode, the user is working primarily in a concentrated and active manner. He interacts with a device primarily without any interruptions and over an extended period of time. He exerts and has a constant and direct influence on the depiction and dissemination of the information.

This situation is less about media and information consumption and more about conscious modification and modification of information and data. The actions are of a rather longer duration. A typical situation in which you are in the lean forward mode is working on the PC. Lean forward is often less relaxing than lean back.

> *The context of use consists of the users, tasks and equipment, and the physical and social environments in which a product is used.*
> Martin Maguire (Loughborough University)

4.2.4 DETAILED QUESTIONS

The aforementioned rough classification handles the most important parameters. The context of use can be examined and defined in a more detailed manner using the following additional parameters:

Users/operators
(see Chapter 3)

- User type(s) (homogeneous or heterogeneous user group?)
- User's role
- User characteristics (age, gender, physical and mental capabilities and/or handicaps, etc.)
- Attitude, frame of mind, behavior, physical state (e.g., tiredness, physical condition)
- Motivation (motives and needs)
- Knowledge, skills, qualifications
- Technological competence, media affinity
- Possible restrictions: (restrictive) clothing, busy hands, movement of the user/device, body posture and grip

Task/activity
(see Chapter 3)

- Type of task
- Goal, purpose, result
- Characteristics (frequency, duration, dependency, steps)
- Physical and mental requirements
- Risks, safety requirements

Time
(see Chapter 3)

- Time frame: When does an action take place?
- Point in time during the daily operations (see Chapter 3, Section 3.2.1)
- How much time does the user have at his disposal?
- Situation

Technical equipment/features
(see Chapter 2)

- Devices (hardware, software, performance)
- What devices are available (TV, desktop computer, tablet, smartphone, feature phone, telephone booth, e-reader, smartwatch, etc.)?
- Network, connectivity
- How is the connection quality (WLAN, LTE, UMTS, EDGE, dead zone, roaming, no connection, etc.)?

- How is the file access and the availability of contents and information?
- Miscellaneous features

External influences (physical environment)

(see Section 4.2)

- Where is the user (physical site, location)?
- Environment/surroundings (where applicable, terrain situation, hindrances)
- Movement
- Body posture
- Weather and temperature (insofar as this is relevant)
- Constant or changing conditions
- Light situation, noise
- Are there background noises and, if so, in what form?
- Are there time pressures? In this case, for example, you must differentiate between shopping with long waiting lines and online shopping on the sofa.
- Is there information or are there interaction options in the surrounding area (through or with products in a shop, film poster, etc.)?

Social environment/social situation (social milieu)

(see Section 4.2)

- Are strangers present?
- Are friends or acquaintances present (personally, via telephone, or not at all)?
- Have these persons been integrated into an information source and do they help during decision-making?
- Relationship to (surrounding) persons (social interaction)
- Number of persons surrounding the individual person (quantity of persons)
- Attitude/behavior of the persons surrounding the individual person
- Attentiveness, distraction, disruption, interruption
- Communication skills
- Aid possibilities

Influence on the interaction

The following four examples help explain the significance and the influence of the various parameters and factors of the context of use on the interaction with a screen and/or device (Feige, 2010):

- User and activity: The degree of alertness and the health condition of the user change dynamically and have an effect, for example, on concentration and motor skills.
- Features: The type of interaction with a device has a decisive influence on the precision of the input and on the type of collectable information (touchscreen with fingers vs. audio input with a microphone vs. use of mouse and keyboard).
- Physical environment: Changing light conditions can have a negative effect on the contrast of visual information on a screen. The contents may then be perceived more poorly—for example, in a dark room with changing brightness (concert/opera).
- Social milieu: Persons who are present can distract or pressure a user so that errors are thus made during the inputting.

4.3 CONTEXT RELEVANCE

An information offering should always fit the situation, the environment, the user, and the device used and therefore the context of use—thus supplying the right information at the right time. Throughout the day, users consume contents on a wide array of devices. It is important to understand the respective context of use in which the various devices are being used in order to create a user experience that fits the motives and needs of the users.

> *Each task has a time, and a place. Be responsive to the user rather than the device.*
>
> Emma Lindahl (2015)

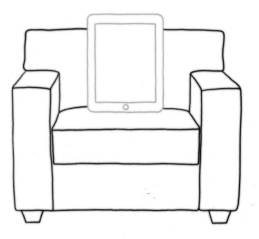

Of course you have to consider the devices used in a particular situation, but you must not ignore the people who use them. The following are important questions in this regard: Who uses the application? In what situation does the user find himself? What information is relevant for him at the moment? Which device does he use, when, how, where, and why? What is his intention? How much time does he have? These and other questions about the user and the context of use are the focus when you conceive an information offering.

Sensibility, awareness, and anticipation

With a good service, contents and information are not simply duplicated. Based on the context, unimportant information is intentionally not displayed; only the truly relevant information is displayed (context awareness). In order to design the context-relevant services, you must know and understand both the context of use and the users' needs in conjunction with the respective screen.

In order to be able to adapt the information to the respective context and the differences between the devices being used, it is beneficial to correspondingly sensibly structure the potential user experiences and to adapt them to the respectively suitable devices in the respectively presumed context (see Chapter 5, Section 5.14). Each device has its own special requirements and possibilities that should be taken into consideration. Each touchpoint with an information offering must be separately assessed from all perspectives (see Section 4.2).

During the course of a day, contents are retrieved and consumed in various contexts with a wide array of devices. You may not transfer design principles from desktop applications on a one-to-one basis to mobile offerings and upscale or downscale the information. The same is valid for TV offerings because the screen resolution, the viewing distance, and the operation of TVs are much different from those of other devices.

It is also not sufficient to simply make contents and information available on all devices (see Chapter 5, Section 5.10.1). In order to obtain the highest possible context relevance, it is most important to offer the right information at the right time, in the right location, and that is thus suitable for the context of use.

Context relevance and contents

Context and service are often directly connected to each other and influence each other. You cannot determine with certainty the information needs of a user. Thus, you should also not differentiate between the information depth of mobile and other offerings. Normally, the same offering is being obtained in a different context.

It can also be the case that the same offering is required based on the situation and the context by different user types. Thus, the respectively suitable contents should be offered.

The contents of a website that is accessed with a laptop must potentially look different on a smartphone because the user may be in a completely different context of use and may quite presumably be imposing other requirements for the information. It is possible (but not guaranteed) that he would like to invest less time on the smartphone in order to obtain information than he would at home on the laptop. It may also be the case that he is in a hectic situation or requires targeted local information (geolocation, guide, and navigation). When contents that he has looked at on the desktop website and wants to retrieve soon thereafter on the smartphone suddenly go missing or are not visible, the user can become irritated.

It is not known with certainty how the context of use will look. The supplying of contents based on assumptions can be useful or hinder the user. The safe variant is to provide the same contents in principle for all devices and to merely depict them in a device-specific manner.

Context first/key device first

Based on the mobile first approach (see Chapter 5, Section 5.1), it can be beneficial to first determine the most important device with regard to the service and the user and then focus on this device. This does not necessarily have to be a smartphone. When determining the prioritized device, you must predict the most likely usage scenario and the most likely and most frequent context of use for a certain service.

Information can indeed be different, but it should nonetheless be supplied and depicted in a coherent, context-relevant, and device-specific manner. A tablet is an optimal device for viewing large photo galleries. It is also suitable (in contrast to the smartphone with a smaller screen) for reading longer articles or even books. On the TV, most users prefer moving-image information (films and videos). In individual cases, context- and device-related functions are used. Each smartphone has, for example, a photo or video camera and GPS position finding. Amazon uses the smartphone camera in the mobile application as a bar code scanner (see Chapter 5, Section 5.9). This facilitates product search and price comparison (e.g., in a shop).

The offering of the *Tagesschau* (a news and public affairs program in Germany) with an app for the smartphone and tablet, TV news, and online portal is an excellent example of context relevance. The *Tagesschau* offers relevant information and options that are respectively suitable to the device and the context of use. For interested parties who have little time or are frequently in transit, there is also a location-independent livestream and a condensed version ("*Tagesschau* in 100 Seconds"). With the mobile *Tagesschau* apps, you can download articles to read them later (including offline). Moreover, the *Tagesschau* app offers breaking news and (push) notifications of important events.

Screen versus information versus context of use

Depending on the context of use and the respective situation, various information is relevant for the user. If you understand the context of use and the device, you can address these various user requirements in a targeted manner. The (desktop) website for an event can display beautiful photos, large videos, all artists, and the event plan. On-site, equipped with a smartphone, presumably other information is the focus, such as location-related information about how to get from the train station to the event location.

There will soon be computer technologies that can automatically address and respond to the context of use. In a 2009 study, Gartner used the terms "context-aware computing" and "situation-aware functions." In this regard, information about the user and the context of use is taken into consideration in a targeted and conscious manner in order to improve the quality of the information and the interaction. "Context-enriched services" use this information about the position, external influences, and the social environment in order to anticipate the user's immediate needs and to offer him suitable, situation-related and useful functions (Gartner, 2009).

4.4 THE MOBILE CONTEXT OF USE

Contexts of use are diverse and varied. The mobile context of use (not to be confused with a mobile situation) is essentially unforeseeable and affects all parameters.

Always and everywhere

You always find yourself in a mobile context of use whenever a mobile device is being used (see Chapter 2, Section 2.3.1). It can occur anywhere: The iPad is used as a substitute for a cookbook in the kitchen, the smartphone is "at the ready" on the couch while watching TV, the mobile telephone is used at the airport or while waiting in line, and even the use of the cell phone while bicycling has been observed. A mobile device can also be used as an interface to the auto interface. And with a smartwatch on your wrist, you are always online and connected.

> *Mobile is not a subset of the internet – it IS the internet.*
> Benedict Evans (2015)

Difference between stationary and mobile

A differentiation must be made between a mobile situation (see Section 4.2.2) in which you are *in transit* in most cases and a stationary situation in which a mobile device is being used (e.g., reading from the tablet at home on the sofa or using the bar code scanner on the smartphone when shopping in a store). In both cases, mobile devices are being used. Both cases concern a mobile context of use.

The conduct regarding mobile information collection has changed. Mobile is everywhere (Google and PSOS OTX MediaCT U.S., 2011). Most people almost always have their cell phone or smartphone with them. A smartphone user is potentially online at all times and in all places (*always on* and *instant on*) (see Chapter 3, Section 3.5.14).

Even if a tablet is frequently used within a stationary WLAN network, it involves a mobile device. When using a mobile device in the bathroom (stationary situation), you are certainly not in a mobile situation and you are (it is hoped) also not in a hurry, but it is nonetheless a mobile context of use.

Compared to users of stationary devices (TV or desktop PC), mobile users have different needs and expectations for a product or a service. Consider the example of a website on current movies. On the desktop, the users presumably want to watch a movie trailer and find out information about the details of the film and its production

(actors, director, crew, shooting locations, etc.). Even interactive specials or sweepstakes may possibly be interesting. On the mobile device, especially in transit, the visitors to the website are probably more interested in a compact overview of the film, hit lists, nearby movie theaters, and show times. The same applies if someone is interested in cooking and recipes. On the desktop PC at home, it is more relevant to decide what one can cook, for what occasions a recipe is suitable, and how costly the ingredients will be. In the supermarket, one is interested in how much the ingredients cost, where they can be found, and available alternatives.

Your own experiences with the mobile context of use

In order to design mobile applications and services, you must understand the mobile context of use to optimally experience it yourself. In addition to the related parameters such as the environment, situation, or device, additional factors influence the use of mobile devices: the user's mental state, his level of skill in using the device, the user's intention, his expectations and motives, network and connection quality, the limitations or possibilities prescribed by the environment or the device, and so on. Each person can understand this from his or her own experience or observation.

THE MOBILE CONTEXT OF USE FROM MY OWN EXPERIENCE

The following text is a narrative of my own experience.

Whenever I am in a mobile situation in a public setting (e.g., when shopping), I am distracted by all types of environmental influences. I am then seldom able to use an application with my full attention. That just simply does not work at all. I operate my smartphone with only one hand. To type in text on the reflective small screen is rather tedious—this applies generally for the interaction with the device.

Naturally, my personal motives and needs at the respective moment influence my behavior. What do I want to do? What interests me? Is a soccer match going on that I would not like to miss? Or do I have an idea that I absolutely don't want to forget? Why am I here and why am I even using my smartphone during shopping (perhaps because my companion cannot decide between three sweaters).

There is a difference whether I am waiting for the next bus or have to quickly complete a banking transaction. Depending on the current situation, I want to access the current bus schedule, find a bank nearby, or directly complete my banking transaction via the smartphone app. Perhaps I want to simply zone out and spend some time playing a game.

The classical mobile situation in the public sphere with a smartphone or cell phone that I operate with only one hand is hectic. I can use a mobile device (e.g., a tablet) at a (temporary) workstation in the cafeteria or the library—with a connected keyboard, sitting in a comfy chair, and with a sufficiently fast Internet connection. I then concentrate exclusively on what I am doing precisely at that time. According to the spatial situation, I may perhaps even find myself in a rather private environment (individual office) and have sufficient time and also electrical power to work for an extended period of time at the same location in lean forward mode. Although I use a mobile device, we can no longer talk about what comprises a typical mobile situation. I use mobile devices, especially my smartphone, everywhere—for example, on the go in the train, with both hands, in a completely relaxed manner, in a concentrated manner, and for extended periods of time. Sometimes, I can even find an outlet to a reliable electrical power source.

Whenever I am sitting comfortably at home in an armchair (private environment) and simultaneously watching TV, I have the smartphone or tablet at the ready—sometimes even the laptop. When my son was younger and I sometimes rocked him to sleep (which occasionally could take a long time), my posture was sometimes even less comfy, but I also often had the smartphone in my hand—naturally, I could operate it with only one hand, but I could also constantly devote myself to a crying baby or other babysitting events.

Exclusively mobile usage

Often, because users sometimes access information exclusively with the mobile device, it is necessary that the complete scope of functions is available on even the small mobile devices and not just an extremely "slimmed-down" variant is offered.

The number of users who go on the Internet first or exclusively with mobile devices is increasing (Meeker, 2010). Even the number of mobile-only users is increasing. "There are no longer the just-look-for-a-second moments" (Cho, 2011). The average visiting time on news pages is only approximately 5 minutes, but on a tablet, the time spent may be much longer (Frommer and Goldman, 2010; Tomorrow Focus Media, 2010a; Uhrenbacher, 2010). For the various user behaviors, correspondingly adapted use cases must be conceived and considered.

Bohram Cho (2011) describes the increasing relevance of mobile devices and why they are frequently preferred to stationary devices: "Whenever I give my mother the iPad, then she will use primarily it at home—instead of the Mac. It is easier for her— she can use it in the kitchen, while watching TV, while talking on the telephone, or at the dinner table." Mobile devices are more convenient and can in principle be operated more easily via the touch interface than a PC with a keyboard and a mouse.

> *Don't cut content or features just because people happen to be on a small screen.*
>
> Cennydd Bowles (designer at Twitter)

When all functions are available only on the laptop, the usage quality of a service declines for users who use exclusively mobile devices because they cannot access some of the information or functionalities. Users cannot be forced to wait until they are sitting at a different (large) screen in order to complete a task. You must examine and observe how people behave in various situations and design accordingly in a targeted manner.

The increasing mobile Internet usage does not necessarily mean that stationary usage is declining and stationary devices are thus becoming less important (e.g., at the desktop workstation or video-on-demand on TV). However, very often a mobile device is being used on a parallel basis or in order to start an action, and sometimes even exclusively.

Mobile does not necessarily mean "in a hurry"

A mobile user is not always distracted and in a hurry. Nonetheless, mobile applications and websites are very often designed to be "slimmed-down" versions of the desktop counterpart. Josh Clark corrects diverse flawed assessments and misunderstandings in conjunction with the mobile context of use (Clark, 2011b; cited in Myers (2011) and Frost (2012a)).

> *Don't confuse context with intent. Core content should always be there.*
>
> Josh Clark (designer and author of "Tapworthy")

Do not mix up context of use and intention

Mobile does not necessarily mean less content, attentiveness, or functionality; rather, it means the opposite. The assumption that users want to do less with a small screen and thus everything must be reduced is simply false. Josh Clark is even of the opinion that mobile applications should always be able to do more than their desktop counterparts. This idea can be complemented to mean that mobile apps should be able to do at least the right thing and should not be overburdened.

Prioritizing relevant usage cases

Because it is almost impossible to take all potential scenarios and usage cases into consideration, you should concentrate on the most probable ones—optimally while taking into consideration the typical behavioral patterns in the mobile context of use (see Section 4.4.1).

Usability and complexity

If an application has been structured to be clean and comprehensible, complexity does not necessarily have to be a problem. Complex information does not automatically have to be complicated but, rather, can also be provided for mobile devices and/or small screens in a user-friendly manner. You do not have to offer all contents at the same time.

It is better if you respectively display only the core idea. Breaking down complex information or applications into small tasks is the actual and most difficult challenge. Additional tabs or clicks are not problematic if the interface is clear and comprehensible and the click process is (mentally) logically set up. The additional menu items, tabs, and clicks must lead to valuable and useful content. "Tap quality" is more important than "tap quantity."

Optimize for micro-tasking! One big idea per screen.

Josh Clark

If you use many buttons and menus, and thus you have a complex interface, a tutorial is important (e.g., as a superimposed level with additional explanations about the actual content). However, the tutorial for interacting with the interface must be displayed only until the user has used it once and understood it. You can also consider whether you are offering the user mobilely the complete scope of functions and how many and which functions are actually helpful or, where applicable, can be left out.

Relation between "mobile" and the desktop

When it involves access, you should not separate the mobile website and the desktop website. Everything is supposed to be accessible under one and the same URL. "There is only The Web" (Stephen Hay, Zero Interface). Josh Clark recommends the following: "Don't think 'mobile website,' think 'mobile web experience'" (as quoted in Frost, 2012a).

An automatic switch to the mobile website is not recommended if you would like to, for example, share links and pass them on (virality of information). A mobile link does not look good on a desktop screen. In this case, the device would have to be recognized, and the layout of the page would once again have to be adapted to the desktop screen (optimally while keeping the same URL).

Reducing content to display on mobile devices not only makes sense due to the smaller screen, but also because too much unnecessary content is often already offered on desktop websites. A shortened form is recommended in this case and has nothing to do with the mobile website. There is much to be said for examining contents and reducing them to the necessary scope.

Mobile information offerings

The conception of mobile services includes not only apps. To have an app is still no (mobile) strategy. By having one, this does not automatically solve all your problems or fulfill all your requirements. The product is always the service (and the supplied information and functions) and not only an app or a website.

Exploiting the technical possibilities

Mobile devices can improve and/or expand the user experience, service experience, or multiscreen experience by sensibly utilizing their special features and capabilities, such as the camera, GPS sensor, or voice input. Sensors and localization have enormous potential. If the user "plays around" with the interface (service, app, information offering, and device) and can exploratively interact with it, he can become involved even better. At the same time, you can increase your fun during use (see Chapter 5, Section 5.13–5.16). Despite all options that mobile devices and especially smartphones offer, you should, in the sense of a good mobile application, concentrate on what is essential and the basic functions that take into consideration the actual needs of the mobile users and design the application to be as simple as possible.

In this regard, the device fragmentation is a major challenge. It is difficult to develop permanent apps for all device classes, platforms, and operating systems and to keep them updated (narrow the focus on all versions). Much more important is flexible content that can be delivered and displayed in various containers (website, app, or via interfaces). The key terms are "fluid experience" (see Chapter 2, Section 2.6.2) and "content like water" (see Chapter 5, Section 5.10).

Device fragmentation

Fragmentation means to cut up or divide into small pieces. Device fragmentation generally means that there will also be more and more devices which will be increasingly diverse. You must keep in mind that the more fragmented the device landscape is, the more diverse the features of the target devices will be for which you develop an informational offering; it will ultimately be even more difficult to create a cross-device and consistent user experience.

Fragmentation craze

The increasing fragmentation as a result of the various devices, platforms, user types, and contexts of use will continue to increase challenges. You must take the various platform cultures into consideration. It may be helpful to create platform personas or platform prototypes and to reconcile them with the device and/or user prototypes.

What makes a Windows phone user tick? What differentiates him from the typical Android or iPhone user? What platform fits which device and user type? In other words, What platform will be most likely to be used by my target group? How and why do the users use a certain platform? What differences must you take into consideration when you develop a service, an app, or generally a concept for iOS or Android?

Subconscious and subjective user decision-making

The conduct of the users on a platform is heterogeneous. They use the devices and services on the platform very differently. Accordingly, the *mobile experience* of the users is also different. On the various mobile platforms (e.g., from Apple, Google, and Windows), you thus navigate differently because many devices have other hardware buttons, a different layout of hardware buttons, and a different number of hardware buttons. This again results in the fact that the number, layout, and placement of the software buttons (on the touchscreen) differ among the various operating systems.

Various platforms, devices, and services provide different experiences, feel differently, and are operated differently. Tastes are different. That has a lot to do with emotion and psychology. Due to this fact, the users, based on their individual motives and needs, usually subconsciously choose a certain platform, a suitable device, and the services that they consider to be helpful and interesting. It must be assumed that people who use the same services, platforms, or devices, device types, or models have at least some things in common and would presumably also act similarly in comparable contexts of use.

4.4.1 BEHAVIORAL PATTERNS IN THE MOBILE CONTEXT

In the mobile context of use, there are five typical interaction and behavioral patterns:

- **Completing smaller tasks:** Micro-tasking with Evernote, managing a to-do list, accessing e-mails, travel route tracking, documenting events, blogging, writing SMSs, talking on the telephone, using Skype, mobile offices.
- **Doing repetitive tasks:** Obtaining a status update about subjectively important information that changes regularly (e.g., live sports ticket, stock prices, weather, eBay auction).
- **Seeking a diversion or "killing time"** (due to boredom, while waiting in line, while traveling on a train, or during free time): Surfing the Internet (browsing), social networking, reading e-books or articles, watching videos or films, taking and sharing photos (Instagram), playing games, general free time activities.
- **Location-related information** is frequently important in a typical mobile situation (quite concretely related to the user's current geographical position): Timetable of the local public transportation network, route planner, events

nearby or points of interest (restaurant, theater, movie theater, disco), augmented reality. In this case, the personalization and the usage of user profiles are beneficial.

- **Handle what is urgent:** In many cases, you urgently need a piece of information or you must quickly do something—for example, find the route to the airport, complete something that cannot wait (send an urgent e-mail), or write a memo that you would otherwise forget to do.

Literature references: Mobile First (Wroblewski, 2011d), Tapworthy (Clark, 2010), and Google Mobile UX Strategy (Wellmann, 2007).

4.5 CONTEXT PROTOTYPES

Identifying and modeling contexts of use

In order to be able to identify and predict the potential and relevant contexts of use in which a service is used, you must examine the aforementioned parameters and detailed questions as well as the corresponding characteristics and special features. Based on these findings, an adequate context of use experience (*context experience*) can be conceived.

With the aid of scenarios, use cases, and other methods, situations can be described in which the corresponding service will presumably be used. The *context prototypes* for which you are designing the service can then be modeled and formulated.

Context prototypes are generally described contexts of use in which an information offering or a service could be used or situations in which users have a need for information or a service (Ballard, 2011). A wide array of features and parameters define the various context of use in which we find ourselves every day.

For the various contexts of use that are not only restricted by the form factor of the screen or the device but also may be differentiated through additional parameters and special features, you need corresponding contents. These should flexibly respond to the respective conditions and/or be able to be adapted to these conditions. We call this smart content (see Chapter 5, Section 5.10).

Thinking from the user's perspective

Contexts of use are different and not equally relevant. Whether they are suitable for the characteristics and needs of the relevant persons must be examined in individual cases. If necessary, a new or modified persona must be created for a special context of use. Conversely, if no target persona can be found in the context of use, it is possibly not relevant.

OPEN DISCUSSION

The discussion of the definition of the "mobile context of use" and/or the context of use and its various forms in general and the suitable methods for mastering this challenge is not complete (Lustig, 2012) because, among other reasons, the device landscape and the networking of the devices, services and people among themselves will continue to change.

The digital society finds itself in a transitional phase and/or in a constant and continuous change process (e.g., device fragmentation, new device classes, Internet of Things). What is important and where the focus should be placed depend on the individual project requirements, the various parameters, and the perspective. For more in-depth ideas, approaches, and discussions, see the website for the project at http://www.msxbook.com/en/contextofuse.

4.6 CONCLUSION AND TIPS

1. **Context is king.**
   Know, understand, and define the relevant contexts of use. They can be very different and depend on various parameters.

2. **The context of use can be very complex.**
   It is defined primarily via the five parameters of user, device, usage mode, situation, and environment. All parameters are not always equally relevant.

3. **The right contents at the right time.**
   A good service recognizes or anticipates the context of use and supplies the suitable information for the user (context relevance).

4. **The mobile context of use is quasi everywhere.**
   Whenever a mobile device is being used, you find yourself in a mobile context of use. It does not necessarily have to be a mobile situation.

5. **Use context prototypes.**
   It is helpful to anticipate the potential context of use and to model it. Of course, not everything can be foreseen, but whenever you work with representative scenarios, it is easier to design multiscreen-capable concepts. It is important that you think from the user's perspective in order to develop a suitable content strategy.

Strategies and Examples

5

In multiscreen experience design, you should take into consideration above all the users' expectations. Moreover, there are a wide array of cultures, user types, platforms, contexts of use, and devices that you must reconcile and take into consideration in the concept. The previously discussed device, user, and context prototypes can help to master these challenges. In this chapter, important and helpful patterns, methods, principles, and approaches are introduced for the development of strategy and are discussed in detail with examples.

OVERVIEW

There are various patterns, principles, methods, and approaches that you can rely on during the conception of cross-device and cross-platform services. The basis for this is the information presented in Chapters 2–4 regarding device classes, user types, and the context of use. With the aid of the previously described device, persona, and context prototypes and the ideas presented in this chapter, sensible and user-centered concepts and strategies can be developed for various screens. Some of the following patterns are based in part on the classification and definition of *precious design studio* from Hamburg (Stoll and Schardt, 2010). We have expanded, aggregated, and adapted these patterns.

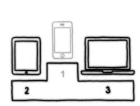

5.1 Mobile first
When you first develop for small screens, this results in a better structuring of the information due to the necessity of reduction.

5.2 Simultaneity
Various devices or information offerings are used on a parallel basis whereby the pieces of information can reciprocally complement each other.

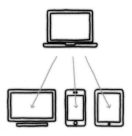

5.3 Social TV
Spatially separated viewers can quasi *watch TV together* or directly participate. Broadcasts are recommended by user profiles.

5.4 Device shifting
The displaying of contents and information can be shifted from one device to another device.

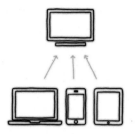 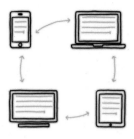

5.5 Complementarity
Both the devices and the information depicted on the screens reciprocally influence, control, and complement each other.

5.6 Synchronization
Information is always synchronized across devices and thus kept updated and to the same degree.

5.7 Screen sharing
An information (source) is displayed across multiple screens and shifted or expanded to them.

5.8 Coherence
A user interface should be comprehensible and understandable across devices as well as displayed similarly and in a logical visual connection.

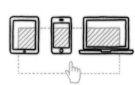 

5.9 Fluidity
Information offerings should function similarly across devices and offer an unchanging and fluid user experience.

5.10 Smart content
The more granular the contents are, the more flexibly they can be utilized and published across devices.

5.11 Mashability
Platform-independent and flexible information can be combined with (application programming) interfaces to create new added-value services.

5.12 Communification
Social networking can make a service more attractive to its users. They can create, share, assess, and comment on contents.

5.13 Gamification
Game mechanics simulate a competition. A game factor can motivate if it is challenging and sets a relevant goal.

5.14 Storyfication
With a story, you can create an engaging cross-device user experience and increase understanding of the product.

5.15 Emotionality

Services are emotionally more appealing if they are fun, support a device-fragmented daily routine, and adapt to and meet a user's needs.

5.16 Microjoyment

Due to the increasing information density, you must simplify small and important subtasks. Focus on details to enhance the user experience.

5.17 Hybrid media

The cross-media combination of analog and digital media for a cumulative information offering is the expansion of purely digital approaches.

The following are two supplemental areas that you should consider during realization:

5.18 Technical challenges

As with all digital projects, you should be familiar with and take into consideration the technical challenges.

5.19 Legal issues

There are various valid legal directives that you should responsibly follow.

5.1 MOBILE FIRST

Studies from Morgan Stanley Research and Gartner Research show that Internet-based services are accessed mainly or at least increasingly with mobile devices (Oschatz, 2010; see also Meeker, 2010, and Gartner, 2010). Studies also show that there is an increasing number of mobile-only users (Lipsman, 2015). Thus, it can make sense to take an approach according to the principle of *mobile first* (Wroblewski, 2010d) and to develop concepts first for mobile usage and/or primarily design them for the small screen. Depending on the project scope and potential usage of any user interface and/or service, the small screen can be a smartphone and/or a smartwatch (see Chapter 4, Section 4.4).

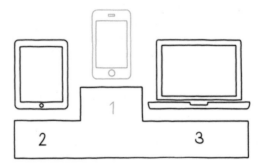

Clarity and usability

On a small screen (typical feature of mobile devices), there is substantially less space (than on the desktop PC) to arrange contents. Good mobile information offerings are thus more focused and frequently better adjusted to the user's needs. The actual limitation leads correspondingly to an improvement in quality. Whereas landing pages on desktop screens are frequently overloaded, good start pages on small mobile screens are frequently more transparent and more user-friendly. Moreover, because of the reduction, less data must be loaded, which results is generally shorter loading times and faster websites. This has a positive effect on the usability of the information offerings.

> **NOTE**
>
> The usage and relevance of devices are dependent on the target group and the context of use. With a TV service (e.g., Apple TV), the large screen will assume the main role. The same is valid for services and applications that have been designed for a designated context of use or a designated target group and thus for a screen that is best suited for it.

Expanding the first principle

The various screen sizes, screen resolutions, and device parameters influence both the layout and the content-related concept. Based on which devices are included in the concept, you can expand the *first principle* by initially concerning yourself with the screen that offers the least space for contents or is the most complicated to operate. In many cases, such as with social TV and second screen concepts (see Section 5.3), an approach based on the TV first principle could also make sense because you are rather limited due to the size of the screen in comparison to other screens. The fonts and menus are relatively large, and the navigation options (with the currently popular remote operation) are limited and thus comparable to the navigation options on feature phones (see Chapter 2, Section 2.5.4).

Mobile as an opportunity for innovation

It is not exclusively a matter of making everything smaller and maximally easy. In addition to many restrictions, mobile devices offer possibilities for innovative application concepts that other device classes cannot offer in this form. Localization, orientation, audio input, intuitive touch interface, camera, inclination sensor, and other options can be intuitively and sensibly utilized for new (mobile) concepts (see Chapter 4, Section 4.4).

One of the critically important limitations of smartphones in comparison with the desktop PC is the screen size. The small screen offers approximately 80% less space. That forces a focusing and restriction to the most important information and actions that you offer the users.

> *Thinking "one eyeball, one thumb" forces you to simplify mobile designs.*
>
> Luke Wroblewski (author of "Mobile First")

Desktop already there: Mobile second (as a latecomer)

Not each project begins at zero. Often, there is a lack of resources, time, or budget to begin completely anew. The mobile first principle can also help if there is already a desktop website or a desktop application that was originally developed without a mobile strategy (Fedorov, 2013). The layout and contents must then also be (belatedly) dynamically and flexibly prepared and/or supplied for all device classes and eventualities, and the existing interface must be examined for potential adaptations (see Section 5.8.1).

You must determine which relevant layouts and layout elements are needed, which you must focus extra attention on, and which you can adapt directly in the code. Next, the breakpoints are defined, and various device features are identified (resolution, camera, etc.). The interface for the small screen can be designed independently of the existing materials and, on this basis, an optimization for the larger screens can then be undertaken quasi retroactively. In this regard, you can proceed as follows:

- Identify and analyze use cases. What do visitors to the website actually want to do? What is their focus?
- Simplify the navigation, layouts, and the existing functionality. What can you leave out? How should you change the layout on mobile devices?

- Critically scrutinize interaction. Information offerings on touch devices are used differently. The screen area offers less space. Thus, you must adapt the navigation and content concept for mobile devices.
- Utilize responsive design patterns. Often, it can suffice to work with well-known and established layout patterns and to change the arrangement of the content elements only slightly (e.g., changing a two-column layout to a one-column layout).
- Remove unnecessary elements, aggregate similar ones, and simplify the user interface (e.g., reduce and simplify the input fields on the contact forms).

You can begin this approach relatively quickly. It is important that you do not rigidly hold fast to principles but, rather, respond collectively to conditions, have an iterative approach, and perform many tests (see Section 5.18).

A good example of Mobile First are the (former) website and smartphone app of **Southwest Airlines** (Wroblewski, 2010b and ZURB, 2010). Luke Wroblewski also used that example in his talks and in his book to explain his "Mobile First" principle. The landing page for the (large) desktop screen is totally overloaded and not very comprehensible. Conversely, the start page on the mobile screen has been reduced to what is essential and is more user-friendly.

> **TIP**
>
> Whenever you design layouts and user interfaces for mobile devices (as the first action), it is beneficial to define two or three reference sizes and/or reference resolutions, to create a standard draft, and, based on this, to create a flexible layout for various screens. With touch interfaces, for example, gestures and the content can be used for direct navigation (content = user interface). The sensitive area should be sufficiently large so that it can be operated with one's finger or stylus (the dimensions in centimeters are relevant). A hover function is often not available. In return you can utilize several different touch gestures (e.g., press, long press, tap, double tap), which however won't probably be available on all devices. Whether a native or web app is the better solution depends on the respective project (see Section 5.18). Also consider that a huge variety of different (mobile) devices are available (mobile is not just iPhone). It is nearly impossible to design perfectly for each device. Thus, you should also think about a more generic and flexible approach such as Atomic Design with your reference target devices (or device classes) in mind (see Section 5.9.1 and Chapter 7). The different devices and their definitions are described in Chapter 2, Section 2.3.1.

5.2 SIMULTANEITY

In a typical multiscreen scenario, various devices and/or screens (and thus also information offerings) are used at the same time (see multiscreen definition in Chapter 1, Sections 1.1 and 1.2). The information on both screens can reciprocally complement each other and are in more or less direct connection with each other.

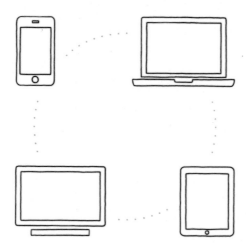

According to a Google study, we usually devote our attention to various activities on the individual devices during *simultaneous use* (Google et al., 2012). Contents that are watched on one device can trigger an interaction or user behavior on another device. Thus, you should not restrict yourself to the device on which the information is initially displayed and consumed. The various screens are potentially always related.

> *TV no longer commands our full attention as it has become one of the most common devices that is used simultaneously with other screens.*
>
> Google et al. (2012)

Parallel users and the second screen

Currently, every second TV viewer surfs the Internet parallel to watching TV (Google, 2012; TNS Emnid, 2011). Additional information can be displayed on the screen that is being used on a parallel basis.

Second screen refers to an additional digital device (e.g., tablet or smartphone) that allows TV viewers to interact with the consumed TV contents (shows, films, music, and video games). This is also referred to in this context as a "companion device" or (if it concerns the software being used) as a "companion app." On the portable device, additional complementary information about the TV contents is displayed.

The simultaneous use of various screens is also possible without the consumed information having a direct correlation to it. Additional useful options for devices being used on a parallel basis are microblogging, a chat, and/or generally allowing the viewers to participate in the TV program broadcast or tickers as a complementary information stream.

While you watch soccer, you can, on a parallel basis, also communicate with friends about the match on your tablet via Twitter and Facebook, write a short message with your smartphone, and read your e-mails on your laptop.

In the future, the TV will increasingly more rarely receive your full attention. However, it will act as the catalyst for the online search. Consumers search in a targeted manner for things that they see on TV (Google, 2012):

> *I'll be watching a movie or TV show and I'll look up the actor or actress on IMDB or I'll Google image them, or I'll see when it was made or how it was filmed. I'm always doing that. And I use my phone a lot for stuff like that.*
>
> (typical TV user; Google et al., 2012)

With the **Walkers Kill Count companion app**, which can be obtained on a complementary basis for the TV series *The Walking Dead*, viewers can predict—with/on the second screen—the number of zombie kills while watching the current episode at the same time. The app is synchronized with the broadcast both live and on-demand (thus time-delayed). At the same time, fans can discuss the broadcast with other fans via Twitter (for more in this regard, see Loo, 2012).

ABC's Grey's Anatomy Sync app allows viewers to interactively participate in the action. While the broadcast is running on TV, viewers can—at the beginning of an episode parallel to the broadcast—chat with others via iPad in real time or participate in surveys and small Q&A sessions. When so doing, the iPad app registers the audio signal of the TV so that the interaction can take place as synchronized as possible.

Some users search on the second screen for additional information about the film currently being shown. TV formats such as **The Voice of Germany** logically anticipate the increasing simultaneous usage of the devices and integrate, for example, the Twitter stream with the corresponding hashtags (#voice) or other communication platforms directly into the mobile apps for the tablet or the smartphone (see Section 5.12). Also see the example of Zeebox (re-branded to beamly in 2014) in Section 5.12, in which an app on a tablet or smartphone provides additional information to the TV show.

The **Sting 25 app** celebrates the life and the musical works of Sting. In combination with AirPlay, you can use two screens at the same time. While you watch exclusive concert clips on the TV screen, you can rummage through the complementary content on the iPad. Based on your perspective, the TV can serve as the complement to other devices. On the big screen, streamed contents or photos can be displayed from the tablet, or you can use a stereo system to improve the sound quality.

MetaMirror & The Future of TV from Notion is a concept that is already somewhat older (but was innovative when it was developed and remains innovative today) and that analyzes the changed situation in the digital household and changed viewing habits. Additional information about a TV program can be superimposed on the iPad that is being simultaneously used (Notion, 2010).

5.3 SOCIAL TV

With social TV, two or more spatially separated viewers can reach agreement on a collective audio video offering via an electronic communications channel and quasi "watch TV together." The users can communicate with each other while watching TV, discuss a broadcast, or directly participate.

By means of user profiles, the users are provided with corresponding recommendations for potentially interesting broadcasts (personalized electronic program guide [EPG]). Among others, viewing habits, personal preferences, the behavior of network friends, and the devices used are evaluated. Actually, watching TV has always been social. In the *social TV* concepts, the earlier family situation is actually only emulated.

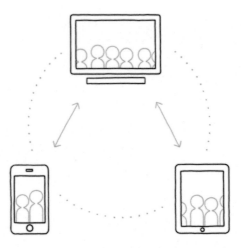

Basically, social TV is the linking of simultaneous use (see Sections 5.2 and 5.12). Additional information about social TV can be obtained via http://msxbook. com/en/socialtv.

TV revolution: The smart channel

Social networks are conquering the TV, and tablets and intelligent apps are revolutionizing the way we watch TV (Cohrs and Rützel, 2012). A typical situation in which the entire family sits together in front of the TV is becoming increasingly rare. The central TV in the living room (see Section 4.2.1) and/or the device class "TV" is losing its significant unique status as a moving-image medium (Hannemann, 2012). Films, videos, and broadcasts can also be accessed on the other devices. Each person can watch when and where he would like. In the future, users will expect that contents (broadcasts, films, and series) will always be available (see Section 5.6).

In the current age of personalized TV, classical TV broadcasting companies must rethink their business model. Linear lean back TV is competing with multimedia libraries, online video libraries, video platforms, and interactive TV participation formats. The people of "Generation YouTube" are accustomed to both self-produced amateur video clips and special-interest channels, which include the offerings of the large broadcasting companies, the official channels of prominent brands, and special niche themes for various interest groups. Regardless of whether it involves a large TV broadcasting company, semiprofessional producers, video bloggers, or amateurs, everyone will become a producer and a broadcaster. By means of profile information, TV offerings can be customized exactly to the users' needs and habits.

I turn on the TV and it is so cool. It's always exactly shown what I want to see. Although I really didn't even know at all what I want.

Conrad Frizsch (cofounder of tape.tv)

The big screen will remain the biggest, and it will perhaps get even bigger (e.g., as digital wallpaper). But its future role as a part of the multiscreen world will be changing.

Today the "TV" for many people is still a device which is located in the coziest room in your home. For us, it is the relaxing consumption of all possible high-end contents and regardless on which device.

Marcel Düe (founder of Tweek)

TV-optimized websites from YouTube to Vimeo and Clicker exploit the possibilities of the current web technologies and offer a fast and first-class user experience without colored buttons. The sites are fast and can also be operated easily from the PC in "couch mode" (see https://www.youtube.com/leanback, http://www.vimeo.com/couchmode, and http://tv.clicker.com).

Truly interactive TV

During the age of social TV, it is no longer a matter of where a licenseholder publishes his contents but, rather, of the contents themselves and their quality. Content must and should be able to be shared. It does not necessarily have to appear on the provider's channel or (web)site (licenseholder) (this applies for all contents—not just for moving-image contents).

The new media users "like," comment on, and share TV contents. However, it largely does not matter to them from where the contents originate. The broadcast or the format is the brand itself, not the broadcasting company. Broadcasts must be entertaining, captivating, informative, and funny—that is, they must be so good that the audience will gladly like and recommend them to others (see Section 5.12).

Some ideas and examples of interactive TV are presented next.

Combination of social TV and communification: Via corresponding apps, you can directly purchase music, furniture, accessories, and clothes depending on the broadcast and theme. Based on the profile information, personalized advertising can be superimposed on the large screen or the second screen.

The **TV broadcasting company joiz** offers its viewers the possibility of interacting, including during TV advertising, 24 hours a day.

At **Tape.TV**, the users can like or dislike rate videos and have videos recommended by friends. By means of the profile settings and user information, the offering can be customized to the users—with personalized playlists and interactive supplemental functions. A win–win situation is created. The provider learns which music videos which users like and can offer targeted and optimized contents (see Section 5.12).

Rundshow: In the TV experiment by Richard Gutjahr and the Bavarian Broadcasting Company, viewers could express their opinions via e-mail and the social networks or participate in the broadcast via Skype or Google Hangout. With a supplement app, "The Power," the viewers could directly comment on the occurrences on the screen, rate them live, and even upload photos or videos. With the like and dislike buttons, the users could trigger live "YEAHs" or "BOOs," which were also visualized with a green or a red bar.

Couchfunk and TunedIn are typical second screen apps for iPhone and/or iPad through which the users quasi "watch TV together" and (can) discuss a program during its broadcast. Based on the user profiles, the applications will send recommendations for potentially interesting programs and analyze the TV-watching habits, personal preferences, and the user behavior of the network friends. Moreover, users can rate programs. The social TV services also use popular social networks such as Twitter or Facebook.

With **Shazam for TV**, users get supplemental information about each program. Moreover, they can obtain information about their favorite programs and interact with their friends. Via a direct connection to Facebook and Twitter, this information can be shared and discussed in one's personal network. The interaction functions of the second screen are also used for the commercials (Hohenauer, 2012). In this case, the audio signal is utilized in a targeted manner as an interaction parameter.

5.3.1 CLASSIFICATION OF SOCIAL TV

In addition to the content area, there are other aspects, segments, and issues concerning social TV—for example, with which technology contents and platforms are synchronized, why and how users can obtain and supply the most accurate data possible, or which offerings the users want to find on their second screen devices.

TV is no consumption and one-way medium any more. It is a communications medium.

Mathias Menzl (Head of Music at joiz)

Based on these questions, Mathias Menzl classified social TV into three layers. All layers correspond to each other and are intermeshed. No layer functions without the other layer, and all three work together (Menzl, 2012).

1) CONTENTS LAYER

TV contents are altered or created through social TV and user interaction. For example, tweets can be displayed and/or commented on by the users during the broadcasts. In the second case, user contributions are directly addressed. References to social media accounts or the superimposing of hashtags are the easiest and most obvious form. Taking it a step further, it concerns transmedia storytelling (see Section 5.14) in order to attain multiway communication, transparency, and communication with each other as equals. One should live this and integrate it authentically into a broadcast.

2) ADVERTISING LAYER

Through interactive TV advertising, helpful information (especially for advertisers) can be obtained about user behavior. Through direct participation of TV users, the value that a Facebook Like box should have that appears synchronized to the TV commercial on the TV broadcaster's website can be evaluated. Moreover, you can examine whether a buy link is used on a second screen and whether, when, how often, and perhaps even why users view TV commercials. Finally, whether the users actually land on the website being promoted and trigger the action being promoted (purchase, subscription, participation, registration, etc.) can be evaluated.

Shazam permits the user to identify a music title based on its audio track with his smartphone within a very brief period of time. Newcast used this technique for a Toyota TV spot. When the viewer sees the spot in the advertising block, he is requested by an icon to activate Shazam. The music recognition application recognizes—in only a few seconds—the audio track and links immediately to the Shazam tag result of Toyota. There, the user has the opportunity to access diverse links and social media channels in order to participate in a sweepstakes, to book a test drive, or to find the address of the nearest Toyota dealer (Middelhoff, 2012).

The **red button from joiz TV** integrates clickable TV advertising into the program. In a trailer from the broadcasting company joiz, the moderator tells her audience to click "Press the red button!" and points to a red button that appears in the upper right corner of the screen. Behind this feature, there is clickable TV advertising integrated into trailers, an editorial program, and normal advertising spots. Via a smartphone app or a desktop website, the registered viewer can participate in sweepstakes, other competitions, and various campaigns with a click. Everything is tailored to the program that is running. The direct access is triggered by physical purchases and closely coupled to the program. The red button can be used by everyone who has registered at joiz via the app or the Internet. By means of the red button, according to joiz's Managing Director Alexander Mazzara, it is possible to supply anonymized sociodemographic information about the people who interact based on this TV spot to advertising clients (Schräder, 2012).

3) TECHNOLOGY AND THE USER-INTERACTION LAYER

The following are fundamental questions about the technology and the UI layer: Which platform will be used for social TV (HbbTV, Connected TV, apps, website, etc.)? With which technology will the synchronization of TV programs/TV advertising and interaction platforms be implemented (audio/video fingerprinting, EPG synchronization, or audio detection)? Does the provider have his own second screen for the interaction or does he use existing platforms? What contents will be offered on the second screen and how do the contents, which are input by the user via the second screen, come back to the TV? How do the interactions influence the TV program broadcast (or not), and which contents does the user and/or TV viewer want to find at all on the second screen? Which does he really use and which make no sense? Most important, how can the viewer profit from what he does with his interaction? How can he be rewarded (see Section 5.13)? If he does not want to be rewarded (but he definitely wants to interact in some other form, even if it is merely participating in communication), for what reason does he then interact?

Each program offers other possibilities. TV producers, website operators, and advertisers must try to identify potential and integrate interaction options into future TV concepts, offer the viewers an interactive experience, and allow them to participate in an organic and authentic manner in the product "TV" (Menzl, 2012).

The **MTV Video Music Awards** have firmly integrated the Twitter service into the event. In so doing, "promoted trends" are used to strengthen the communication about the event. The viewers are asked to twitter with the hashtag #VMA, can participate in the live broadcast, and can actually influence it. In 2012, more than 10 million tweets were sent for the event (Twitter, 2012).

The social TV monitor from Goldmedia shows the **social TV practices** for TV broadcasting companies and TV broadcasts in Germany. The Facebook pages for the broadcasts that were evaluated reveal **five different concepts** (Goldmedia, 2012):
- The simplest form is the pure announcement with program notes or program-supporting information.
- This concept is also realized by the news broadcasts (e.g., ZDFheute, RTL and Aktuell), expanded by additional news content (second concept).
- A third group is formed by broadcasting websites that focus on discussion and communication (e.g., Galileo and Sat.1 Breakfast News).
- In addition, there is the concept of the vertical show expansion (e.g., GZSZ)—for example, through a look behind the scenes.
- A very highly successful concept is the horizontal show expansion (e.g., *Berlin Day and Night*). In this case, the show becomes part of the social reality of the viewer. Similar to status updates from friends, the fans see news about the show characters in their private streams (parasocial interaction).

X Factor cooperates with the social media experts from Mass Relevance in order to more strongly involve the audience in the show. In addition, Twitter contents are displayed in real time (http://twitter.thexfactorusa.com) and directly aggregated, filtered, and integrated into the broadcast. The tweet counter, graphics about the Twitter frequency, Twitter streams, and a photo wall have been integrated into the website in order to increase the participation of the fans on the second screen (Mass Relevance, 2012).

Text adopted with courtesy of Mathias Menzl (2012).

5.3.2 SOCIAL TV: THE FIVE STAGES OF INTERACTION

The possibilities for social interaction during TV consumption are varied. A classification from Bertram Gugel (2012) breaks them down into five stages. The classification concentrates on the content-related, editorial portion of the interaction between TV producers and TV viewers.

1) USER-TO-USER INTERACTION

Interaction among users: On their own initiative, viewers comment on the TV program—either with their friends on Facebook, in a check-in app, or publicly via Twitter. In this scenario, the broadcaster does not participate.

Tatort, a German language crime thriller and police procedural television series developed by the German television channel ARD, is a good example for this stage. The viewers had a lively discussion at #tatort on Twitter without ARD participating in the conversation. ARD (full name: Arbeitsgemeinschaft der öffentlich-rechtlichen Rundfunkanstalten der Bundesrepublik Deutschland) is a joint organization of Germany's regional public-service broadcasters.

2) MODERATED INTERACTION

Interaction between the users and the producers: On this level, the broadcasting company participates in the communication and the interaction by actively interacting with the users and/or generating its own contents via the social media accounts of the broadcasting company, the actors, or the program. For example, ZDF supports the program impeccably with @ZDF on Twitter. The users have a starting point and experience something live about the program. ZDF (Zweites Deutsches Fernsehen; English: Second German Television) is a German public-service television broadcaster.

MTV participated actively for the first time in 2008 in the communication about the Video Music Awards. At that time, the stars were equipped with smartphones in order to send brief messages from the backstage area.

3) MIRRORING THE USER INTERACTIONS

Displaying the interaction on the TV or online (e.g., tweets and voting results in the graphical form as TV graphics or online): The broadcasting companies curate and aggregate the messages and comments from the users and thus mirror the interaction either on the TV program or on its own website.

The easiest form is to integrate a **Twitter Widget** or a Facebook chat on your own home page, which has been done for the Eurovision Song Contest and similar events. It is slightly more time-consuming if selected comments are to be seen during the TV program as a band or screen shot, as is the case with *The Voice of Germany* and other show formats or in the case of **MTV**, for which data visualization is used. In 2009, MTV decided to no longer just be active in social media but, rather, to mirror the interactions of the users in a data visualization on the Net.

4) ENGAGEMENT OF THE USERS

Interaction as a mood barometer and opinion survey during the broadcast: Whereas the previous stages were based on the fact that the intrinsic motivation of the users and/or the opportunity to get on TV with a tweet were sufficient for interaction, the deliberate engagement of the users goes a step further. The users interact not only because they would like to interact but also because they are given creative tasks or are asked for their opinion. The answers and results once again flow into the broadcast.

In 2010, **MTV** once again expanded its integration of social media and relied not only on Twitter moderators and gigantic visualization but also on entertaining hashtags such as the legendary #IfBieberMetGaga.

ProSieben has, for example, with the TV show "Pop Stars" with the hashtag #NelaOnMyCouch, offered the incentive of a visit from the TV moderator Nela.

Fox has gone somewhat further by analyzing political debates with the aid of Twitter. In order to participate, users could state via Twitter whether they thought the speaker had dodged the question (#dodge) or had answered it (#answer). The approach is similar to visualizations and rankings on TV that are updated in real time on the basis of user interactions.

5) INTERACTION WITH THE TV PROGRAM

Interaction defines the broadcast and the result: This last step is the most difficult because not only does it involve the users interacting with individual parts of the program and discussing them but also they have an influence on the program's outcome. That means that the interaction of the users guides the program, which is possible with only great difficulty for many programs. However, especially for events and shows, several approaches for this type of interaction can be considered. Votes are the easiest answer, as the *MTV Movie Awards* show. Another option for designing formats that are really interactive is to get users to the program via social media—as occurs with *Rundshow*—or to at least supply contents to them. How interaction can be sensibly integrated into the narration without losing the non-active viewers, is still another major challenge of social TV that must be solved in the future.

In 2012, **MTV** included social media as a decision-maker in the *MTV Movie Awards* program. Via Twitter, users could vote to determine the winner of the award for Best Hero.

Text adopted with courtesy of Bertram Gugel (2012).

5.4 DEVICE SHIFTING

The displaying of contents or information can be shifted from one device to another device. In so doing, the display is alternated between the participating screens. The advantage for users is that they can use as many devices as they desire and/or the currently available devices and the information can be displayed on the preferred device—always suitable for the context of use. The users thus remain very flexible when obtaining information.

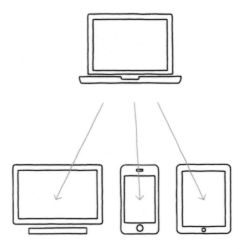

If I'm watching TV I won't go upstairs to grab my laptop to follow up on a product I see, I'd just pull out my phone.
Sophie (Google et al., 2012)

Of course, each user has preferred devices for certain activities. Nonetheless, the closest or available device is often used because it is simply more convenient.

Device shifting is also relevant in conjunction with time-delayed information. For example, if you find an interesting article or video during work or on the go, you can bookmark it for later (watch/read later) and continue to read it later or read it in its entirety at a later suitable time. The watch later function has been directly integrated into the video players of YouTube and Vimeo. Bookmarking services with the read later function are Pocket or Instapaper.

Instapaper is a web service that you can use to bookmark online articles in order to read them later on any device of your choice (read later function). To use it, you must merely install a bookmarklet in the browser. The bookmarks can be managed and sorted in a folder. There are also clients for mobile devices. All articles are stored locally on the device and can also be read in pure text display on the go and without an Internet connection. You can change devices at any time and decide on what screen you would like to read your articles. The synchronization (see Section 5.6) takes place automatically as soon as you call up a client or use it and indirectly supports a modified form of device shifting—a type of virtual, time-delayed shifting between the devices (device switching).

With Apple AirPlay (in conjunction with Apple TV), you can change devices in the middle of a film and continue obtaining information on another device. The film is shifted from one (e.g., the iPhone) to another device (e.g., the TV) in order to continue obtaining information on it at the same point. In order to transmit videos via AirPlay to a TV, an Apple TV receiver box is required. For wireless music streaming, Bluetooth can also be used. You can also shift images or the iOS screen to the AppleTV screen.

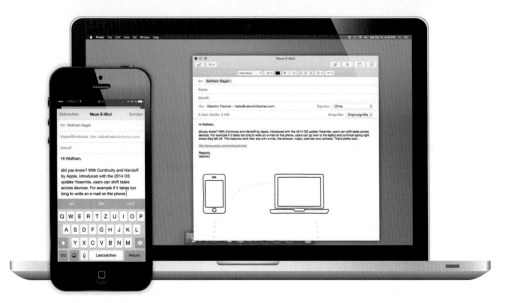

With **Continuity and Handoff by Apple**, introduced with the 2014 OS update Yosemite, users can shift tasks across devices. For example, if it takes too long to write an e-mail on the phone, users can switch to the laptop and continue typing from the point at which they left off. This feature works inter alia with e-mail, the browser, maps, calendar, and contacts.

Flow from Samsung is similar and lets you move tasks from one device to another or put them off to be completed later (see also Sections 5.9 and 2.2.6).

With **Continuum**, it is possible to connect a smartphone to a normal desktop PC monitor or a TV screen in order to use it like a desktop PC. With this **Windows 10 feature**, smartphones are able to scale up to a full PC-like experience (Welch, 2015).

With **Deep Shot** (a prototype project by Google), you can move an interactive map by simply taking a picture of it with the camera of a smartphone. The map stays interactive on the phone (Li, 2011).

Google Chromecast is quite similar to Apple TV. You can also switch videos or films (e.g., from YouTube or an online TV recorder, **"BONG.TV"** as shown in the image) easily from your smartphone (or tablet) to the TV screen with one button push. You need a Chromecast dongle that can be plugged into your TV. You can also mirror content from the Google Chrome web browser running on a laptop or PC, as well as from a screen of some Android devices.

Google's Copresence enables users of Android devices to share information (e.g., maps, music, photos, and websites) with others nearby across devices and operating systems, even if they use iOS devices. This feature is similar to Apple's AirDrop on iOS, which works only in the Apple ecosystem.

Tablets are optimal reading devices due to their form factor and operation. **Pocket** (similar to Instapaper) represents a good example of how you can maintain a consistent multiscreen experience with the aid of a tablet. While surfing the Internet with the desktop PC or the laptop, whenever the user finds something interesting that he would like to watch or read later, he can simply put it in his pocket. The pocket stores these articles and displays them in a clearly arranged, reader-friendly layout on the tablet or smartphone and generates a type of personalized, individualized magazine (Itzkovitch, 2012).

AllRecipes is a good example of a cross-device application concept that offers a fluid multiscreen experience. You can search online for recipes on the desktop PC and add the ingredients to a virtual shopping list. While shopping, this shopping list can be accessed on the smartphone. With the app, you can also scan products with the camera and display other recipes. The iPad app serves, among other things, as the cookbook and has a cook-friendly interface with large letters and large buttons that can be operated easily, which is very helpful when you are working in the kitchen and have wet or dirty hands. There is a supplemental app with video cooking instructions (see Section 5.6).

If the **auto interface** is coupled and/or synchronized with the mobile device, the information is mirrored on the car's display and the interface can be navigated via the car's operating controls (Kuehlhaus, 2011; Trapp, 2011).

5.5 COMPLEMENTARITY

If various devices can communicate with and respond to each other, the interaction quality can be increased. The devices can reciprocally influence, control, and complement both each other and the information depicted on the screens.

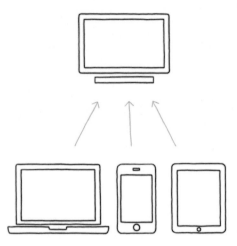

Depending on the service, target group, and use, it can make sense to be able to influence the screen of one device from another device. The user can control the displaying of the information on one screen from another screen.

Often, a second device serves as a type of remote control for interacting or navigating with another device. For example, a smartphone can be used as a remote control for a TV.

In addition to the provided remote control, you can also operate Apple TV with the remote app for the iPhone, iPod Touch, or iPad. **The smartphone (or tablet) serves as remote control** and controls and influences the display on the TV.

Padracer is a good example of how different devices can complement each other. With the racing game, the iPhone serves as the steering wheel while the race track is displayed on the iPad.

Adobe Nav is a supplemental app for the iPad and serves to complement Adobe Photoshop. Via the app, opened Photoshop documents can be searched through and selected, and Photoshop tools can be activated. Accordingly, you control the tools on the desktop PC via the iPad screen. The iPad can then be used as a quasi-remote control.

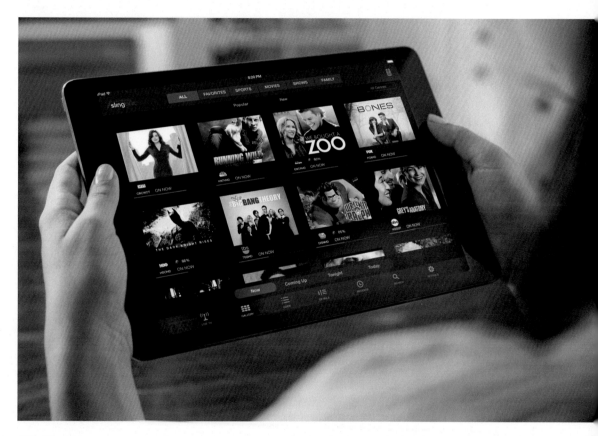

With **SlingPlayer**, you can watch or record programs quasi remotely regardless of where you are at the time and play everything back on mobile devices that you could watch on the TV at home (see Section 5.4). In combination with the corresponding Slingbox (supplemental hardware), the programs can be streamed "from your living room" to the mobile device. In so doing, via the smartphone, you can, for example, change the channel or control the digital video recorder remotely. The principle functions both for live and for recorded programs. Each device complements the other. The complementary multiscreen experience functions only with multiple devices.

Scrabble Tile Rack is a supplement to the iPad app by means of which you can use the iPad in the multiplayer mode as a gameboard. iPod Touch and iPhone serve as a quasi-personal tile rack that the other players cannot see from which you can flip tiles to the iPad.

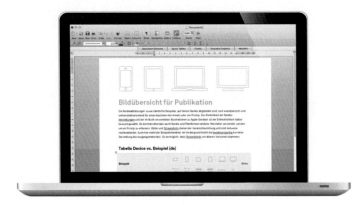

Vigour platfrom: See explanation on the following page.

The **Vigour platform** (formerly Brisk.io) offers innovative options with regard to the interaction with contents and the type of multiscreen media consumption. With Vigour, you can edit and influence the user interface, the interaction design, and the information design (see Chapter 2, Section 2.6.2) and combine and apply various patterns and principles in one single application.

Contents can be broken down into pieces, allocated across multiple devices, and controlled from various screens—for example, the UI elements of a word processing software or various video feeds of a sports broadcast. All changes are replicated in real time across all connected devices and the database. Applications can be coherently depicted and implemented on various devices and platforms.

The Vigour developmental environment creates a bridge between traditionally separated back-end and front-end components (server and client) and provides a good and scalable basis for the creation and operation of multiscreen applications (see http:// vigour.io; see also Sections 5.4 and 5.6–5.9).

Super Sync Sports from Google is a multiplayer browser game in which you can control the main game and/or the game piece in the desktop browser with the smartphone or tablet via WLAN. In order to do so, you must visit the corresponding URL at https://chrome. com/supersyncsports and/or g.co/super via the respective browsers (both on the desktop and on the mobile device). On the desktop web page, you will receive a code by means of which you can register on the smartphone. You can then synchronize the devices with each other. The mobile device then quasi becomes the game controller and serves for the controlling of the browser application. Up to three additional players can participate (multiplayer mode).

There are three sports disciplines offered: running, bicycling, and swimming. For each type of sport, there is a multitouch gesture that you can use to move your game piece forward. For example, for the running game, you must move two fingers on the display from up to down, and for the bicycling game, you move your finger in a circle.

DIAL ("*d*iscovery *a*nd *l*aunch") is a simple protocol by means of which you can search for and start apps on the first screen and then shift them to second screen devices. By so doing, any app can be used for the remote control and operation of the TV (for more information, see www.dial-multiscreen.org).

Cube Slam is a video game that can be played against others on different devices. Opponents do not have to be in the same room. There is a link that has to be shared. This Chrome experiment uses a WebRTC, an open web technology that is normally used for video chats without the need of installing any plug-ins.

And take control of the website
with your smartphone

 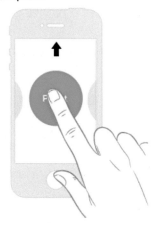

On the **Diplomatic-Cover** website, you can connect the smartphone with the desktop browser. Once connected via a distinct URL, the screen on the desktop computer can be controlled and the website's content navigated by using the smartphone. To start browsing, you have to swipe a picture representative for each content topic to the desktop screen. Illustration taken from the website at http://www.diplomatic-cover.com/multi.

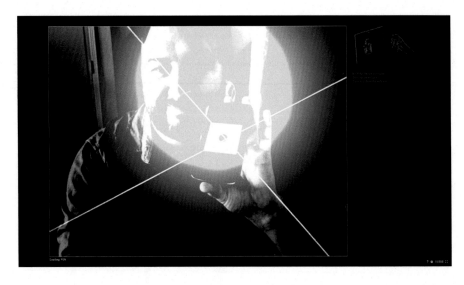

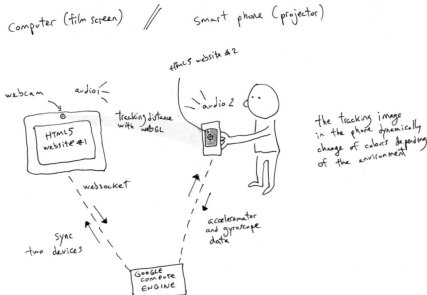

"Just a Reflektor" (justareflektor.com) is an interactive short film directed by Vincent Morisset and featuring a song from Arcade Fire. This Chrome experiment uses the camera of the desktop PC to actively influence the film. To let the story begin, a smartphone or tablet has to be synchronized with the desktop browser. Then a virtual projection on the computer screen can be casted by holding up the mobile device in front of the computer's webcam. That way, all of the visual effects in the experience can be controlled by moving the phone or tablet through the physical space around oneself (Arcade Fire, 2015). Above you see the "Just a Reflektor" interactive instructions screen and an original sketch of the technological setup of justareflektor.com.

Tado is a smart thermostat for the heating system with location awareness. The system can be controlled remotely (wherever you are, not just at home) by a smartphone app or via web application in the browser. The system learns how you live, knows when you are at home and therefore adjusts the temperature depending on your daily routine. It adjusts the temperature automatically depending on how far you are away from home, or reduces temperature when you go to bed and checks the weather forecast. Tado is comparable to the Nest thermostat.

You can search, find and show details of a restaurant on your smartwatch. If you like to reserve a table (for example), you choose the phone number on the watch and make a phone call with your smartphone. Thus the **smartwatch controls the smartphone**. You start an action on one device and continue and complete it on another (the example shows the Yelp Apple Watch smartphone app). See Section 2.6.2 "Continuous Experience."

Remote-control release from your wrist: **ProCamera** turns the Apple Watch into a remote shutter with a few other features (e.g., taking multiple shots and setting a timer). Images can be displayed on the watch screen, too. The app also has editing features if you want to do that from your watch.

5.6 SYNCHRONIZATION

In an increasingly networked and device-fragmented environment, information should always be synchronized and thus always kept updated to the same extent on the relevant devices.

When you start building your multiscreen applications stop and think about these things for a second. You may want to offer the user a way of syncing data across multiple devices. I'm sure your user will appreciate it!

Serge Jespers (Adobe Evangelist)

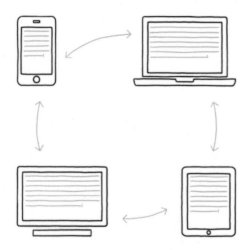

    As is the case with many fans of casual games, Adobe Platform evangelist Serge Jespers (2010) wishes there were a better synchronization of popular multiscreen applications:

Like many of you, I am addicted to Angry Birds. I installed it on my smartphone and on my tablet. But both are not connected to each other. Wouldn't it be great if you could simply open the app on your tablet and continue to play at the same level which you had previously attained on your smartphone? In order to then perhaps once again continue to play on the desktop at the same level? Or on the TV?

Independence and interoperability

Like Jespers, users expect that the identical information or data can be retrieved and processed at any time and in any place with various devices and spontaneously (thus without any preplanning). In order to do this, they must be synchronized across devices. Sensible multiscreen and cross-platform services are not conceivable without cloud computing and data sharing.

The better the various services, software, and data formats can be combined with each other and the more easily and more efficiently that information can be exchanged between various systems, the better interoperability. If data are regularly synchronized and/or their statuses are updated and synchronized, users can be independent of the device type, time, or place.

You can then switch the device at any time, easily and without any disruptions, and continue to obtain information or your activity on another device—provided that the information is in principle available. Simple examples are saved (and synchronized) shopping baskets when doing online shopping or logging in.

With **Amazon Kindle**, you can interrupt your reading of an e-book at any point you want, switch the device, and continue to read at the same point on another device because the application remembers where you stopped (which is an example of a continuous experience as described in Chapter 2, Section 2.6.2).

"ChromeBooks (web based laptops) took the principle of synchronization to an extreme in 2010 with a series of ads that showed you working on one device, it getting destroyed in a gruesome manner, yet you can just pick it up again effortlessly on another one," as Scott Jenson mentioned in his preface.

One-way and two-way synchronization

A frequently encountered synchronization of digital media is that of appointment programs which, for example, manage a calendar at the workplace on a computer. Synchronizing this calendar with the stationary appointment calendar on calendar-compatible smartphones can be done using synchronization programs via various options. With one-way synchronization, all appointments are sent from one device to the other device; with two-way synchronization, all data are reciprocally sent from each device to the respective other device. By so doing, this can lead to redundant entries, which the synchronization software must then identify.

Problems and challenges

To date, a perfect synchronization scenario has been very difficult to realize due to major technical challenges. Even if an application contributes all the required functionalities, the synchronization can still fail due to a lack of network coverage. In conjunction with synchronization and cloud computing, you must also make reference to the theme of data protection, which has still not been satisfactorily solved and/or communicated by many providers (see Section 5.19).

Issues that arise during data synchronization and that must be solved in conjunction with the cross-device multiscreen information offerings include the following: When does the user know which data are "syncted" where? Which device has been updated? Do you have to ask the user to actively synchronize? Does the synchronization automatically function (does it work at all and, if so, how)? Are there information offerings that can serve as a reference with regard to data synchronization (e.g., Instapaper, Dropbox, YouTube, and Evernote)? What can be improved?

"Watching a Film" Scenario

Sometimes and depending on the service, it is possible to continue to watch a film begun on the TV on another device or to watch it to the end (and vice versa). If the information and the position on which the film has been interrupted are synchronized, there is nothing preventing a fluid experience in which the user can move back and forth between the devices randomly and as he so chooses.

With the set-top box from **Apple TV**, you can play back various media contents (mainly video but also audio and photos) on the TV. The contents can be retrieved from the Internet or the local network—for example, from an external PC, on-demand as a streaming rental video, or from an iOS device. The standard functionality is the renting out of films via Apple's online video library. You can also use video sharing portals (e.g. Vimeo) and access the bookmarked films and/or the general offerings there.

You can connect Apple TV via the Internet and/or WLAN to a computer. By so doing, you can play/show films, music, and photos from the private iTunes media library on your TV. Third-party providers such as the online TV recorder **BONG.TV** offer RSS feeds for recorded programs that can likewise be played via Apple TV. In combination with the AirPlay technology, you can stream contents from an iOS device in a wireless manner to a TV.

Meta-data sharing: On the Internet video portal **YouTube**, users can upload, watch, and comment on video clips for free. In principle, there is no direct access to the video file; that is, the videos cannot be stored locally but can be watched online in the web browser or on various devices.

Each user can set up a free-of-charge account and save videos as favorites. Profile information, the favorites list, and other meta-data are stored in the cloud and are available across devices. YouTube videos can also be accessed via Internet TV offerings and streamed (e.g., from Apple, Google, Samsung, or Sony). Videos can be posted in blogs or integrated into websites via a programming interface (application programming interface [API]) (see Sections 5.10 and 5.11).

Google Calendar is an online calendar for which a Google account is required. The information can be shared with others (calendar sharing). The calendar can be viewed through RSS and iCalendar feeds with suitable programs and synchronized via Google Sync with mobile devices and programs.

With the network file system **Dropbox**, files can be synchronized between various computers and users. The service can be used for file sharing or backing up your own data. After the installation, a folder is stored on the respective device that is linked to the Dropbox account on the web server and synchronized with the server. You can access the virtual dropbox folder online from anywhere. With an active Internet connection, it will immediately be mirrored on a central server. Via the programming interface (API), other applications can also access the dropbox. Numerous applications, such as iAWriter and Plaintext, use the service as a cloud interface for the cross-device storage and synchronization of text files.

With the **iCloud from Apple**, appointments, addresses, documents, music, and photos can be saved in the cloud online on Apple servers. All personal devices are automatically synchronized and thus kept up-to-date. Similar to the Amazon Kindle, since iOS 6.1, positions in musical pieces or films are also saved and automatically loaded onto all devices for which you have already registered with the same account. If a film, a podcast, or an audio book is played on a device, all other devices automatically "know" where the broadcast was interrupted.

The music-streaming service **Spotify** can be synchronized and used across devices. Based on which device you use when utilizing the service, the broadcast pauses on the one device and continues in a quasi-seamless manner on the other device. Community functions have also been integrated. An interface to Facebook tells friends which music you are listening to right at that moment and also provides information via e-mail about newly created lists and albums (see Section 5.12).

Wunderlist is an online task manager. The list of tasks is managed locally and can be synchronized via a web server. The list can be retrieved and managed by means of various devices. The synchronization is often done automatically, but it should be undertaken manually for security purposes. It entails a classic client–server synchronization.

iOutBank serves for mobile online banking on the iPhone and the iPad. On the go, the account balance can be obtained or transfers can be done. The app retrieves the encrypted data on the bank server and stores all bank data such as account and bank routing numbers from previous account transactions locally on a contact list. With online banking, high standards for data security and data encryption exist.

Evernote, a digital notebook, serves for the archiving and categorization of various types of notes/memos—text, websites, photos, videos, audio and/or voice memos, and handwritten notes—that are stored in the cloud and are provided by means of various clients and a web application in a device-independent manner. The notes/memos can be processed at any time on any device of your choice and, as a result of cloud computing, are in principle always synchronous (depending on the various synchronization settings).

The application indeed appears slightly different on various screens and devices, but it always operates similarly in principle and is also modified for use on the respective devices. The smartphone app has been optimized for inputting photos and audio and, through the aid of GPS position finding, saves the location where the notes/memos were created (see Section 5.8).

Device synchronization: In order to use an Apple Watch in a sensible way you need a constantly synchronized (Bluetooth) connection to the iPhone that in turn is connected to the Internet via wireless LAN or cellular phone network. Bluetooth is a wireless technology standard for exchanging data over short distances. If you leave a room (without the phone) or if the distance is too long the smartwatch loses connection and therefore the capability to obtain information (comparable to a dead zone). That has to be considered when developing applications that rely on these devices and depend on such usage paradigms.

Synchronizing internet connection: If you have several devices (e.g., a smartphone, a tablet, and a laptop) and only one has access to the internet (e.g., the phone) you can connect the other devices via tethering and therefore "borrow" or share the internet connection with other devices. The connection of the phone or tablet with other devices can be done over wireless LAN, Bluetooth, or by physical connection using a (USB) cable.

Just an example how **information is (or could be) synchronized across devices**
(see Chapter 2, Section 2.6.2 "Continuous Experience"): You can search for and book
a flight on the desktop website (you can do that on a smartphone as well, of course), get
and check status updates on a smartphone and get notifications or check status on a
smartwatch. All the information is synchronized and displayed in an appropriate manner
(examples show screenshots from Lufthansa).

The day I **felt like Knight Rider**. In the car it's difficult to interact with screens. Recently I
just talked to my watch to start a phone call with my family through the microphone and
speakers of my car. The watch was synchronized and connected with the smartphone that
again was connected with the interface of my car. All connections start(ed) automatically
when devices and interfaces are in operating distance. I just needed one finger tip on the
watch and start the phone call by voice command to activate the action and to involve three
different "devices" and their screens, that's all. Situations like this will be and are already quite
normal. Some years ago that was a future scenario, now it's common reality in a connected
multiscreen world. Some thoughts on automotive and synchronizing device(s) with the car are
mentioned in Chapter 8, Section 8.2.

5.7 SCREEN SHARING

There is often not enough space on a screen to display all information satisfactorily and in a large enough size. In this case, it may be helpful to combine multiple screens and to have the information displayed across them. With screen sharing, primarily the size of the screen space is increased and the display of a piece of information or an information (source) in general is spread across multiple screens and moved or expanded to them.

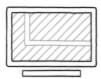

Each additional screen serves as an expansion of the platform and/or the main screen. The individual contents and information on the various screens are in a direct correlation, but the screens do not display the same contents and information. In many cases, this pattern can overlap with the complementarity principle.

With many desktop programs, the graphical interface can be displayed and used on multiple screens. The display can be allocated across multiple screens and/or moved to other screens. With **Photoshop**, you can, for example, move pallets, windows, and control panels to a second monitor.

Junkyard Jumbotron, a project from MIT Media Labs, shows how you can combine multiple, very diverse displays to form a large virtual screen area. You place the corresponding devices next to each other as desired and visit the corresponding project website that depicts a visual marker (QR code) on each display.

You photograph this scenario and send the photo to a designated e-mail address in order to quasi calibrate the overall display. Then you can send any desired photo to the server, which will immediately display the photo conformed to the screens. Even interactions such as scrolling or zooming function as expected. More information on this is provided at http://msxbook.com/en/jubtrn.

With the slot car racing game **Racer** (a Chrome experiment), you can build a racetrack across up to five phones and tablets. To start a race, devices have to be synchronized. Various colored cars are then able to race around the track, from screen to screen (Cipriani, 2013; see g.co/racer).

With **Adobe Nav**, you can move the Photoshop toolbar from the desktop PC to the iPad and conform it so that it can be better operated via the tablet (see Section 5.5) and create more space on the main screen.

In the **Couple Up to Buckle Up** campaign from Scandinavian Airlines, the members are asked to jointly book a trip while using a smartphone. The "2 for 1" offer can be seen only if both of you are using both screens together (Carlsson, 2012; for video, see http://www.msxbook.com/en/cutbu).

Llévalos a la escuela is a project cooperated by ING DIRECT and UNICEF. There a two screens involved. The story begins on a desktop website and ends on a smartphone. The website shows children who are waiting to go to school. The smartphone app acts as a virtual school. When the smartphone (respectively its camera) is held over an orange smartphone-shaped space on the website, one by one the children come off the website and jump into the phone in order to go to school. **All the profits raised via app downloads go to UNICEF's educational projects. You can support it at** http://www.llevalosalaescuela.com/en.

Brass Monkey is a complementary game in which the browser serves as a console and the smartphone as a controller. Once the browser is synchronized with the phone, you can choose between various games and play them on the desktop browser (see http://playbrassmonkey.com).

5.8 COHERENCE

A (graphical user) interface does not have to look exactly the same on different platforms and different screens, but it should be similar. Despite all differences between the various devices and screens, the contents should be displayed coherently, consistently, visually uniformly, comprehensible and in a logical visual connection to the greatest extent possible. With regard to coherence, the focus is on the *graphical user interface* (GUI) and the *visual design*. The principle is complemented by Section 5.8.1 on adaptability and Section 5.9 on fluidity to create the meta-principle of *fluid experience*.

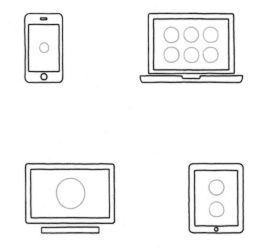

To gain more mainstream users for the service, design equilibrium is more important than anything else.

Nick Bilton (journalist, *The New York Times*)

Visual consistency

Films and other broadcasts that, for example, are made primarily for the TV screen can in principle also be watched on other devices. Because users are changing their location and thus potentially also the type of device with increasing frequency (also sometimes spontaneously), cross-device user interfaces are required that support the users' needs regardless of the location and device.

It is important for a service to be in equilibrium across all screens. Cross-device visual consistency is more important than designing a separate and individual user interface for each screen that is not suitable for the interface on the other screens and is difficult to understand. A consistent visual language across different screens supports recognition, orientation, and brand identification.

Concerning visual design and layout, you will have to decide if you prioritize corporate guidelines or the guidelines of the operating systems for which you are designing and developing. It depends on the specific project scope and definitions. Try to determine if a service is used more in the service context itself with a prioritization on a fluent cross-device experience or as a single app in the context of an operating system.

Twitter, in comparison with previous versions, has started using standardized layouts for the smartphone, tablet, and desktop PC. By so doing, the sometimes very appealing individual interfaces have indeed been lost, but the user can operate across devices much more easily.

The **video provider Netflix** supplies its on-demand service in a cross-device and device-specific manner for the TV, tablet, smartphone, and laptop. The interface appears similarly across the devices and also functions similarly. The information obtained from the work on the TV interface was also subsequently applied for the desktop interfaces. The contents were made into the interface. You can directly interact with the contents.

Windows 8 also undertakes the approach of a fluid platform (see Section 5.9). The interface has a similar look on all devices and is designed in such a manner that it can be conformed to the container in which it is displayed (Punchcut, 2012d).

Metaphors and learnability

It can be helpful to use familiar (analog) metaphors and operating elements (e.g., on the touchscreen) instead of confronting the user with new paradigms that are difficult to learn. This makes sense only if it involves an application that is used often and regularly or if no helpful visual metaphors or interaction paradigms can be utilized. Only then is the user willing to work with this in a more in-depth manner (Wilson, 2011).

Pseudo-realism and the "uncanny valley"

Skeuomorphic design imitates real objects. Examples are imitating screen displays and user interfaces (UI), physical devices, or objects such as with the leaf metaphor with iBooks or the design of the calendar or notebook in previous versions of iOS, which have been very strongly influenced by real products (Vogel, 2012).

The advantage can be that these visual metaphors are easily understood by the users. However, the problem is that the user also then expects that it will function just like the real model. Otherwise, it will have a mysterious or "uncanny" effect. If graphical (digital) interfaces that imitate real objects or products do not fulfill expectations, this can quickly devolve into a negative user experience. This is called the *uncanny valley*.

By using Uncanny Valley, you are generally referring to an empirically-measurable effect that appears to be paradoxical with regards to the acceptance of the depicted fictitious figures by the viewers. The acceptance of the technically simulatable, nonverbal behavior by the viewers depends upon the reality-based content of the presented media (robots, avatars, etc.). It does not constantly increase upon a linear basis with the increasing similarity of the figure to humans, but rather indicates a strong decline within a certain range.

While you would like to assume at first glance that the viewers or computer game players accept the avatars offered to them even more so the more realistic the figure is, the reality shows that this is not accurate. People find highly-abstract, completely fictitious figures to be more appealing and more acceptable than figures which become increasingly more realistic. The acceptance falls abruptly starting from a certain level and only then increases again from a certain, very high level. The acceptance is highest at that moment in which the avatars can no longer be differentiated from the film footage of real persons. The same is valid for graphical (digital) interfaces which (only) imitate the real objects or products. If this is not done well, corresponding expectations are created which can quickly deteriorate into a negative user experience if such expectations are not fulfilled. Wikipedia provides a detailed explanation.

The **contact app on the iPad** formerly looked like a book, but you cannot page through it and thus it breaks completely with the visual metaphor.

Flat design

It also works without metaphors. With Windows 8 (released in 2012), in contrast to Apple iOS 6 (at that time), a skeuomorphic user interface was not used. Microsoft used no metaphors whatsoever but, rather, relied on "digital authenticity" (Punchcut, 2012c). The design of Windows 8 is called flat design. The advantage of a flat design in comparison with pseudo-realistic displays is that it imitates nothing, awakens no (false or unfulfilled) expectations, and is limited by no metaphors with regard to interface and interaction (Greif, 2013).

Other companies followed and changed their design as well to a flatter visual design language. With iOS 7 (released in 2013), Apple replaced its skeuomorphic design with a flatter operating system with a function-led, unobtrusive, and minimal interface. The skeuomorphic design philosophy is to replicate physical counterparts. With a flatter design, you must try to make functionality on screen obvious and easily accessible (Watson, 2014). The design language Material Design developed by Google and released in 2014 is comparable to this mainly anti-skeuomorphic flat design philosophy.

However, skeuomorphism did not disappear completely with the emergence of flat design. The motion and behavior of interaction elements are strongly borrowed from the physical world (Bodeit, 2014).

If the interface is too flat, it will possibly lack critically important visual aids for the user that are important for usability. Discreet shading, adumbrated three-dimensionality, or sparingly used gradients (e.g., for buttons) can make an interface more user-friendly. You must decide in the individual case whether and when a flat design, a skeuomorphic design, or, as required, a compromise is the right solution. Completely flat will probably be very difficult to understand for users in most cases.

5.8.1 ADAPTABILITY

In order to keep the expenditures for the multiple outputting on various devices to a minimum, paradigms are required for adaptable layouts and contents. To simplify cross-device information management, layouts and contents can be dynamically and flexibly adapted to the respective device features. With regard to adaptability, the focus is on the user interface, layout, and (the display of) content. The subprinciple is complemented by Section 5.8 on coherence and Section 5.9 on fluidity to form the meta-principle of fluid experience, and it forms a bridge to Section 5.10 on smart content.

Layout adaptability

A modern information offering should be able to be displayed on each relevant device. Layouts must be designed for all screens: They must be fluid, proportional, and relative. Even within the individual device classes, there are sometimes major differences with regard to display size and screen resolution (see Chapter 2). Furthermore the screens of the tablet and the smartphone are also used in the landscape and portrait formats. In order to come to grips with this challenge to at least some extent, the use of responsive or adaptive web design is recommended—flexible, scalable, and adaptable layouts that respond to the respective devices and/or screens and their features (Marcotte, 2010; Tran, 2011). Columns, rows, and image and text sizes are dynamically conformed to the various screen formats (with the contents remaining the same). In this context, the term "responsive (web) design" has attained general acceptance.

CONTENT ADAPTABILITY

In addition to the layout and design, the contents must also be adapted to the context of use, the various needs of the users, and the respective device and its special features. (See Section "Responsive or Adaptive Content.")

We can design for an optimal viewing experience, but embed standards-based technologies into our designs to make them more adaptive to the media that renders them.

Ethan Marcotte (author of "Responsive Web Design")

Responsive or adaptive web design

There are different approaches. Either the layout of the content constantly fits the changing layout width when the browser is reduced or you define two or more breakpoints for the output and display of content on various devices. Breakpoints are threshold values. If they are exceeded, other or new layout standards, rules, and definitions apply. In general, you determine the maximal and/or minimal dimensions of a screen format (e.g., of tablets). The respective styles, definitions, and parameters are then applied for this area. The approaches can also be combined.

Based on this, for example, photos are constantly being reduced in the existing proportions and texts are wrapped as desired or the individual content elements always have a fixed width and are also not scaled until a breakpoint is attained that defines the layout differently and/or redefines it. From a certain breakpoint that has been set, the respective elements receive new values. The layout or the alignment is redesigned and redefined for optimal display.

The following is an example of breakpoints: As soon as a website is displayed smaller than 960 pixels, the right-hand column will be displayed under the main content and the navigation that is shown to the left will move to the upper edge of the screen.

There is no common breakpoint rule that you can apply identically in each case. You cannot rely on a definition for a specific device class that fits every need. For each case, it depends on the layout, design, and primarily the content. You have to decide and define from the content out and not based on screen size. Check it in the browser and on different representative devices. Resize it. Start with the small screen first and expand it until the layout and content do not fit and look good anymore. Then it is time for a new breakpoint for that specific combination of layout and content.

NOTE

There is no exact definition and consensus of what responsive and adaptive web design exactly means. There are different interpretations. But I think that is not that important. Call it how you like. More important is to choose the appropriate approach to each project.

Both approaches—responsive and adaptive design—are time-consuming in a way. Expenditures and costs cannot be absolutely determined on a lump-sum basis but, rather, depend on a wide array of factors (Bartel, 2012; Frost, 2012c). For projects, it is seldom the case that the budget and time are limitless. Thus, you must pragmatically decide in most cases how you would like to proceed.

An excellent explanation of responsive web design and information about the approach with media queries is provided by Ethan Marcotte (2010). He thoroughly describes the technical background and solutions and how you can apply responsive web design with standard web technologies in practice. For interested readers, his book is highly recommended (Marcotte, 2011). Kayla Knight (2011) explains in a detailed article what responsive design is and how to apply this method.

Adaptive mostly means that there are fixed layouts and breakpoints (e.g., foodsense.is). Responsive layouts are fluid and normally use the whole screen width (e.g., bostonglobe.com).

An adaptive website uses and offers several (static) layouts for various screen resolutions based on breakpoints. It detects the screen size and loads the appropriate layout. Advantages of adaptive layouts are that you can more easily work with wireframes and sketches, the grid is more static, it is not that complicated, content must only be optimized for specific resolutions, and the realization is more time-saving. It provides the opportunity for a specialized user experience for a specific device. But it is just optimized for specific devices or layout-widths and probably does not look that good on other devices content and user interface (UI) are not tested and optimized for.

With responsive layouts the layout is more flexible, adjusts automatically to each screen size, and no space is wasted. The information stays in the foreground. You have less screen size design control and it is more difficult to work with mock-ups, wireframes, and sketches and often it has to be realized and tested with prototypes, to show the behavior of the website to clients. It is more complex to design and to develop and can be more time-consuming (explanation based on Erdmann, 2013 and Hellwig, 2015).

You find a lot more links and additional information to that topic in the mentioned sources and via msxbook.com/en/responsivedesign.

Layout categories and layout patterns

If the device features change, this will usually have effects on the layout. It can be some-what adapted to the various screen sizes and screen resolutions if you, for example, define corresponding rules, templates, and (resolution) breakpoints based on the resolution and the layout categories that are suitable for the device type (Wroblewski, 2011d).

> **HINT**
>
> When developing a multiscreen strategy, you should consider that you must not rely just on screen size because that could lead to wrong decisions. For example, there is currently no reliable relationship between screen size and bandwidth or input methods (see Chapter 2, Sections 2.2 and 2.3).

Brad Frost opines that you should design for the breakpoints and not for the devices (Frost, 2012b). Furthermore of course, you design primarily for the user. Nevertheless, the device class plays an important role because not all resolutions are the same. For example, 1000 pixels on a laptop are completely different than 1000 pixels on the TV screen or smartphone. Despite the sometimes huge variations between devices and even within device classes, their classification is still relevant concerning usage mode, context of use, device availability, interaction patterns, and possible combination of devices.

> **EXAMPLE**
>
> A high-resolution smartphone display with a resolution of 960 × 640 pixels cannot display more contents than a display of the same size (with the same dimensions) with a smaller resolution of only 240 × 160 pixels. The contents indeed become sharper, but you cannot scale them as desired. The same applies for a TV. Regardless of whether it is a high-end display with full HD resolution or an old CRT TV, the font size that you can still read at a distance of 3 meters does not change as the result of a higher resolution. The same applies for the laptop screen whereby this, in principle, can display the most information. Thus, whether you should overload it is another question.

With the aid of the responsive web design gallery mediaqueri.es, Luke Wroblewski (2012a) has identified five generally valid layout patterns: mostly fluid, column drop, layout shifter, tiny tweaks, and off canvas. These patterns differ from each other in the arrangement of the individual layout elements depending on the changing screen width. With some, merely the content area is reduced; for others, layout elements are gradually arranged under the main content or completely different upon the attainment of the respective resolution break points. In the following illustrations, the darkest area is a respective example of the most important contents.

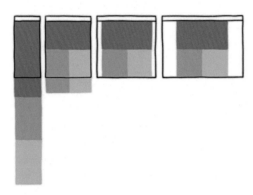

Mostly fluid

The multicolumn layout is based on *fluid grids* and photos that are dynamically adjusted. On large screens, the edge distance is larger. The basic structure only changes for the smallest screen (columns are stacked on top of one another). Otherwise, the layout is fluidly adapted to the respective screens.

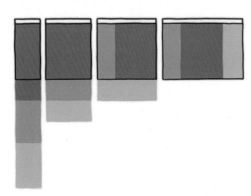

Column drop

The number of columns is reduced with screens that are becoming smaller. They are successively stacked on top of one another. The size of the individual elements remains tendentially the same. Generally, the navigation or the content is placed at the top.

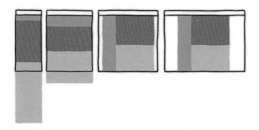

Layout shifter

With this pattern, the layout is most frequently adapted to the various screen sizes. Different layouts are used for the respective screens. This causes more expenditures than with other patterns.

Tiny tweaks

The easiest form of adaptation is when you must make only small-scale optimizations (e.g., font size or picture layout). This functions with very simple information offerings that use only a few elements and single-column layouts.

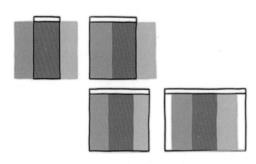

Off canvas

Content or navigation can be placed outside of the visible area as long as either the space on the (larger) screen allows it to be visible or the user takes action to expose it.

Advantages and disadvantages of responsive design

With responsive (or adaptive) web design, you can lay the foundation for a *fluid multiscreen experience* in order to then incrementally optimize the layouts or adapt them to the respective and individual device features and/or device possibilities. In any case, it is a good approach and a beneficial method; however, it is not a cure-all that always functions and it is also not the "be-all and end-all" solution.

In most cases, the contents are thus not adapted to the various contexts of use but, rather, are merely arranged differently on the screen. It is often not sufficient to merely adapt the design and layout. The content must also be adapted to the context of use, the device, the user, and the user's potential interaction behavior. It's recommended to design with content (structure) in mind (see Section 5.10 and Chapters 6 and 7).

A wide array of devices and contexts of use can be optimally supported with responsive design only with great difficulty. In order to create context-relevant user experiences, it is furthermore necessary to ponder this extensively and to use suitable methods. An overview and additional sources, ideas, and suggestions regarding the theme of responsive design can be found on the website at http://www.msxbook.com/en/responsivedesign.

PERFORMANCE MATTERS

When you design and develop responsive websites and layouts, you must also consider the website's performance (loading times, page weight, speed, bit rate, file size, and latency). "RWD may make your pages look better on a variety of devices, but it doesn't automatically make your pages load better on a variety of devices. It's all about implementation. Performance is a requirement not an extra feature" (Wolfermann, 2015). You can incorporate "performance budgets" to limit page weight and reduce loading times (Kadlec, 2014). Limit the maximum page weight (or file size) of your website and portion it to all elements, components, files, and assets as needed.

Define how long it shall take at the longest until users can use your site. Determine for which devices and with which connection this applies for (consider context as well). You can deduce the maximum file size from that. Dispense that size to all elements used on the page (HTML, CSS, JavaScript, images, fonts, etc.). Weigh up if you can remove other elements (such as heavy CSS definitions or scripts) when you want to add an additional image to keep to the performance budget. Make performance and loading time part of the project definition.

Responsive navigation patterns

On large screens, it is typical to use a top-left navigation, but on smaller screens it is quite challenging and there is need for various navigation solutions on websites. There are different responsive navigation patterns that you should consider and compare depending on your content and UI requirements (Frost, 2012d).

You can simply keep the navigation on top or use a simple anchor link in the header that points to a navigation list in the footer. A similar solution is to use a menu button that opens a menu in the header section. That menu can slide in from the top of the site or from the side like an off-canvas menu. You can also put all the links of the main navigation into a select menu on smaller screens. The so-called Priority+ pattern exposes the most important navigation elements and tucks away less important items behind a "more" link. The less important items are revealed when the user clicks the "more" link (Frost, 2012e). The smaller the screen, the more links that are tucked away.

There are many more possibilities to display navigation on small and medium screens. It is important to keep this in mind and to think about it at the latest when starting with the layout and user interface (UI) in general.

UI modeling

When developing concepts for an unpredictable variety of screens, you should also think about the process of constructing a design system using a methodical approach. Atomic design is a methodology introduced by Brad Frost (2013a) for creating (and describing a systematic approach of) design systems based on the chemistry metaphor. This method focuses more on production than on the user and user needs. There are five distinct levels in atomic design: atoms, molecules, organisms, templates, and pages.

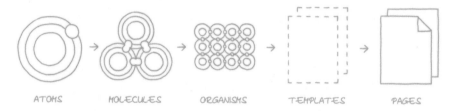

ATOMS   MOLECULES   ORGANISMS   TEMPLATES   PAGES

Atomic design principle based on the chemistry metaphor. Figure based on Brad Frost's illustration (Frost, 2013a), just converted into the illustration style of this book.

Web or any other digital user interfaces (UI) can be stripped down into the smallest possible elements (atoms). These basic building blocks can be combined to more complex components (molecules) and segments (organisms). Templates consist of groups of organisms put together to form pages. Templates are more generic and wireframe-like, whereas pages are specific instances of templates. In the fifth stage, the placeholder content of the template is replaced with real content. For a detailed description of using a building block approach for designing content and constructing user interfaces, see Chapter 7.

Frost's atomic design approach—and the ideas, methods, and tools behind it—are described in an article on his website (Frost, 2013a) and in his book (Frost, 2015a).

With an adaptive user interface that is built based on bricklike elements, you are more flexible for the future and prepared for fluid and liquid layouts that may work in most imaginable contexts. Thus, it is less difficult to react to new devices such as smartwatches, smartglasses, or any other future developments (see Chapter 7, Section 7.1.2).

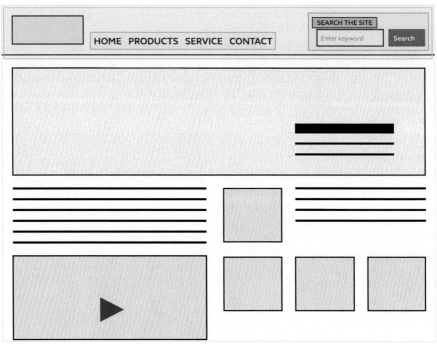

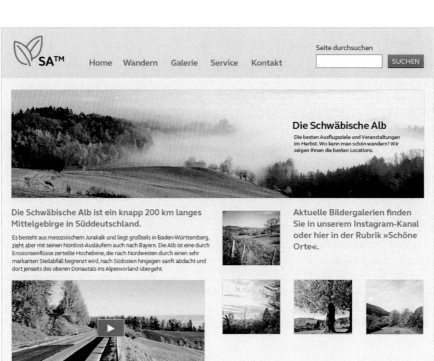

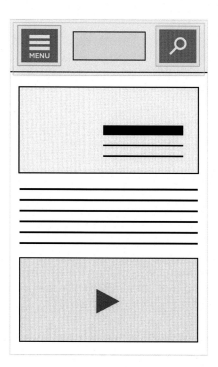

The two wireframes (exemplary desktop layout on the left, smartphone layout on the right) show the **example of a structured brick-based atomic website UI** (this example is based on Brad Frost illustrations, cf. Frost, 2013): The red form label is an atom, the smallest possible element of aUI. Together with an input field and a button it can be combined to a larger UI component (the green search form), called molecule (referring to the atomic metapher Frost uses). A main navigation (blue) can also be such a component (or molecule) that can be combined to an organism (neutrally I'd call it UI segment or layout area), e.g., a header of a website (yellow). Other sections could be main content area, navigation area, footer, etc. Finally, the whole wireframe (or UI Template) of a webpage consists of different organisms, that are built of molecules, that again are built of atoms.

If you insert real content and apply color and style to it, it is the specific and unique page (an Instance of the generic template, compare colored website screenshot on the left with specific and unique content, and concrete visual design, typography, logo, color, and images).

When you use a styleguide that is based on that principle you can define how each element (atom) or component reacts to different viewports or media characteristics, for example a smartphone.

In the small smartphone wireframe the search field transforms into a single button (that – when pressed – opens a search field) and the main navigation is reduced to a single button as well. If you press that button a menu can slide in from the top or from the left (as an "off canvas" menu). Thus that UI element or component also encompasses interaction, transition and animation (see Section 5.16).

More thoughts about the brick-based approach are explained in Chapter 7.

Living style guide

It is often difficult to keep style guides and manuals up to date. They are often outdated and not maintained and updated regularly. With a living style guide (or a pattern library) based on the atomic design principle, you can solve this problem.

> **NOTE**
>
> This book focuses on the user and the overall user experience of digital services. It is not important for your users how you build and maintain your user interface. However, UI modeling (or the atomic design approach) and the implementation of a living style guide are helpful methods with regard to production topics.

Many companies and services use and deliver information on a number of digital touchpoints, websites, and apps (e.g., a large company with different country-specific local websites that must all be visually coherent and consistent). To deliver a consistent user experience across all digital touchpoints, it is important that design patterns and visual styles are based on one general definition. To achieve this, you need to have a single point of reference for all the patterns you use so that everyone who has to produce digital media and content for the company can refer to them.

In the style guide, you do not provide just typical UI elements such as color, typography, and buttons. You also define transitions, animations, flows and user dialogues, wording, and labeling of buttons and elements.

A shared vocabulary of UI elements and code allows teams to collaborate and communicate with each other in an efficient way. A well-structured style guide helps teams refer to particular single definitions as efficiently as possible. For example, you could use anchor links to specific and detailed definitions (for each heading, subheading, text size, button variations, etc.).

One of the main goals and benefits is to encourage reuse of code, provide guidance on correct usage of all definitions, and reduce redundancy to a minimum. The underlying approach of such a style guide is to use a design system instead of page-based designs.

If you approach a project as just described, you are more flexible for upcoming devices or whatever touchpoints may appear in the future, and the viewport does not matter as much as when you rely too much on device-specific templates. Thus, it can also assist a device-agnostic approach.

The style guide can use the same underlying CSS and markup. It is a "living document" that will be updated when new code or elements are added, implemented, or updated.

It is helpful to use the atomic design methodology (Frost, 2013a) to structure, combine, assemble, and classify UI elements and patterns. Think of this approach as using Lego-like building blocks designed to be combined together. The atomic explanation is a good metaphor. However, you can also use other more generic and universal terms for these atomic bricks.

At SETU GmbH, we used the following definitions and classification for a large client project based on and inspired by Brad Frost's approach:

Basics (no equivalent in the atomic approach): We added a basic level (as the very first "element") that describes more abstract elements such as color, logo, grid, interactive states, and typography. All other and the following elements refer to these basics.

Elements: "Atoms" are the smallest possible elements of the interface, such as a form element, a label next to an input field, or buttons.

Components: "Molecules" are small groups of elements that function together as a unit—for example, a search combined by an input label, text input form element, and a search button.

Layout area: "Organisms" are groups of molecules and atoms (components and elements) joined together to form a distinct section of an interface, such as the footer, main content area, or header area (e.g., the header includes the search functionality as described previously).

Layout "templates" are generic combinations of different layout areas with components and elements. Pages are concrete unique shapes of these templates that also provide examples of specific content.

See also the five-stage building block principle in Chapter 7, Section 7.2.3.

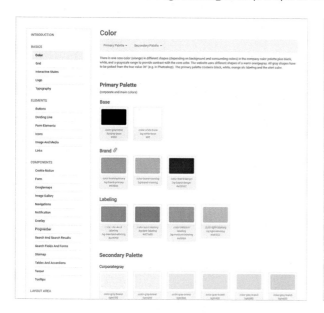

This is an example of a **living styleguide** (or UI pattern library) that we developed and implemented for our client "Lapp Group" (www.lappgroup.com). All important information about color (basics) and navigation (components) is provided, including a function to view and copy (and paste) the source code.

Agile design process

Workflows must be as agile and flexible as possible. Instead of spending a large amount of time on elaborate and pixel-precise drafts—especially at the beginning of a project—and in order to understand the client's wishes, you can jointly work on a design approach with *style tiles* (similar to pattern books and color guides used by interior designers) and develop a visual language without having to go into too much detail and without having to design various screen layouts.

Style tiles function regardless of the screen sizes and are restricted to the essentials. Style tiles are comparable with the elements and components used and described in the Atomic Design approach. Style guides and other visual guides or libraries with reusable and easily modifiable design elements and building blocks, which are stored in a central file, are likewise flexible and correspondingly helpful (style tiles are discussed in detail in Zillgens, 2012). See Chapter 7 for a more detailed discussion on processes.

For easy, simple websites, good results and **adaptive layouts** can be obtained with CSS3, flexible grids, photos, and media queries, which are all based on the same HTML5 basic structure.

> *The modern website fits the device, instead of commanding that the device fits the website.*
>
> Jamie Appleseed (Baymard Institute)

COHERENT INTERFACES

Not only visual interfaces (graphical user interface, GUI) have to be visually coherent but also audio interfaces. For example, if you have to develop a solution for automotive interfaces that are also controlled by voice (which is nearly the same when you control your smartphone by voice recognition, compare "Hey Siri" or "OK, Google"), you have to ensure that the visual input and output on any screen are coherent to and in correlation with the audio input and output options. See also "Automotive and Connected Cars" in Chapter 8, Section 8.2.

The website I conceptualized and designed for Architect Peter Fischer uses different breakpoints. Based on these the layout, images, position and arrangement of UI elements and content adapt to various screen sizes and devices. You find it at http://www.architektur-peterfischer.de. You can see a back end screenshot of the website in Chapter 6, Section 6.3.4. We used a customized form according to the output independent brick-like building block principle that is discussed in Chapter 7.

At http://mediaqueri.es, there are many **adaptive and responsive design examples** with various content and design characteristics and focuses. As representative and exemplary, we show the website here from http://foodsense.is. The contents of the website are gradually made smaller and stacked on top of one another with a screen that becomes smaller. Another great responsive design source is "responsivedesign.is" from Justin Avery with lots of examples, tips and details on design, development and strategy.

The information offering of **The New York Times** is displayed differently on the screens of the tablet, smartphone, and laptop. On the smartphone, the texts are shorter, and on the tablet, series of photos and photo galleries are very sensibly arranged.

5.9 FLUIDITY

With fluidity, the focus is on the areas of *information*, *interaction*, and *service*. The principle is complemented by Section 5.8, Coherence, and Section 5.8.1, Adaptability, to form the meta-principle of *fluid experience*.

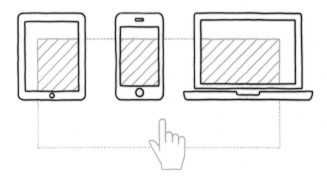

Users expect (subconsciously) that the same service can be operated on various devices similarly—and thus intuitively. Information offerings on all devices should be seamlessly integrated into the context of use and offer—across devices—a constantly high-quality and fluid user experience. The transition from device to device may not pose major obstacles. A type of common thread must exist. Users should be able to begin an activity on one device, continue it on a second device, and then complete it on a third device. Sometimes, it is recommended to analyze and incorporate certain device features and user interface components in order to determine whether the service can be operated better and the user can profit from this.

If, from the very beginning, you take into consideration all platforms and their unique features and possibilities in the design work, you will create the prerequisite that an information offering can be realized both in a cross-platform and in a platform-specific manner and is harmonious overall.

A service and the use of an application should feel similarly on all screens and/or devices. The information offering must be optimized in the sense of a suitable and *continuous service quality* (continuity). See Sections 5.4 and 2.6.2 "Continuous Experience."

Native experience versus corporate guidelines

An information offering should also be logically integrated into the native experience of a platform. For mobile offerings, this means, for example, that the button layout that is typical for the operating system (OS) is retained so that the user can use the application in his customary manner. If the use of an individual offering (an app) deviates (too much) from the customary use of all other offerings within an operating system, this may irritate the user. An iPhone app must in all cases feel like an iPhone app and not like a website or Android app. This means that the button layout, size, interaction, and screen flow should be designed to conform to the iOS. At the same time, the offering must also still fulfill the visual standards (corporate style guide, corporate language, icon language, etc.) of the respective brand and/or the provider.

In various contexts, various functions are useful and appropriate; this again depends on the respective device. The three parameters—context, function and device—always influence each other and must be taken into consideration if you would like to expand the service experience to multiple devices. It does not necessarily and dogmatically mean that there must be uniformity and that everything has to be kept absolutely identical but, rather, is a matter of continuity.

However, in some cases it can be better to first focus on corporate guidelines and second on an operating system-conform user interface and interaction paradigm. For example, if your service is an app that is used for inspection and car analytics in a garage on different screen types (e.g., smartphone, tablet, and desktop PC) by the motor mechanics and if that multiscreen usage is the main use case, it is better to focus on a fluid and coherent experience of the "motor vehicle garage service" than matching and fulfilling all the OS guidelines because they are less relevant and other applications are seldom used in this special purpose.

On the other hand, Google with its Material Design attempts to implement some kind of a cuckoo operating system in all other (non-Google) mobile operating systems. If it is not applied on Android devices, it is a kind of an operating system within an operating system. Google undercuts these different operating systems by recommending or specifying a style guide for all apps that are built on the Material Design language and are also available on non-Android platforms.

Whether native or corporate guidelines should be prioritized concerning interaction and visual design patterns depends on the specific project scope, definitions, and goals. Thus, you have to decide for each project if the operating system or your app must subordinate or to consider both in an appropriate manner.

Channel-optimized shopping experience

The users' usage and/or purchasing behavior during (online) shopping is different from device to device. Thus, the respective shopping experience must be precisely tailored to the corresponding channel and optimized for the respective device. The shopping experience of one service should also be similar and comprehensible (as much as possible) across and on different devices. Whenever a customer would like to shop, he should be able to quickly and easily find and buy the relevant product.

The camera installed in the smartphone serves in the Amazon app as a **bar code scanner**. Device-specific functions are used as an input mode in order to upgrade the generally identical offering.

5.9.1 SERVICE EQUALITY

A service should always offer equivalent information quality. In principle, information must be the *same* and *adaptable*. Content structure and information architecture should be as identical as possible. To ensure a coherent *app quality* an application must have the same functionality on all devices and platforms—provided that the devices offer this functionality (Workman, 2011). Features should be available and work as similarly as possible across devices. The user experience of a service should be comparable and consistent on all screens. Visual quality (GUI, transitions, etc.) and usability should deviate from each other as little as possible.

When developing apps across mobile platforms, there should be
no devices left with a poorer user experience.

Steve Workman (IT consultant at PA Consulting)

The **National Football League (NFL) commercial** "Anytime. Anywhere" shows how a fluid
experience should function in principle. Regardless of place and device, the person in
the video watches a football game absolutely seamlessly and without any interruptions. As
soon as he grabs another device, the livestream is already on the screen. Wouldn't it be
beautiful if it were so easy (NFL, 2010; see also http://www.msxbook.com/en/msxnfl.

Applications (e.g., smartphone apps) should generally offer the same functionality. That
was previously not the case with the **Facebook apps for the iPhone and Android** due to the
different smartphones and operating systems (Workman, 2011). Thus, the user experience
was not uniform across devices and platforms.

Regarding optimization potential, the former Facebook app for Android 2.2 (*left*) offers only
six functions. The iPhone app (*right*) offers substantially more functions (and even a memo
function on an additional page). The app for Android 2.3 (*center*) is indeed closer to the
iPhone experience. However, the icons for notifications and the designation of the Inbox
(and/or messages) were different. This situation has recently improved, but this is still a good
example of the challenge of having to provide service equality across devices and platforms.

5.9.2 FLUID INTERACTION

Interaction paradigms and comprehensibility (seamless interaction)

The interaction with an application or an information offering must be cross-device, logical, and comprehensible. Users do not want to have to adapt to new things. When changing devices, they expect that an already learned interaction (pattern) will at least function similarly on a different device (disruption-free interaction).

> *Content and experiences that move seamlessly from one screen to another are an absolute must.*
>
> Jeremy Lockhorn (Razorfish)

The user must be offered comparable, similar, consistent, logical, and comprehensible interaction options on the various devices. They improve the cross-device operability. When the user first comes into contact with a website or an app, the mental model is formed (especially with regard to navigation and interaction).

If there are still no paradigms for a certain application, it may be helpful if the digital user interface is based on already learned analogous interaction paradigms (see the discussion of advantages and disadvantages beginning in Section 5.8). The interaction should also be suitable for the respective platform and the system's own interaction paradigms.

User behavior and inputting methods

For cross-device user interfaces, you must also take the respective user behaviors into consideration, which may vary in various cultural circles. Experienced and inexperienced users likewise interact differently (Wroblewski, 2010d). If possible, you should try to consistently use (touch) gestures across devices and platforms.

Device-specific inputting methods can be taken into consideration and beneficially utilized on a complementary basis. This refers generally to options that offer a certain device class (e.g., touch interfaces). The camera or the microphone for the smartphone can be beneficially utilized: In the area of TV entertainment or for TV broadcasts, you could, for example, also use the microphone for recognizing the audio signal for online votes in addition to the superimposed Internet address (and instead of a QR code) in order to directly guide the user to the corresponding Internet site (which has been optimized for smartphones) (see the example of a Toyota TV spot with Shazam in Section 5.3.1).

The **_cover flow_ metaphor** in previous iTunes versions was a good example of coherent cross-device and comprehensible interaction. It is visually conveyed to the user that he can flip horizontally through the information offering. Cover flow functioned the same on all devices (and also looked almost identical), regardless of whether you navigated with your mouse (laptop) or with your finger (iPhone). The cover flow technology was available in Apple iTunes and in the iTunes desktop application, on the iPhone, and on various iPod models. In the meantime that interaction paradigm has been replaced by _album wall_ which shows tiles of album art.

5.10 SMART CONTENT

It is becoming increasingly more important to enable people to have the easiest possible access to digital services and information. They should be provided in a context-relevant manner for each situation and optimized for the respective device. To be able to provide relevant information you should consider its semantic meaning.

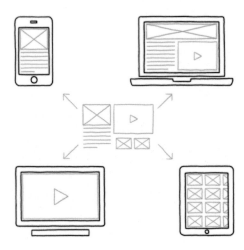

Responsive or adaptive content

The content should be adapted to the respective conditions. In principle, the depth of the content should remain the same because many users access information exclusively with mobile devices (Cho, 2011). Thus, no differentiation should be made between mobile and other offerings and/or contents. There is only the same offering once, which is retrieved, depicted, and used (differently) in different contexts of use (see Chapter 4).

Content first

In order to design a sensible layout, you should (at least roughly) know the content with regard to scope, type, and format (content first). It is a critical difference whether you must display long or short texts, photos, galleries, or videos and in what quality and quantity these contents exist. Conception, design, and implementation must go hand-in-hand (see Chapter 7 concerning content design and its correlation to UI modeling).

Flexible information and contents

An information offering must flexibly respond to and address the interaction behavior, bandwidths, performance levels of the devices, and other parameters. Thus, the options of the various (especially mobile) devices can be sensibly utilized (see Section 5.1).

The **Teletext of ARD (Germany)** is an example of smart content and adaptability. It is provided on the website with the same length and the related video text table (see http://msxbook.com/en/ardtxt). At the same time, the focus on the website is automatically on the digit-input field (you can thus navigate directly via the block of digits). On the mobile-optimized website, the digital layout opens directly during inputting (also a user-friendly solution).

Ideally, complex data constructs, platform-independent and flexible contents, and data and information can be automatically and intelligently aggregated and arranged based on the meta-information in a user-, context-, and device-specific manner.

Whenever contents are fluidly and flexibly adapted to devices, layouts, and the respective context of use, content is smart. Josh Clark uses the metaphor "content like water" to explain the idea taking the example of water. Regardless of whether you pour water into a cup, on a plate, or in a glass, it always adapts exactly to the container form. The contents should also be provided in a correspondingly flexible manner (Clark, 2011c).

Content like water: You put water into a cup, it becomes the cup. You put water into a bottle, it becomes the bottle. You put it in a teapot, it becomes the teapot. Empty your mind. Be formless, shapeless, like water.

Josh Clark (2011c)

Future-oriented contents

Future-oriented contents are accessible to everyone, adaptable, findable, convertible, connectable, reusable, and archivable. Contents shall not be withhold from the user, and he must be able to adapt them to his needs and requirements (voice output, layout, contrast, and font size). Through meta-data, contents can be found better.

Good content can be easily modified and easily linked to other services. It is format-independent or can at least be easily converted into another format. It is flexible with regard to aggregation, combination, dissemination, and preservation (read later) and archiving (Erle, 2012).

Central data maintenance

Cloud computing, content management systems, and interfaces (API) play an important role during the flexible outputting and dissemination of contents. "The API runs the show," opines Josh Clark (2011b). In order to create and maintain multiscreen-capable information and data, back-end systems with flexible content management structures are needed.

Contents should be stored and maintained in a central location (see Chapter 6, Section 6.3 and Chapter 7). With a collective back-end and/or content management system (CMS) for all contents, redundant and inconsistent data and additional expenditures can be avoided during data maintenance (see Sections 5.8.1, 5.9, and 5.11).

The more elegant and granular the contents, data, and information that are to be published, the more flexibly they can be used, edited, and displayed. The formatting is the task of the presentation system. Formattings are part of the data storage system in only a reduced manner. Unformatted texts can be much more easily integrated into other information (app, software, and news) and displayed on many different devices, screens, and applications.

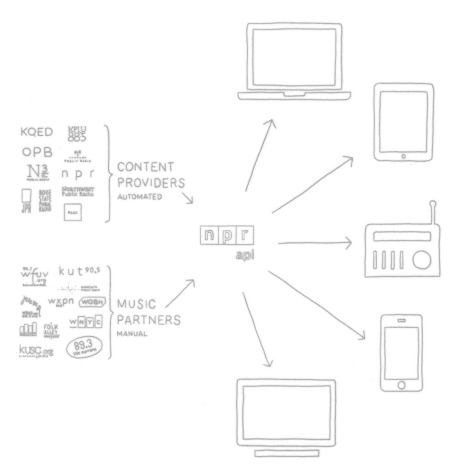

National Public Radio (NPR) uses and provides an open API (application programming interface) according to the COPE principle—create once, publish everywhere (Jacobson, 2009). Since the introduction of this philosophy, NPR can disseminate already-created contents quickly and efficiently as well as everywhere that is desired. The new interface had above all a big influence on the mobile strategy because it was no longer necessary to separately develop a service or an app for each individual platform and each individual channel.

Condé Nast has an approach that is the opposite of the NPR approach. The problem is that print design principles do not function for the iPad and/or in a fragmented device landscape. The sales figures of the iPad magazines from WIRED, GQ, and Co. have declined substantially. However, in contrast, the page visits at NPR have almost doubled. The question is whether the open API vis-à-vis a cost-based platform and/or application also earn (sufficient) money (via McGrane, 2011).

Other examples of companies that employ the independent use of flexible and neutral content formats are the providers Twitter, Facebook, and YouTube and content aggregators such as Flipboard, Pulse, Flud, or Storify (see Section 5.11 for more information).

Separating content, structure, and display

Whenever possible, you should keep the contents, their structure, as well as the display and output strictly separate from each another. The following three-part classification is recommended:

- Creating and maintaining the contents
- Information architecture, structure of the content elements, and meta-data
- Display and output depending on the medium, device, and context of use

The more independently the contents are collected from their subsequent usage, the more flexible you will able to be with regard to the dissemination of the information on the various media and channels—regardless of whether it involves print, TV, or the Internet (see Section 3.2.1).

Structure more important than design

Before you develop a layout or a design, you must determine which type of contents are supposed to be published and disseminated. Because information is not only consumed on a certain platform but also aggregated into other applications to form new information packages, it is critical that the focus is placed on the design of the information instead of the design of its display (content vs. visual design). With the method of "content wireframing" (McGrane, 2011), you create flexible contents based on the principles of message, meaning, logic, and structure—without paying attention to the typography and design. It is important to consider (and describe) the semantic meaning of information (e.g., with meta information).

> *You don't know where your content is going to appear next year.*
> *You probably don't know where it's going to appear next week.*
> **Karen McGrane (author of "Content Strategy for Mobile")**

The most successful information systems offer the possibilities of networking pieces of information with each other. This can be or can become a problem for established, conservative content providers. Accordingly, suitable monetarization models must be found that take this increasing networking into consideration.

In order to optimally depict or aggregate information as best as possible, it must be clearly structured, among others, in the form of meta-data or meta-information. They are data that contain information about characteristics of other data (e.g., file name, file size, file type, date, author, descriptions, and key words). Meta-data help during the improvement of search mechanisms and search results or during the sorting of contents on the basis of a wide array of information (e.g., price, size, color, manufacturer, or assessment of a TV in an online shop). Ethan Resnick, UX designer from New York, opines that meta-data is the new art direction (as quoted in Clark, 2011b).

Structured information can be beneficially accessed only via an (application programming) interface. The structuring of the information is again the basis for a media-neutral content strategy.

The future of mobile is structured content.

Karen McGrane (2011)

Likewise and according to Karen McGrane the future of multiscreen is structured content, as well. You can find a checklist and more tips and suggestions for the creation of multiscreen-ready content via www.msxbook.com/en/smrtcnt.

Atomic content (or content modeling)

Structurally, information consists of the single smallest possible elements that are combined to a larger meaningful information object depending on context, viewport, channel, user interface (UI), layout, surrounding content, and other parameters.

Comparable to the atomic design principle by Brad Frost (2013a)—a systematic approach that describes the atomic composition of UI elements—content elements can be treated and put together in a similar way. There is also a correlation of UI and content elements, components, and segments (for a detailed explanation, see Chapter 7).

A content model is a representation of the types of content, simple attributes, and data types and their relations with each other. Content modeling is the process of creating content models that describe structured content (Gibbon, 2015). Only with structured content are you able to deliver it independently to whatever channel in the future may be relevant for your business. Smart and structured content and its future are also discussed in several sections in Chapter 6 on the future of content (management) and other topics. Small content snippets consisting of a very minimized and radically reduced combination of content elements are especially relevant and interesting for notifications and mini-updates on a smartphone (lock screen) and smartwatches. The better content is structured in small pieces and content bricks, the better it can be used and delivered for this purpose.

Future content flows

In the future, content must be able to be obtained from a multitude of sources on various devices and channels. How content will be created, managed, and consumed is one of the main challenges in a multiscreen world.

The needs of the users and of the content creators and editors must be taken into consideration as best as possible. These are the first (input/creation) and third (output/usage) steps in a three-step content flow, in which a centralized content hub should be in the center. This topic is explained in Chapter 6.

5.10.1 CONTENT STRATEGY

Content strategy aims to create, structure, edit, and publish information and contents logically and based on the communication goals. It involves offering a cross-device, context-relevant, and comprehensive user experience on all relevant channels.

> *Content strategy is the practice of planning for the creation, delivery, and governance of useful, usable content.*
>
> **Content Strategy Consortium**

How to do it?

You develop a suitable strategy sensibly on the basis of jointly defined project goals and the respective target group (e.g., with the aid of personas). Not till then can you plan, create, and publish the contents and then ultimately manage and update them after publication.

In order to sensibly implement this process (Tiedtke, 2012), you must focus on the potential users. Detailed tips and information in this regard are provided in Chapter 3. Which contents are relevant for the users? When (time frame), where (context of use and environment), and how will they use them? What content needs do the users have? The devices, media formats, and channels used must likewise be known.

With a *content audit*, you can assess the scope and the current quality of the contents and, where applicable, design optimization measures. In order to do this, all of the contents must be collected and assessed (Leibtag, n.d.; Tiedtke, 2012). If you know what type of your own or third-party contents are being read, commented on, assessed, or recommended to others and how often, you can set priorities (for information regarding the checklist, see http://www.msxbook.com/en/cntadt).

When the contents have been roughly determined, first the *information architecture* and then the wireframes can be created. Important principles that you should keep in mind in this regard are content first (discussed at the beginning of this chapter), adaptability (see Section 5.8.1), and responsive design (see Section 5.8.1). See also Chapter 7 concerning content design and UI modeling. In addition to the visual guidelines, guidelines should also be determined for the contents (style, tonality, messages, content types, content size, and content structure). By using various *usability testing* and research methods, you can check whether the contents function, are understood, and trigger an action as required.

The Coca-Cola Company's content strategy serves as an example. The Coca-Cola website actively links to third-party contents. It does not host videos on its own but, rather, integrates them via YouTube. Techniques are used which you are familiar with from blogs. After logging in via external accounts such as Facebook, Twitter, or WordPress, you can leave comments (Knüwer, 2012; see Sections 5.12 and 5.14).

> *Content is the creation of stories that are to be expressed through every possible connection.*
>
> **Coca-Cola Company**

Action-relevant content

Meinald Thielsch and Rafael Jaron (2012) researched the interplay of website contents, usability, and aesthetics with regard to the four typical stages of website usage. They documented that the content plays the decisive role and that it is accordingly (even) more important than usability or the pure design. The four stages are as follows:

- First impression
- Overall impression
- Willingness to visit again
- Willingness to recommend to others

The study showed that the aesthetics have the primary influence on the first impression and sometimes on the overall impression. In all other phases, conversely, the content plays the decisive role. It is action-relevant: "The contents take on a central role as soon as a longer interaction or continuous use of a website takes place" (Thielsch and Jaron, 2012). With corresponding tests, you must analyze all four stages because the analysis reduced to the initial impression is not nearly sufficient.

Information and data management are the core of all information services. The "recommendation" (social web, community, networking, and information dissemination via social networks) is a decisive factor for (assessing) the website quality.

Content availability

An information offering is of no benefit if it cannot be used on the preferred device. Contents and information should in principle be available and retrievable on all platforms and on all relevant devices (information availability). The access to the information is more important than its ownership (Kaltner, 2012; Nagel, 2012a).

The platform- and device-independent and consistent availability of information or applications is a quality criterion. Regarded technologically, the theme of *cloud computing* plays the central role (see Section 5.6).

The quality and the scope of a service also increase if data are integrated into other offerings. If information is stored and supplied in a usage-open manner (i.e., if third parties are granted access to it), it can be aggregated into various offerings. That is the basis for all kind of "content mashups." An application programming interface (API) provides access to an information package. Other offerings can access them, and the accumulated information can be combined to form a new offering (with added value) (see Section 5.11).

Innovative services

On the basis of the most flexible and open contents possible (open content), interfaces, and meta-data, new business models can be created that specialize in offering services with freely available and accessible data (open source, open data, etc.) for which no (new) contents, platforms, or devices must be created. The existing ecosystems and the existing infrastructure are sufficient.

Information visibility

In the digital information age, the actual information becomes invisible, but the standard for the visual quality of the information (full HD TV, retina display, etc.) also increases. Simple examples are music and books. Previously, each record or CD had a lavish record cover, and comprehensive information was in the included booklet. Books attracted and competed for customers with their titles and covers. MP3s, streaming music, and e-books are today database objects and quasi-invisible (in any case, but not haptically). They are sorted and found through good indexing, meta-data, and linking information. The visual form is often reduced to thumb-sized photos (thumbnails). It is suspected that the emotional connection of the users to this information is waning (Siebert, 2013). A future question will be how the invisible digital information is visually upgraded, made visible (again), and enabled to be experienced visually (and possibly haptically in terms of gestural interaction).

Taking the analog media into consideration

For analog processes or if the target group rarely uses digital devices or does not use them at all, you should also take into consideration analog or classical media during the conception of an information offering or a communications strategy (print media, placards, and multichannel publishing). Alternatively, the combination of digital contents and analog media makes sense (see Section 5.17).

5.10.2 EXTENSIBILITY

A future-oriented information offering must be flexibly extensible and able to be adapted to changed requirements. You can never absolutely predict in which direction an information offering will develop. The extension at a later point in time can cause unnecessary and high costs and additional expenditures. In the extreme case, a scaling or extension is not possible because, for example, it would not be economically feasible—with corresponding consequences for the project (to the point of termination).

Take it into consideration early

Extensibility and platform independence must be taken into consideration during the conception (even if only one medium is relevant at the beginning of a project and supposed to be involved). Flexibility is system-imminent and can be complemented later only with great difficulty or not at all.

Thus, from the beginning, a concept should be flexibly designed for cross-media (digital and print), cross-device, and cross-platform information dissemination. These days, each project is potentially a multiscreen project. The information must be available on multiple platforms, devices, and screens as well as frequently also in various languages. If the requirements change, an information offering (e.g., software, data stores, and information) must be able to be extended and adapted as flexibly as possible. The 2012 Google study recommends that not the complete but at least the essential portion of the "content experience" for a "smartphone experience" must be conceived and designed.

Scalability or extensibility is a core requirement and must be considered for multilingualism, device independence for the selection of technology (e.g., *flash* restriction for the iPad and the iPhone), or increasing server loads as the result of increased access figures to a website or webserver (e.g., if you permit user-generated content or host storage-intensive data such as videos).

The mobile devices from Apple with the operating system iOS can display no **flash contents**. Other platforms and browsers also sometimes have compatibility problems or block flash content by default. Another (some type of designed) page also then shows merely the note that the Adobe flash player is supposed to be installed. In this case, al least **fallback solutions** (replacement contents for which you need no flash plug-in for their display) should be provided.

Losing control with user-generated content

By integrating the social networks or developing a community and the related active participation options of the users and their influence on the contents (user generated content), you give up control (see Section 5.12). The project can develop its own unforeseen dynamic. When you take such factors of uncertainty into consideration in the concept, you can respond flexibly to influences and changes.

Content management

For the multilingual, device-independent, and context-appropriate outputting of information (see Chapter 4, Section 4.3), structured content management systems (CMS) are suitable in which information about one and the same database can be collected in different ways (e.g., short and long texts about outputting onto mobile devices or laptops, with or without images, high resolution, or minimal data size) (see Chapter 6, Section 6.3).

Cross-media publishing

With cross-media publishing, contents are managed and stored in a media-neutral manner (Wikipedia, n.d., "Cross Media Publishing"):

Texts, photos, and other graphical elements are stored in an unaltered and unformatted form. For photos (and also videos), this means that they will be stored in the best available quality and only then be reduced for actual use; for example, to the required quality level within an Internet website.

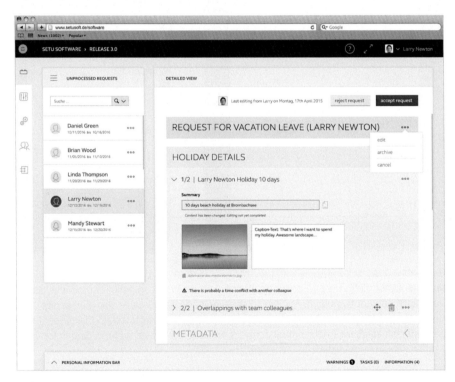

SETU is an information management software for intelligent data storage and flexible structures. Using this software, contents and meta-information can be flexibly collected and handled for multilingual and device-independent outputting—for all channels and markets. Through its architecture, SETU supports many of the principles described in this book and is based, among others, on the ideas described in Sections 5.10 and 5.15 and in Chapters 6 and 7. For more information about SETU, see http://www.setusoft.de. The moodscreen shows an impression of the user interface of a demo use case of the SETU 3.0 release.

5.11 MASHABILITY

Users no longer use certain sources in exclusively a targeted manner. Information is more aggregated today than ever—via news or RSS reader, *read later*, or magazine concepts; social networks; or other platforms in which the sender of the information is no longer clearly classified. An article is no longer mandatorily read where it was originally created (see also Chapter 7, Section 7.1).

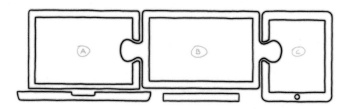

It is increasingly more important to generate and supply contents that are as flexible as possible. The basic requirement for this consists of an existing and suitable content strategy and platform-neutral data. Even in this context, meta-data are increasing in importance. The sources are becoming more heterogeneous. Editorial contents, user-generated contents, (application programming) interfaces, and profile information are being used to set up customized information constructs (see also Chapter 6, Section 6.2 and Chapter 7, Section 7.1).

Using interfaces (API) intelligently

Those who use (application programming) interfaces intelligently can save much work and generate added value for their information or publications. It does not always have to be a proprietary solution. Often, added-value information can be created with relatively few expenditures and without having to develop software completely on one's own, via aggregation or a mashup that cleverly combines and synchronizes the various services. With a mashup, new (media) contents are created through the seamless (re)combination of already existing contents. There are currently many tools that intelligently and almost perfectly solve a task. The decisive challenge is to skillfully combine these tools and synchronize them with one another. The information offering of the future is an intelligent, personalized mashup service that aggregates relevant and purposeful content.

Some mobile applications use, for example, Dropbox (a web-based file hosting service) as a cloud interface in order to store data or information and to synchronize them in a cross-device and device-independent manner.

Combination and democratization of contents

Mashups have great innovative potential for the intelligent networking of information. Platform-independent and flexible contents, data, and information can be combined through the use of corresponding interfaces (API) to form new added-value services. Such mashups are a challenge—perhaps even a "problem" or a risk—for journalism and publishing houses and/or generally for established, conservative, and past (e.g., advertising-financed) content models.

Aggregation of contents and services

For information, news, articles, or photos that are aggregated in services such as Google News, Google Reader, Pulse, or Flipboard, the sender and/or the author is no longer clearly identifiable (see Chapters 6 and 7). Often, the origin of the information is no longer clear (classifiable). Conversely, copyright issues may arise if the original sources are not properly named or cited (see Section 5.19).

With **Apple iTunes**, the origin of the audio contents is, for example, not relevant. Songs and albums do not have to be purchased on corresponding sound carriers but, rather, are aggregated on a platform and can be directly purchased and downloaded in the iTunes Shop without the "detour" via the producers (in this case, the interpreters or music label).

> *The reader no longer wants news from a single source. The only killer app (for news) which has existed up to now is the browser.*
> **Oliver Reichenstein (Information Architects)**

The usage and availability of APIs enables integration of services with other screens and additional device classes (e.g., automotive displays). They also support the communication and information exchange among services. Beyond that, all devices that are able to connect via any type of technology (e.g., WIFI or Bluetooth) can be part of the Internet of Things.

Open news platforms

Various news services offer interfaces (API) for their contents. They can be used for free subject to certain requirements and can be integrated into other services. The daily newspaper has become a platform. The following are examples:

- *The Guardian*: http://www.msxbook.com/en/guardian
- *USA Today*: http://www.msxbook.com/en/usatoday
- *The New York Times*: http://www.msxbook.com/en/nytimes

The New York Times (2013) states the following about its news API: "You already know that NYTimes.com is an unparalleled source of news and information. But now it's a premier source of data, too—why just read the news when you can hack it?" In other words, "It's not a newspaper; it's a platform" (Josh Clark, 2012c).

Added value through availability

Services with corresponding interfaces (API) such as YouTube can be integrated everywhere. The video platform has also been integrated into many smart TV platforms. This has given YouTube an enormously good market position and has substantially upgraded the service (see Sections 5.9 and 5.10). Conversely, there are smart TV providers that integrate popular services such as YouTube into their offerings and are thus more attractive for potential buyers.

Fundamentally, it does not matter from which manufacturer you buy a TV. The technical features are almost identical. Solely the form factor decides, and that is a matter of taste. In the future, the most important factor for the buying decision will be the availability of and the access to information. The elementary question (and this applies for all device classes) is whether certain apps or services that are important to the potential buyer can be used on the device and with the related platform.

It is the same with TV service providers and network appliances, for example, from Amazon (Fire TV Stick and Instant Video), Apple (Apple TV), Google (Chromecast), and other services. The one that integrated the most APIs and offers the most services are in the pole position when the customer has to decide between a giant offer and variety of services or "TV sticks" (as extension to TV devices). Services that offer and use more (application programming) interfaces to other services (e.g., media libraries of television broadcaster) are potentially just more appealing than the ones that offer less. It is just as simple as that. Can I get and use a service on that device or not? It is about access to information! Furthermore it is also important how smart the application feels (the User Experience of the Service), of course, and how easily and user-friendly it can be combined and used with other convenient and popular (standard) devices, such as, a smartphone or tablet. Some services additionally even offer smartphone and tablet apps that can be used as and replace their physical remote controls.

The principle of the **Qwiki iPad app** consisted of a mashup of a search engine, a lexicon, and a video portal that, via corresponding interfaces, aggregates information from various sources to form a new information package. The provider is currently pursuing a different strategy and has discontinued the service.

about.me is a platform on which you can aggregate information from various online profiles, social networks, and websites to form a one-page user profile (you can see my profile at http://about.me/wnagel).

The **contacts app with the Windows Phone** accesses information from Outlook, Exchange, Facebook, and other social networks and bundles it all into a single application. The user does not need to switch applications in order to receive comprehensive information about a contact.

The music streaming service **Spotify** offers an interface for developers for integrating music into other online services. Thus, Spotify can be integrated well into communities and other platforms. The same is conceivable for TV service providers in conjunction with broadcasts and films.

iAWriter and Plaintext use Dropbox as the interface for the storage and synchronization of text files. Dropbox is a web-based file hosting service, that offers data storage in and file synchronization via the cloud.

With **Storify**, information can be combined from as many Internet sites and social networks as desired (e.g., tweets, status notifications, photos, and videos) to form a new story.

Smart TV or hybrid TV platforms aggregate a wide array of information and services and integrate them via corresponding interfaces. For example, **Samsung SmartTV** offers apps from tagesschau.de, YouTube, Facebook, and Twitter. Social TV options are likewise integrated like a web browser or offer the possibility of communicating via Skype.

5.12 COMMUNIFICATION

A social network or the creation of a community can make information offerings more attractive in many cases. Moreover, it can make sense to integrate existing social platforms into an information offering via corresponding interfaces (API).

Involving users and upgrading information

How can you upgrade and dynamically design the content of an information offering without your own involvement in this regard? How can you animate users to create contents, to assess information or products, or quite generally to participate?

Two factors for the success of the social Internet (Social Media, Web 2.0) are the community-driven approach and user-generated content.

User-generated content (also abbreviated as UGC or referred to as user-driven content) constitutes media content which has not been created by the provider of a website, but rather by its users. In this regard, the content must fulfil the following criteria according to OECD: Published contents, creative personal contribution, and creation outside of the professional routines. It is (as explained on Wikipedia) defined as any form of (media) content that was created by users of an online system or service, often made available via social media websites, for example, blogs, wikis, discussion forums, posts, chats, tweets, digital images, video, audio files, and any other forms of media produced by user. Community-driven means that a project is pushed and edited by a group of people (community). The member of such a community work together on a project (networking).

The community and its members are responsible for the information. The users create, comment on, and correct the contents on their own. Social networks are a phenomenon of the masses and are very relevant for search engine optimization. Many media also integrate the contents and opinions that have been provided by the users into their printed products.

Social involvement, user-generated content, comments, personal recommendations, and user ratings provide information (message, data, and products) with a higher, personal, and sometimes subjective quality. Each comment to an article or blog post (for example) is an additional element of a specific content object that has to be stored and managed (see Chapters 6 and 7 concerning "Content Flows," "Content Modeling," and "Content Hub").

Whenever users have a direct influence, the offering is better tailored to their needs and they will use it in a more motivated manner and more frequently. In order to benefit from this effect, the suppliers or the manufacturers of a product must largely sacrifice control over the information offering and be open to the community-provided input, which is unpredictable and not plannable in detail. (Compare the Sobooks-example in Section 6.2.1 where readers of these social ebooks become quasi co-authors of the original and initial content.) This entails legal risks (see Section 5.19) and the risk of the loss of quality through, for example, so-called Internet trolls (Lobo, 2011).

Win–win situation

If you develop an information offering as a community or "dock" a community to it, you can increase its value to the users. If you can animate them to create or modify contents themselves (user-generated content) and/or to participate in the development of products, everyone will profit. A win–win situation is created for service providers and users. The service provider receives useful and valuable feedback from the users, and the users can exert influence on the products. Via the community, an additional communication channel is created for the direct dialog between the service provider and the user and also for the dialogue between the users—the users can interact with each other in the community.

The community must be accessible and available on all relevant devices. Which devices are relevant can be determined via target group analyses, surveys, access statistics, and user-centered methods in general.

User profiles and personalization

Another aspect in this context is profile-appropriate information. When users create user profiles (which you must first motivate them to do), you can create specially adapted and very individual information offerings—exactly customized to the user's potential requirements. Conversely, this supplies helpful information about user behavior that you can once again take into consideration during the optimization of the offering. In the end, no information offering is the same as another one. However, it may nonetheless result in a collective usage of individually selected pieces of information if the interests of both user profiles overlap.

Recommendations from friends and automatic recommendations via an evaluation of the user profiles can be combined. A prominent example of this is the purchasing recommendations at Amazon for which user profiles and behavioral patterns are evaluated ("People who bought X also bought Y.").

Relevance and ramifications of social media

It is not a matter of only developing a (new, one's own) community but, rather, generally having a presence in the social media and on corresponding networks, platforms, and devices. You must be able to be contacted via them, to (be able to) communicate via them, and to integrate them into your own offerings and to link them to your own contents. Lobo (2012) states: "The structure of the social media makes it attractive for large brands to assemble their target group there and to directly reach them without any intermediaries being required. At the end of November 2012, Lady Gaga has a Twitter account with more than 31 million followers. With this self-controlled range, why does she still need media, let alone expensive advertising for her products? Social media and presentation intelligence reduce advertising budgets. Thus, the refinancing of journalism needs additional tools."

Information worth sharing

With regard to social media, it is a matter of whether users would like to recommend a piece of information, share it, and disseminate it virally. How can a mere event be presented as a company event with news value? An example is Felix Baumgartner's stratospheric leap from a balloon. With the spectacle followed by millions of people worldwide, the sponsor Red Bull obtained advertising value that exceeded the estimated cost of approximately 50 million euro by many times over (Zeit Online, 2012).

The blogger and journalist Sascha Lobo (2012) writes in this regard (see also Section 5.10): "At the moment, all the groups of companies in the world are probably considering with their agencies how they can imitate Red Bull's stroke of genius. The functionality of the social media simplifies this enormously to present a mere event as a company event with news value: Whenever so many people twitter about it, you must probably also report on it. From the perspective of groups of companies doing advertising, the future of advertising lies not only next to the contents, but rather also in the contents."

Shareable information

Information that is worth sharing is just one aspect. The other one is if and how information can be shared technically, flexibly, and easily. It's about how information can be published, integrated into or combined with other information offerings (see Section 5.11). The more and easier content can be shared on various platforms, the more it will be spread.

Facebook Music Stories is a post format which enables music discovery and sharing on its social platform. It allows people to stream and listen to a 30-second snippet of the shared song (or album) from different streaming music services (Cerda, 2015). If a user likes a song from a particular streaming service he can copy that link to add it into the Facebook timeline, where a preview automatically appears.

Content must be structured and prepared for that kind of usage. You need **shareable content elements**, at least an audio snippet of that content and a content element that can appear as preview (see also Section 5.10, and Chapters 6 and 7). One thing is clear: The better that service is, the more music will be shared (and used, and paid). That shareability requirement is relevant for all kind of content and media types: articles, books, videos, images, etc.

Next, examples of cross-device social involvement and the combination of social profiles with added-value information are given.

Social TV is fundamentally a combination of entertainment, simultaneous usage, and communification (see Sections 5.2 and 5.3).

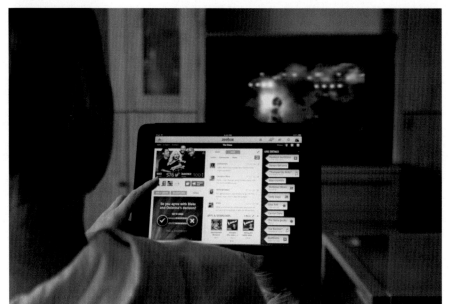

Zeebox (re-branded to beamly in 2014) morphed from a TV guide and utility app into a social platform for talking about TV shows. It is now an interactive social networking and social TV service for mobile devices that offers textual information about the TV program that is being shown. For example, there is information about which friends are currently watching the same program or supplemental information about the actors, music, or certain themes. There is also a corresponding desktop website for the service, with a program overview and articles from social networks. Zeebox has set the goal for itself of being the starting point for the TV experience (see Sections 5.2, 5.3, and 5.11).

With the **Nike+iPhone app**, running routes can be determined via GPS, synchronized with the online portal https://Nikeplus.com, and shared with other runners in the community. All running routes are listed in the online platform and displayed there graphically. They can be commented on, rated, shared with other networks, and recommended to other runners. It is also possible to compare yourself with other joggers in a competition or to break personal records (see Section 5.13). The Nike+ running app also works with Apple Watch and offers updates and running data on the wrist.

Eventbrite is an excellent example of a fluid multiscreen experience. Users can register for an event on the Eventbrite website and receive a ticket that they can print out themselves. There is also a mobile app for accessing tickets and event information even more easily. The mobile application is optimal in the context because the users will most likely have their smartphone with them at the events and thus can utilize a personalized QR code displayed on the screen as a ticket, which can be scanned well even in poor lighting conditions.

Another offering goes even farther. **Bizzabo** is an application that places the social aspect of conferences very much in the forefront (direct eye contact, shaking hands, and personal meeting). With the app, event organizers can import information from Eventbrite (see Section 5.11) in order to involve the participants in meetings and conferences, to come into direct contact with them, and to make networking more efficient.

5.13 GAMIFICATION

How can you get people to use a certain offering, an application, or a service with enthusiasm?

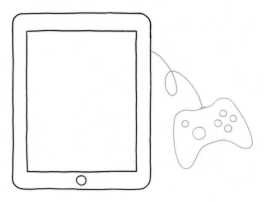

The difference between play and work lies in the "must." Playing is voluntary. A play factor can motivate people when it is fun, challenging, prescribes a relevant goal, and the user can in principle voluntarily decide. Thus, it makes sense to have the information or application concept run via a gaming approach (Ferrara, 2011).

Work consists of whatever a body is obliged to do, and play consists of whatever a body is not obliged to do.

Mark Twain

Game mechanics simulate a competition

With *gamification*, gaming approaches are intentionally inserted into an information offering (Crane, 2011). When they are used correctly, game mechanics can motivate people to more frequently use an application. They imply or simulate a competition, look good, vividly display information, and reward the user for what he does. The approaches must be sufficiently relevant, sensible, and challenging. The software must be fun and entertain the user. Four factors are in the forefront in this regard: It must be entertaining, competitive, visual, and rewarding (Dole, 2010).

Often, however, three essential ingredients are lacking in the applications and/ or the definition of the term gamification: challenge, relevance, and autonomy. Deterding (2011) advises, "For a genuine gaming experience instead of flat progress wars, create exciting challenges with a relevant story and gaming flexibility. Pay attention to the ancillary effects and the social contexts. Learn the game rules and be a good designer."

Thus, overall, you should take seven parameters into consideration.

1. FUN AND ENTERTAINMENT

Make it fun and entertaining. An entertaining offering can be more fun for the users. Training programs on the Wii game console motivate the participants, for example, through an entertaining game experience and promote the immersion of the users. The drills then feel less like work or simply better.

2. COMPETITION

Make it competitive for users. With the running tracking tool Nike+ (see Section 5.12), a competitive character is implemented in order to (reciprocally) motivate users. Nike+records, among others (via GPS), the running route and the speed. The performances, running routes, and experiences can be shared with and commented on by other runners in the community.

3. VISIBILITY

Make it visual. Toyota visualized the fuel consumption in the Prius models and started a type of game for saving fuel. The driver could follow in real time how his driving behavior had an effect on fuel consumption. The experiment was known as the Prius Effect. Similar suggestions about fuel consumption are offered by the Honda Insight, in which eco-points are awarded and a green eco leaf is shown in the display, and the electric car Leaf from Nissan, in which the fuel consumption is sent to a website and compared with that of other drivers in a ranking list.

4. REWARD

Make it rewarding. Financial or material rewards influence user behavior less than rewards that generate societal and beneficial added value—for example, rewards in the form of discount tickets or the possibility of indirectly supporting aid campaigns through your own behavior (Dole, 2010; see also Section 5.15).

With the **karstadt** sports app, users can collect trophies through use of the app. They can then redeem the trophies for vouchers.

5. CHALLENGE

Fun is created not (just) through rewards but, rather, through an exciting challenge based on four elements: the goal, rules (collectively producing an exciting challenge), feedback, and a successful experience.

6. RELEVANCE

It is of critical importance whether the information offerings or applications indeed provide content-based quality or whether gamification is offered as the sole added value. Game mechanisms should not be the core. You must determine and support the users' goals and, via a story (see Section 5.14), tell of the relevance behind a goal. This has a lot to do with psychology (see Section 5.15).

With the web-based financial management service https://www.mint.com, users can, for example, create a budget and define goals that can be personalized.

7. AUTONOMY

Games must always be voluntary. You must try to create incentives, offer informative feedback, communicate the voluntariness, and also ensure that your own activity is not devalued.

Whoever must play, cannot play.

James P. Carse (philosopher)

User in the focus

The following are important questions: What does the user get from the implemented gaming principle? For what and why is he rewarded? What constitutes a sensible reward for the user?

An advantage of good gamification is virality or the combination with a social dissemination approach.

Examples of this are the geo-check-in services such as **Foursquare**. With the aid of the GPS compatibility of mobile devices, users can check in at various locations via websites or applications in order to receive rewards. Whether these rewards are awarded at all and the manner in which they are awarded and are sufficiently relevant depend on the respective user and his needs and interests.

Learning incrementally

Josh Clark recommends that when developing apps, you should think in levels, with the easiest possible start. The application should begin easily and then become more difficult. Clark (2011d) advises, "Think about your app as levels. What's your first level? … Think about the whole journey from novice to experts." It is optimal when the usage is fun and adapted to the user's skill level (leveling up). Playthings are important and help during research (Clark, 2011d).

Do not blindly follow gamification

Game elements do not automatically and mandatorily result in a more successful and better service. They are not equally well-suited for all types of applications. Banal elements or irrelevant rewards can turn the desired effect into the opposite. Games are not always fun per se.

Real games prescribe goals and offer the player a truly interesting challenge (Robertson, 2010). To master a situation is the appeal of real games. Game fun is created from the satisfaction of your inner basic needs (see Chapter 3, Section 3.3.1). You must understand the users and know their motives and needs. Intrinsic motivation cannot keep pace with extrinsic incentives over the long term. It is optimal if the users are already motivated to use a service and it has a certain relevance even without game elements.

A well-founded service, a functioning community, and a good website are the basic requirements. Gamification as an additional element—used correctly and conscientiously—can also add a positive complementary effect. It is a matter of motivating people in their own sense (Schätzle, 2013).

With the **Heineken Star Player iPhone app**, viewers can predict live the outcome of individual game situations during a soccer match and accumulate points. The app expands the live event on TV with offerings that are beneficial exclusively parallel to the game (see Section 5.2).

The principle fulfills some of the aforementioned seven parameters (fun, competition, visibility, reward, challenge, relevance, and autonomy). Above all, the app has been appealingly designed. Points are awarded for the correct predictions or answers to questions.

During the game, general questions about the teams that are playing or about soccer are posed. When the correct answer is shown, the results of the virtual opponents are also displayed.

The challenge of answering questions about soccer is obviously relevant for persons who are interested in soccer. It is about the theme. The participants can decide, on their own and consciously, in what phase of the game they are using the app in order to accumulate points.

In order to further increase the gamification approach and the incentive of participation, one could offer not just points and badges but also rewards such as vouchers for Heineken products, soccer fan items, or items that one cannot buy (e.g., a day with a soccer star or a backstage pass). That would certainly motivate the user to participate in the game (even) more.

5.14 STORYFICATION

If you tell the story of a product or an information offering across various media, you can create a uniform, cross-device, consistent and pleasant user and information experience. With the storyfication approach, the users' understanding of the product as well as their identification with and loyalty and commitment to the product can be increased. *Storyfication* is a mix and an expansion of the approaches of storytelling and transmedia storytelling.

STORYTELLING

Storytelling is a narration method by means of which explicit, but above all, implicit knowledge is conveyed in the form of a metaphor and received by listening (source: Wikipedia). If the listeners are integrated into the story being told, they can understand it more easily and think along on their own. By so doing, the information to be conveyed will be better understood and ultimately also accepted.

It is substantially more difficult to learn if you do not understand the correlations. If no correlation is recognizable, humans construct one or they just forget the subject matter. The knowledge that human and/or the users are constantly trying to devise a story when using a product can be helpful when conceiving informational offerings because the stories can influence each other in the users' minds.

When conceiving interaction processes, time sequences are formulated in causal correlations. This has an influence on the stories which the users tell themselves anyhow respectively make sense of them and ultimately also on their user experience.

The interpretation leeway of a user is often greater than suspected. However, the parameters and indicators in the stories can be defined. The content (texts and images), design (GUI: graphical user interface), and interaction set the tone for a story and form the dialogue between the user and the product (information).

In the area of interaction, there are three different parameters by means of which a story can be influenced: Rhythm, level of freedom, and mode. Does the user interact quickly and in a choppy manner or in a steady manner? Is the process heavily guided or can the user interact freely (or more freely)? What can the user do and how and with what inputting methods does he/she uses a system and what associations are evoked by so doing? Ultimately, it is important that the product and/or the service or an informational offering tells a (suitable) story. And you can and should influence it. (Sackl, 2011)

TRANSMEDIA STORYTELLING

Definition according to Riedel, 2009 (sometimes cited according to Jenkins, 2007) and Jenkins, 2007. With transmedia storytelling, a story—as the name already implies—is told across multiple media. Transmedia storytelling refers not only to various digital devices, but rather also to all other media and informational offerings (computer games, social media platforms, POS, print, etc.).

Personas can help to tell the correct and/or suitable stories for the target group being aimed for. By so doing, you receive insights into their media usage (what devices and what media they use when, where, and how?). The better you know the potential users, the better the informational offerings can be tailored to their requirements, wishes, and needs via storytelling (user-centered).

The story which you conceive and/or analyze for a user and formulate into a scenario must likewise show correlations. It must be coherent. Stories can be used during the entire design process in order to create a consistent and pleasant user and information experience.

In his blog (Riedel, 2009), Christian Riedel explains the theme of transmedia storytelling and refers on his part to the MIT convergence expert Henry Jenkins which lists the basic concepts of transmedia storytelling in his blog. We would like to discuss Riedel's article at this point which is also cited below in abbreviated form.

Jenkins describes transmedia storytelling as the process of telling integral components of a fiction systematically across various media channels in order to create a coordinated and interdisciplinary entertainment experience.

"It is not important to disseminate the same story in all channels (like in the sense of 360-degree communication). Instead, the contents should complement each other. Jenkins' favorite example of transmedia storytelling is the franchise around the film Matrix. In this case, the film, comics, a computer game, and an animated cartoon series respectively tell their own stories. Together, they give a comprehensive experience in the fictional world to the consumer who knows them all. The secret of the success of transmedia storytelling lies in [...] creating a fictional world which serves as a resource for stories that are always new. Naturally, in addition to the fictitious world, the quality of the generated stories is of critical importance. Because only if the stories are truly in harmony with each other and each story intelligently reveals a new aspect of the fictitious world do they hold the recipients' interest. [...] If a fictitious world functions well, it even captivates the consumers to tell their own stories. Jenkins refers above all to fan fiction which is written and published regarding Star Trek and Star Wars."

Product, story, experience

Storyfication means telling the story of a product and communicating (about) the product by means of a story. The storyfication of a service is less about minor details or about disseminating the same story in all channels. Rather, it entails the entire whole—that the contents complement each other and that all touchpoints (device touchpoints) and interactions form a user experience that is closely related to a product and first rate (Doody, 2011).

> *So whether you are at a small start up or a large organization, whether you are a founder, executive, technologist, designer, manager, or marketer, ask yourself this: do you know your product's story? And perhaps more importantly, who creates your product story?*
>
> Sarah Doody (2011)

(Transmedia) storytelling

Whenever the listeners are integrated into the story being told, they can thus identify with it more easily and think along on their own. By so doing, the information to be communicated is better understood and ultimately also accepted. The users are more strongly involved in an information offering. They can directly participate in the creation of a product and ideally also influence it themselves. Stories can be used in order to create a consistent and transparent *information experience.*

With transmedia storytelling, a story—as the name implies—is told across multiple media. Transmedia storytelling refers not just to different digital devices but also to all other touchpoints, media, and information offerings (computer games, social media platforms, point-of-sale, print, etc.).

Henry Jenkins (2007) describes transmedia storytelling as the process of "telling integral components of a fiction systematically across various media channels" in order to create a coordinated and comprehensive entertainment experience.

Sarah Doody argues that product storytellers play a central role. They should be the lynchpin and the interface between the product, marketing, and technology in order to ensure that a correct, suitable, and always consistent story is told. Before developers, marketing people, and designers set to work, it must be decided what story the product is supposed to tell. Moreover, she writes that a product is more than an idea, website, transaction, or a list of functions. A product must deliver an experience or offer added value and help the user to fulfill a need or a wish (Doody, 2011).

User behavior-oriented

If you understand how people use a product or a service, you can tell suitable and supportive stories and design the decisive features and the distinctive features. This ultimately results in an improved user experience.

If, for example, a company determines for its online website that the creation and sharing of photos is supposed to be **an important element for increasing the user's participation**, the camera can be the decisive element in combination with the smartphone app.

With the smartphone, the camera is always with you. The photos can be synchronized with all other devices, edited on the tablet or desktop PC, and viewed on the smart TV when friends visit. The easier the use and the more fluid the transition to the various devices functions, the more high quality and the more relevant the service will be for a user.

Telling user-centered stories

Personas can help to tell the suitable stories for the targeted user group. They supply insight into their media usage behavior by inquiring about which devices and which media the users use when, where, how, and why. In our user prototypes (see Chapter 3, Section 3.5), we also describe the life's motives, the life circumstances, and other personal details. The better you know the potential users, the better the service will be able to be tailored to their requirements, wishes, and needs with a story and by means of storytelling (user-centered design).

> **IMPORTANT**
>
> If a brand or a product has no story, then you must search for it. Just making up a story does not work. You cannot artificially add value to a brand with a story that has been made up. The story is then not authentic.

Cross-media and user-specific

Stories can be told in a wide array of ways via various screens, channels, and media. Assuming that a film or a series (trilogy) is shown in a movie theater or on TV, then the information about the main film, complementary comic books, or video games can be told with a different focus and a different depth (based on the target group, device, and context of use). There is not just one single source in which all information about the film or theme is told.

The story can be respectively told and packaged in a different way based on to whom you would like to appeal. For romantics, this could be a novel or a romantic comic; for younger users, you might consider picture books or coloring books or, alternatively, corresponding digital offerings (website, comic series, or apps for various devices).

The information and stories (and/or the entire story as a common thread) will complement each other to form a greater whole. No user must know everything, but he should be provided with the relevant information that corresponds to his interests, needs, competences, and his prior knowledge.

Based on the openness, it can also make sense to directly involve the users, to offer a direct communication channel, or to request that they themselves contribute contents and information to the story (see Section 5.12).

Who Will Save Dina Foxx" was initially broadcast on ZDF (a German public-service TV broadcaster) as a 50-minute detective program. The case was ultimately moved to the Internet, where it was supposed to be solved within a prescribed time frame. The viewers, who were intentionally integrated into the story being told, could find out the truth and whether Dina was innocent after the broadcast in a multimedia scavenger hunt. They became investigators and had to solve small mysteries, hack passwords, and so on. The information to be communicated about the data protection theme was embedded in the story and could thus be better conveyed to the target audience. The participants learned on a quasi-parallel basis how data protection functions (does not function) (text and image source: ZDF, LfM Nova GmbH, 2011) (For more information on the project, see http://www.msxbook.com/en/dinafoxx and http://www.msxbook.com/en/freidaten.) The media transition from the TV to the desktop and thus the alternation between the lean back situation (allowing yourself to be "sprinkled" with information) and lean forward (urge to want to become active yourself) has functioned very well according to UFA Lab Producer Costa-Zahn (DWDL.de, 2011).

5.15 EMOTIONALITY

What makes a service emotionally appealing? What causes you to use an app or a website frequently and gladly? It is optimal when you have information available to you on all devices without having to particularly think about it and having to, for example, attend to the synchronization (i.e., fluidity).

The information should simply be there and in a good form. It should always be there when you need it. A service should be fun and support a multiscreen-ish daily routine.

Always there and exciting

During the course of the day, I use all devices at various times and in various contexts. I love it if an information offering or digital service supports my multiscreen-ish daily routine. Because it then offers a fluid multiscreen experience. I naturally prefer to use an app which is available on all devices to an app which is available only as a desktop application. If the information offering also appeals to me emotionally at the same time, subjective added value arises for me (subconsciously).
Wolfram Nagel (The author of this book)

Appealing service

A service can appeal to you emotionally in many ways—for example, if it has been well implemented; if it offers a user-friendly layout, a coherent interface (GUI), and logical interaction; and if it tells a story, integrates your own network and friends, "simply" already has place-related and context-relevant information at your disposal, or positively surprises at every touchpoint between the user and the service. It is also important that the app or website is easy to operate, always has information available, or the service is simply fun.

The social photo sharing app **Instagram** is a fast, pleasant, and entertaining way to allow your friends to take part in your life and personal experiences through photos. Thus, it is quite easy to follow what other friends are doing throughout the day. The app is easy to use, fun, and underscores that a picture is worth more than a thousand words. Photos appeal to you emotionally, they are understandable worldwide, and they have a more direct effect than text.

First impression and user onboarding

User onboarding is the process of increasing the likelihood that new users become successful when adopting your product (Hulick, n.d.). "You never get a second chance to make a first impression" is a quite common tip and principle. That applies in a special way to user onboarding, no matter on what device (class) you start using it. It is a very crucial challenge to do the first impression right. The first impression and the first steps (or first-time use) with a product are also affected by the emotional perception and often determine if the user implicitly likes a service (and if he will come back and use it again) or not.

Therefore Samuel Hulick (2015) points out to start designing where the users start using the product. Help people and make it easy to start using a product (for the first time). Welcome them in a friendly way. Do not show blank and frustrating states on the first page; show engaging and motivating progress on to-do lists or during the registration process (see also Sections 5.13 and 5.14). Give them a pat on the back when they mastered a new step. It must be as easy as possible for new users (or customers) to recognize the added value, to register, and to start using the service (e.g., keep initially required registration information as low as possible). The onboarding process has to be tested with potential users. A UI is like a joke. If you have to explain it, it's not really good.

Sometimes apps or products are too complex to keep them self-explanatory. Then user onboarding can be the crucial point for the perceived user experience. Just let users interact with the product and learn step by step. You can ask users to make the first comment or post, to complete the first (demo) task, or to generate the first content object. Emphasize the benefit of your service. A good user onboarding concept can enthuse potential users. Involve them into a story (see Section 5.14), make them part of a game or a mission, and help easily learning the rules (see Section 5.13). The first level of the computer game "Super Mario" is a good example of how gamers are guided and introduced into the functions and options of the game. Onboarding is an important first part of the whole product and service experience and therefore is a crucial challenge for a holistic approach. You can find a lot more information and tips at https://www.useronboard.com.

> *"People don't buy products. They buy better versions of themselves."*
>
> **Samuel Hulick (User Onboarding Expert)**

A personal touch makes a good impression

Personalized communication can support these emotional effects. In general, a pleasant, caring personality (as opposed to anonymity and indifference) is a decisive factor. A personal touch—regardless of whether it is in e-mails, forms, or during a shopping process—appears to be more human and simpatico than cold neutral information.

To address a user emotionally you must know him or at least try to understand his personal needs and motives. To design an appealing service you have to discover and to address the potential motives and needs of your users (in a particular situation) (see Chapter 3, Section 3.3).

Moo, an online printing service that specializes in customized business and postcards, always speaks in the first person with its customers, communicates personally and transparently with them, and, instead of cold product photos, shows the products with people who are using them.

The e-mail marketing service **Mail Chimp** uses a friendly ape as the mascot. On the website, every time you visit a page, it provides a short comment (unostentatiously and different than with the previous Office Assistant under Microsoft Office).

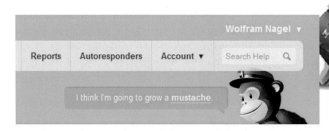

When you know the team behind or the community for a service and can communicate with them, the personal correlation to the service improves. You get the feeling of knowing your unknown counterpart. In order to emotionally appeal to the target group in its language, you must know its needs. When conceiving an information offering, the users' emotional aspects and needs should be taken into consideration as early as possible (see Chapter 3, Section 3.3).

Emotionalizing and offering added value

Whenever an information offering provides added value across various devices and touchpoints and information is available always and everywhere—in an appealing and exciting manner—then the probability increases that users will identify with the offering and use (and benefit from) it gladly and permanently across devices. Game elements (see Section 5.13) and social components (see Section 5.12) can likewise increase the loyalty between the user and the service.

It is not a matter of making little hearts on the screen but, rather, promoting positive emotions in conjunction with a service and its use (intuitively and implicitly). Emotionally appealing interfaces and contents are conceived and designed in a user-friendly manner. They take into consideration psychological knowledge and the ideas and approaches that lie behind communification, gamification, storyfication, and microjoyment. Applications that lack the required UX quality—for whatever reason—most likely are less fun than emotionally appealing ones. The latter are almost certainly used preferably and more efficiently (see also Chapter 5.16).

User experience

Whenever it involves emotions, the user experience (and generally the user experience design) play a central role. When using a service, it is a matter of promoting positive emotions, supporting the user's requirements, and, where applicable, controlling the implicit perception. Additional aspects and approaches regarding the themes of emotions, needs, psychology, and the user experience can be found in Chapter 3, Section 3.3.

(Neuro)psychology and the Emotion Map

Findings from psychology can help to appeal to the needs and motives of the user group in a targeted and sensible manner and to emotionalize information in a target group-appropriate manner. There are interesting approaches and findings from the area of neuromarketing that you can also sensibly use during the user experience design and during the conception of digital services.

As mentioned and explained in Chapter 3 there are different psychological approaches, personality models, and scientific findings that explored various implicit, subconscious "need-drivers," basic human needs and motives. We interpreted and adapted these findings and visualized them on the Emotion Map. The need-drivers are shown in the circle around the map. The motives and needs are located on the map depending on to which need-driver each one is associated with. Thus, the typical user or target group can be classified and appealed to via the respective motives and values (see Chapter 3, Section 3.3.1).

Motives and needs (or rewards and values)

The various research approaches and models regarding essentially the same motives and basic rewards behind human behavior are frequently essentially based on the *Zurich model of social motivation* from Professor Norbert Bischof. Rewards motivate us to do something—to strive for something rewarding (Scheier and Held, 2007). These rewards are comparable to the main motives and emotions from the reward profiles (Scheier and Held, 2007), the Emotion Grid (Roth and Saiz, 2014) and other approaches on which the emotion map (see Chapter 3, Section 3.3.1) and the assessments as well as the daily routines of the user prototypes (see Chapter 3, Section 3.5) are based.

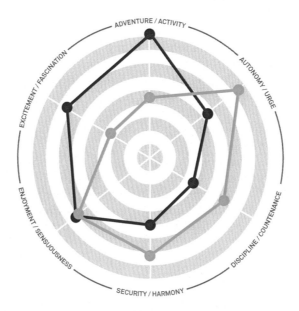

The following comparison between two beer brands highlights the classification of the various motives and rewards. Beer is well-suited as an example because there are hardly objective differences on the product level. The accompanying graphic shows the implicitly measured reward profiles of the brands Jever (green) and Beck's (blue). We have slightly modified the graphic (from Scheier and Held, 2007) and conformed it to the emotion map.

Both beer brands provide the basic reward of enjoyment. That is the practical value that a beer brand is supposed to fulfill. The brands differentiate themselves with regard to other basic rewards. Whereas Beck's appeals to the basic rewards of adventure and excitement with its brand message and young people seeking adventure on a three-master, Jever rewards discipline, harmony, and autonomy with its calming imagery (beach, lighthouse, and sand dunes).

Photos with friendly approval of Jever and Beck's.

Implicit perception and neurodesign

People consciously process only a small fraction of the information that is collected by their sensory organs. The conscious perception can process only 0.0004% of all sensory impressions. Humans subconsciously evaluate the rest. By the time the brain begins to process the tiny fraction of sensory impressions, a person has already subconsciously evaluated enormous quantities of information. He uses the implicit evaluation in order to optimally utilize the consciously perceived information. The conscious perception is thus controlled by the implicit perception. In other words, the subconscious can very quickly process large quantities of information as well as influence and control the conscious perception. Humans can only consciously perceive language and text. Patterns and photos are recognized faster than written words.

Steve Krug recommends providing users with all central information implicitly. The fact that a person cannot perceive more than seven things at the same time is also important. Implicit perceptions can change human behavior. Krug (2005) states, "A fruit juice tastes fruitier depending on the color of the packaging. Test subjects move more slowly when they are confronted subliminally with the term 'age.'"

You can and should take that which is implicit (thus, the findings from neuropsychology) into consideration in a targeted manner in the design process and address the expectations, motives, and needs of the users. The user's expected attitude, the core messages that are to be sent to him, and his implicit perception can be somewhat influenced by neurodesign.

Subconscious actions, perceptions, and motives are difficult to measure and/ or inquire about (because they indeed occur subconsciously). In order to nonetheless examine this, qualitative user tests and analyses can help. These again can be used sensibly only if the person to be surveyed or to be tested indeed works with the theme or contents because subconscious impressions cannot be "outsmarted" through imposed tasks. (This section was inspired by Schulte Strathaus, 2013.)

Privacy as user experience factor

Privacy and security plays an important role when it comes to corporate image, trust, and loyalty—three important factors concerning emotionality. As security breaches, snooping, and third-party data aggregators (see Chapter 5.11) increased, companies should care about secure user data. Journalist and UX strategist Alex Schmidt (2015) explains why and how privacy has to be part of the product design process. User information (can) come from various sources (behavior, messages, click paths, analytics, movement, and location tracking). You must not sell user information to other companies or collect information on behavior that users are not aware of. Privacy can be a selling point. If you want to build a community around your service (see Section 5.12), you require and need to establish trust. On the other hand, lack of privacy could create real danger (e.g., arrests based on erroneous government intelligence, insurances snooping around in health records, and dissenters being punished by dictatorial regimes).

> *"If we believe that treating users with respect and honesty is essential to a good experience, then we owe it to them to ponder these issues."*
>
> **Alex Schmidt (2015)**

Reflect on what kind of information is really required when collecting data (via forms, for example) and consider that every piece of data has a cost (e.g., storage and maintenance, users attention, time, and trust) and can influence the way databases are built. Schmidt recommends to use user stories around a privacy epic, to prioritize privacy (policy) and turn it into a feature, make it an important part of the product, and to inform the users (or customers). Ad-tracking software can delay site load speeds (compare also Section 5.8.1 "Performance Matters").

Collecting information about users is basically not evil. It can help to improve services. But it has to be considered and weighed up how information is being used to enhance the user experience in an appropriate, justifiable, and ethical manner. Think about these topics early and you won't get problems later. For more information concerning legal issues, see Section 5.19. See also Chapter 8, Section 8.2 "Privacy versus User Experience."

5.16 MICROJOYMENT

The information density (also known as information overload, overflow, or burnout) is becoming increasingly larger (Evsan, 2013c) while devices are becoming increasingly smaller. Increasing device fragmentation and the increasing networking of devices and services demand that individual tasks and processes of digital products are simplified and reduced to what is essential and absolutely required (inspired by Feldman (2011) and Saffer (2013a)).

The user experience for these small tasks (*microexperiences*) must be designed in such a manner that the users are neither overexerted nor unpleasantly surprised. These applications—they can also be only subapplications or subprocesses—must be well designed and in detail and be fun (see Section 5.13). You should not be able to see from them that a complex data structure or information architecture possibly lies behind them. They should have a light and simple feel. It has to be uncomplicated to use a service. This applies particularly to mobile applications.

Valuing user experience, polishing visual interfaces (but not only for the sake of pure beauty), and making services and applications easy to use by adding well-designed details, microinteractions, animations, and transitions will increase their value and the emotional appeal in a distinct manner that can make the key difference.

Furthermore, I agree with Dan Saffer that microinteractions can be the bridge between hardware and software—for example, when you have to synchronize data or connect screens (Teinaki, 2015).

What are microexperiences?

Microexperiences are small, easy, simple, smart, focused, comprehensible, transparent, personal, networked, and social and are subjectively perceived to be beautiful. In all cases, it is important that the task is easy to complete (joy of simplicity).

The technical process behind the online micropayment payment system **PayPal** may be relatively complex. For the user, conversely, the workflow with regard to the length of time is rather tiny (log in, click on "OK," and pay). The more seamlessly such a process runs, the more positively it is subjectively perceived. PayPal literally means "Pay friend based upon pen pal."

Regarding visual feedback, for the user, it is helpful if the button during an ordering process displays the progress of the action.

AirPlay is an interface that serves to transmit contents (music, videos, and photos) in a cable-free manner—from Apple devices to AirPlay-compatible receiver devices such as speakers, stereo systems, or TVs. Thus, for example, the current screen content can be transmitted from a compatible device to a TV. Accordingly, browser contents or video games can be displayed on a larger screen (see Section 5.4). The small feature combines things, interfaces (API), information, or screens sensibly and easily.

You can interact with a service per **language or gestures**. Simplicity is important in this regard. Also, it is a very personal interaction with a device.

Chatting or **writing an SMS** are small tasks that should be as easy and uncomplicated as possible. (The conversation is part of a larger social relationship.)

The **weather app** on iOS is minimalist. It does exclusively what it is supposed to do—display the weather forecasts—and does this in a comprehensible, focused, and simple manner. With the **rain app "YES" as well**, very complex weather data are reduced to the most important information and can thus be displayed in a clear and user-friendly manner.

The Facebook "like" button microinteraction is so important that it's become part of their brand.

Dan Saffer (as quoted in Teinaki, 2015)

An **input form** that, based on the e-mail address, guesses the name and fills out the corresponding fields in advance is smart.

Paying by saying your name is easier than paying by credit card or cash. The prerequisite for this is that it functions seamlessly and complicated processes as well as the name and voice recognition run in the background.

On a smartwatch text input is quite difficult and exhausting. A simple solution is if you can use **voice input** instead. After having dictated the text the Apple Watch (for example) offers the option to either send the message as text or in audio format. That's smart. Accurate voice recognition is crucial in that point, of course.

If someone posts something in a foreign language on **Facebook**, Facebook directly offers a translation of it. That is helpful.

Good **navigation applications** (regardless of whether they are for travel, sightseeing, or local public transportation) are focused and only made for a single use case—and indeed in order to find from A to B. Navigation services in combination with geo-location supply, in real time and without you having to interact, information about a route, a transportation situation or the location, anticipate the user's potential goals, and often automatically offer sensible options.

How do you make microexperiences?

You should think only of "the one thing." You must perfect this one thing and/or do it as well as possible. You must not get bogged down but, rather, must concentrate on the main functions and avoid ambiguity. (Less is more.) A clear and comprehensible user interface must be the goal. And naturally it is important to know the respective target group (see Section 3.5), begin early with the prototyping and testing, and reuse patterns.

Avoid cognitive overload for the user.

Darryl Feldman (Product Director)

If you take into consideration the user, the environment, and the time, you can display less contents, but these are at the same time more relevant. This means that the interface will become clearer and, at the same time, more focused. Minimalism and diminutiveness are among the fundamental principles. You must be able to withstand the desire for additional features and concentrate on only the essential core feature. Frequently, these offerings are agilely (continued to be) developed—quickly and promptly published and then optimized often, regularly, and iteratively.

The user should always and directly be rewarded with simplicity and beautiful, sensible content or a feature (see Section 5.15).

Dan Saffer recommends to consider four parts when you build micro-interactions. First, there is any kind of trigger that initiates an action. Rules define what happens in the interaction. Then the user must realize that something is happening and how, he must get feedback by the interface (via a transition, animation, or change of state of an interaction or UI element). And finally, he has to understand and to be clear what next will happen (via Carrie, 2015 and Saffer, 2013b). These four parts and rules (the behavior of the interface) have to be as consistent as possible across different devices and touchpoints, and furthermore should adapt to different situations and the context of use. Perhaps and in some cases they can also incorporate the user and his particular capability and state of knowledge according to the service he is using.

Focus on and improve the little details

When we talk about digital products it is important to focus on the details of the small interaction units of a graphical user interface. Microinteractions are small and subtle visual enhancements of a UI or interaction (e.g., animations, transitions, or a sound). They are always very concrete and well-defined use cases: defining a password, completing a transaction, synchronizing data, favoriting an item, prompting a pop-up message, or regulating volume.

Interactive animations can make an interface more appealing. A well-designed animation can show status and provide feedback, increase the sense of direct manipulation, show the results of the users actions and make an interface comprehensible no matter how complicated and tricky the logic behind it is.

The details are not the details. They make the product.

Charles Eames

Microinteractions are an important factor when it comes to how a product "feels." Good microinteractions are not just for the Joy of Use, they also convey a consistent mental model of what happened with the UI. Animations can explain how an interface works.

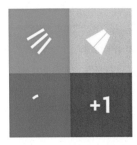 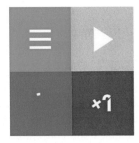 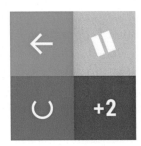

Surprise your users with an **extraordinary transition**. Icons of the *Google Material Design* styleguide change smoothly from one image to another to serve dual functions at different times.

Focus on the details and the little and subtle interactions with your service to boost its user experience (inspired by Svarytsevych, 2015 and Bodeit, 2015).

Keep your user informed about what is going on by showing system status (Nielsen, 1995). They should get an instant response to their action. You can help the user when you indicate what is happening. You can show a graphic in the background, measure the bitrate, or play a sound. Do not let your user get bored and always show them progress.

When you show notifications and emphasize transformation you can ensure that the user sees when something changes. Try to get their attention by using transitions and animations. That could help to prevent them from overlooking important information.

Additionally notifications (in a slightly different meaning) are one of the most important interactions on smartwatches. It is appealing to get the right notifications at the right time. But there are situations where any notification would be annoying (e.g., while watching a movie or during an important conversation). That is why context (relevance) always matters (see Chapter 4, Section 4.3).

Consider that good animations are invisible, they should be smooth and the users main perception should not be that one is looking at an animation. If you can disable an animation and the flow doesn't feel broken, you can probably remove it.

It can be difficult and challenging to show a lot of information on small screens (e.g., on smartphones and smartwatches). Keep context and use an understandable, clear and coherent navigation pattern on different pages (ideally comparable to learned ones on other devices), use animations to show where new content or a new interaction element came from that the user is able to easily navigate back. Elements on the screen should not be (re)moved suddenly, because the user risks losing understanding of the interface.

Microinteractions should help users understand how to interact with unusual and nonstandard layouts without unnecessary confusion. Show and use animations. In a photo album the images can flip forward (instead of just replace each other), charts and graphs can scroll or characters can be rotated.

Microinteractions can encourage users to actually interact with an interface. Use lovingly designed call to action elements if you want your users to keep on browsing, like, or share content. If your service is attractive, users will stay longer on your website (or use your service willingly) instead of leaving it too early.

Data input is an important element for a lot of applications (especially forms, content editing, and data management software), but mostly it is quite boring for users. If you visualize input, use smoothly and helpful transitions to turn this process into something special. Facilitate user interaction. By enhancing user experience of forms you can motivate users and support the ones that are responsible for data input. As today nearly everyone is some kind of author of content it is very important to support these users (see Chapter 6, Section 6.4).

A good interface provides (visual) feedback to the user. If you fill in a form, for example, the input field should give immediate feedback, if something went or is wrong or when the user pressed a button. A good graphical user interface leads the user, shows him or her if and where something happened on the screen and what he or she is should to do next.

A *Nike* app has to feel "fit" and the adjustment of the Nest thermostat feels like turning the heating on. In terms of a consistent and coherent platform wide behavior it is also important to define the duration of animations and transitions as Apple did in its styleguide. You should implement these definitions in your living styleguide (see Chapter 5, Section 5.8.1 "Living Styleguide").

In the styleguide, you do not just document and show how a UI element (e.g., a button) looks like, you also provide code and show different interactive states, how it interacts, behaves, or is animated. That ensures a consistent interface not just in visual design, but concerning microinteractions as well. The flatter the design of a UI is the more you have to provide visual orientation for the user by making functionality on-screen obvious with smooth animations and transitions.

Animations can help users after the launch of an application when you highlight basic features and controls that are potentially helpful for further unobstructed usage. Just show tutorials (and use smooth animations) when they might be relevant for the user and ensure that they can easily reach information and help text whenever needed.

Microinteractions and the focus on microjoyment can make the difference between similar services or products. They can point the attention to the right element. Brands can distinguish themselves from the rest of the market with subtle difference in the behavior of a service. Services, websites, and apps with well-thought-out microinteractions seem to be and are easier, more fun for, and preferred by the users. As digital touchpoints get more and more relevant and often are the first contact with a brand, this is even more important. Coherent transitions and animations (thus microjoyment at large) can support the understanding of cross device interaction patterns and help to optimize a coherent user experience of one service.

One principle you should always keep in mind is "form follows function." The goal is to offer a great user experience that matches the medium and other parameters. Nowadays good microinteractions are as important as good typography, visual design, and wording. That's why it is a matter of course that you should implement them into your styleguide or pattern library as well (Bodeit, 2015).

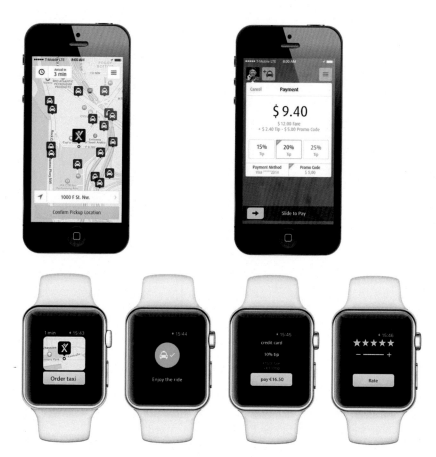

mytaxi is the first taxi ordering app in Germany. The app on the Apple Watch is very simple. You can find and order a nearby taxi easily by turning your wrist. A Google Maps shows the passenger's position as well as nearby taxis. One tap on the order button suffices. When the driver accepted the tour, the passenger gets helpful information about the driver and the remaining waiting time. At the end of the taxi ride the passenger can easily pay by one tap on his watch and rate the driver (cf. mytaxi, 2015).

The challenge for the Apple Watch user interface was to reduce the app to the absolutely necessary, but to keep the smooth functionality and interaction options that users knew from the smartphone app. You do not need to pull out the app from your pocket, but it's always synchronized and uses internet via iPhone. The service is also available for desktop browsers.

As it is difficult to show animations and motion on a static medium, you should have a look at some animated examples on the web, for example, in the Google Material Design Styleguide. Links to examples and resources can also be found on the website via http://www.msxbook.com/en/mcrjmt.

5.17 HYBRID MEDIA

In addition to the possibility of combining digital devices with one another and cross-linking them, digital and *analog media* can also be merged with one another.

Hybrid media is the cross-media combination of analog and digital media and information to form a collective information offering. Analog and digital media that would be in principle also usable alone and independent of one another can be combined in such a manner that reality and virtuality are mixed together.

Digital information that is reproduced on a screen cumulates with real objects that can be experienced haptically to form a new product and/or service. When displaying the information on the screen, virtual objects and processes can be simulated in a quite realistic manner.

Through the cross-media combination, a new (hybrid) medium is created. At the same time, the usage value and informative content increase—otherwise, the combination would make no sense. The principle is comparable with cross-media.

Hybrid media has indeed nothing to do directly with multiscreen because, in addition to a digital device with a screen, another media can be integrated into the information offering without a digital display. It represents a type of transition or expansion to the purely digital approaches and bridges from analog to digital. Also, you may not view multiscreen in an isolated manner because each person also uses analog media in some type of form and can switch back and forth between analog and digital service touchpoints.

The **PhoneBook** is a children's book in which an iPhone has the suitable app installed on it. For every page, there is a suitable little background film. Based on whether the clip for the iPhone displays a window in a train compartment or the view from a U-boat, the corresponding animations can be loaded—for example, a landscape you are driving by or an undersea world and fish (Visnjic, 2010).

Evernote Smart Notebook and Moleskine is based on the idea of linking a notebook made of paper sensibly with a digital medium and combining the advantages of both media with one another. In the paper notebook, collected notes can be digitalized by means of a smartphone or a tablet. In addition, the contents must be photographed in the analog notebook with the Evernote app. It does not always function, but it is generally supposed to recognize both the script and the so-called smart tags. Smart tags are small colorful tags that are stuck into the book and indicate how a note is supposed to be categorized by key word.

With the **AbracadabrApp**, a modified Moleskine notebook becomes a quasi-analog app. By means of a couple of manual changes and a rotating pocket mirror, you can split-screen videos into only one photo with a smartphone. Small plastic filters that can be held on the lens make it possible to add effects. By cooperating with the investors, Moleskine supplies a quasi-analog service for digital media (see http://www.abracadabrapp.com).

The focus of this book is on the methodical, conceptual, and strategic approaches for multiscreen projects. In the following sections, we mention two more challenges that you should take into consideration in all cases when realizing corresponding projects.

5.18 TECHNICAL CHALLENGES

In theory, many things appear to be easier as they are ultimately implementable in practice. In addition to the conceptual and strategic challenges, you must—as with all digital projects—also take the technical conditions into consideration. Of course, they change over time.

Desktop, mobile website, or app?

You are always confronted with the question of whether a pure desktop variant is suitable (clearly not) or whether you need a mobile-optimized version. With regard to whether a native application or a web app (for the browser) is the best solution for mobile devices, you must decide on a case-by-case basis. If you rely on web apps, it depends on the respective project as to whether responsive web design or a separate mobile offering is more suitable (Clark, 2011a). We briefly introduced the responsive design approach and several detailed questions and challenges (e.g., performance, layout and navigation patterns, and UI modeling) in Section 5.8.1. The theme is very complex and comprehensive. There are also additional sources, tips, and suggestions in this regard on the website at http://www.msxbook.com/en/responsivedesign.

With a *mobile-optimized* website (which generally means optimized for smartphones and tablets), you can reach a larger target group because it can potentially be visited from any mobile web browser and be viewed on almost any device. It is found better by online search engines, is normally cheaper to realize, and is always up-to-date because you do not have to take a publishing cycle into consideration in an app store. When a service is offered via browser the users do not have to install an app. All the information is directly available. Information on websites can be linked and shared, which is a lot more challenging with apps and "deeplinks." If you opt for native apps, you must do development work for several different platforms (at the same time) and in various programming languages—provided that you would like to support various platforms. Once again, this depends on the target group.

Ideally, mobile web apps can hardly be differentiated from native or hybrid apps. They are controlled by a mobile web browser and based on web technologies such as HTML and CSS. Creation and maintenance are similar to mobile or responsive websites. You are not dependent on an app store. Changes can be undertaken easily and do not have to be introduced via updates, as is the case with native apps. In contrast with native apps, there are restrictions regarding performance and the use of device-specific functions.

A *hybrid app* is a mix of web app and native app. For an independent cross-platform approach, it is a sensible alternative. Web technologies are utilized. That means that you develop a quasi-web app that is then distributed via app stores. Through this approach, principally standard applications can be developed with certain restrictions for all platforms that are similar to a native app. However, you should avoid imitating a native application with non-native (web) technologies. By so doing, corresponding expectations are created that can quickly turn into a negative user experience when such expectations are not fulfilled (see Section 5.8 "Uncanny Valley").

If necessary, a *native app* will also function even without an Internet connection, it can (intermediately) store data locally on the device, it frequently provides a better user experience (relevant for complex applications), and it can be found by searching the respective app stores and thus simplifies distribution. A mobile app is a good choice if it is used frequently and daily. It enables a rich native integration and the usage of sensors, geo location and camera, for example. With native applications, you must subject yourself to the least amount of technical restrictions, which in principle has a positive effect on the user experience. Native apps are programmed in the individual developmental environment of the various platforms. Based on the platform being supported, this can be very complex and cost-intensive. Each platform is based on various technologies and frameworks. Moreover, you must take into consideration the interaction logics, the gestures and (visual) standards for the individual platforms, and, on the device side, the number and function of the hardware keys. In many cases it is important to allow sharing information that are offered in apps. Therefore you need equivalent information provided and accessible via web browser. In news apps, for example, you should provide a link that leads to a website showing the same information that can be shared via social networks. Otherwise information can just be viewed by the ones that have that particular app installed.

Whether a native app, a hybrid or a web app, a separate mobile website, or a website with a responsive (or adaptive) design approach is the best solution depends ultimately on various factors, such as the purpose of the offering, the target group, and technical requirements. Due to the mostly multiscreen-ish user behavior a *standalone mobile-only* website (just for smartphones) won't be recommendable in most cases.

If the offer is rarely used and, from a technological perspective, contains merely simple information (e.g., an article or an annual report), probably a mobile-optimized website (that supports smartphone and tablets) will suffice. No one will want to download an extra app for it. For frequent usage, you must evaluate whether the app must also function offline, whether you would like to earn money with it (which is in principle easier via app stores), whether it is supposed to be found more via the online search or distributed via app stores, whether device functions (e.g., camera, localization, or tilt sensor) are supposed to be used, and whether the performance and user experience play an important role. You must weigh these criteria when you decide between the native app, hybrid app, and web app. As Jenny Gove (2015) insists, neither web nor apps are dead. It is all about bringing them in a good way together. Apps and (mobile) websites move closer. There are advantages for each approach.

An approach based on the principle of "code once, deploy everywhere" is in principle possible. However, you must carefully analyze the individual platform cultures, paradigms, and patterns. Björn Oltmanns describes these challenges during the development of cross-device applications in the documentation of the Usability Professionals Conference (Oltmanns, 2012).

Requirement, target group, technology

The following are additional questions that you must clarify: What requirements exist for the information offering? What experience should the application deliver, and what standards must it fulfill (user experience, corporate guidelines, and communication goals)? What is the goal of the service, the app, or the website? What contents should be displayed? How is the business model? What is the budget and the how much time is available? How is the target group defined? What user types belong to the target group? What platforms and devices do the potential users use?

Then there are the questions of the relevant platforms, maintenance, and so forth. What technologies are being used? For apps and/or software, the questions would generally be as follows: What developmental environments will be used? Will the devices and device classes (desktop, tablets, smartphones, TV, and any other potential devices such as "normal" cell phones or smartwatches) be correctly and exactly recognized? Will the layout and contents be output in a correspondingly adapted form? Have the contents been optimized for outputting on the various devices, screens, and applications? For an optimal layout adaptation in HTML, you must correctly set (utilize) the various media queries. In many cases, the event adaptations (e.g., menu handling and native input masks for the selection of the date) must be undertaken for the various output devices, and various and device-specific interaction patterns must be taken into consideration (Hover, Click, Swipe, etc.).

It is a major challenge to uniformly guarantee the supporting of the current web technologies across devices and platforms. It must be clarified which features will be supported in the area of HTML5/CSS3/Javascript and which bugs exist in the individual operating systems and the various versions. Each platform has certain features that must be taken into consideration. The development of an efficient and broad-based testing environment can minimize risks as well as the testing and developmental expenditures, but problems can never be completely prevented. We recommend at least two or three devices per category of various quality from low to high end. Ultimately, it is a matter of minimizing the unknown factors as much as possible and learning something new with each new project. From a technical perspective, the requirements, restrictions, and possibilities sometimes change very quickly.

Mobile device management

Via mobile device management, mobile devices such as smartphones, tablets, or sub-notebooks can be centrally managed with the aid of software. The management by one or more administrators is comparable with a company internal app store for the software and data allocation as well as the protection of data.

Many mobile devices are primarily designed to be consumer products and, in contrast to laptops, are not designed for mobile device management. Frequently, users want to access company software and company data with their own device (i.e., BYOD—"bring your own device").

In this regard, among other things, you must pay attention to the following:

- Security needs of the organizations (requirements-appropriate version of the operating system).
- Unblocking the devices while activating PIN entry.
- Data and software on the devices must be protected against loss.
- Access rights to central data must also be managed via the mobile devices.
- Problems when personnel join or depart from the company.
- Where applicable, deletion of company data and company software on the devices.
- Private use or separation between private and business use.
- Legal framework conditions and restrictions as well as, for example, adherence to telecommunications secrecy policies for IT divisions (access to private data on the mobile device is not permitted).

5.19 LEGAL ISSUES

The digital revolution took place at a speed which did not follow many processes in the society. The legal framework conditions for the operation of our current modern information landscapes essentially originate from a time in which messages needed weeks to go around the world, letters were answered in 3 days and in which people pursued their learned trade their entire lives.

Since then, the legal directives have been gradually adjusted in order to try to keep pace with the latest developments. Thus, the legal patchworks to be followed for current IT projects are diverse and unclear. It would certainly completely exceed the parameters of this book if we attempted to do justice to this thematic field.

Multiscreen projects are frequently projects in which issues are addressed which for a long time were neither discussed nor adapted to the current legal situation. Thus, this type of project often identifies already existing painful problems. However, because we consider the legal aspect to be of importance in practice, we want to highlight some of the related legal directives (even if they are not multiscreen-specific) and their lurking pitfalls as examples in order to sensitize you to these aspects.

Thus, we would like to integrate you into and welcome you as a new member of our Sales21 project team and brief you first of all; this is the first project outline for our project as it was agreed between two employees from the Corporate Communication Division and the IT Division.

Project outline

Sensing Devices Inc., manufacturer of top-class sensors, has 2000 employees worldwide and publishes a top-class customer magazine every quarter. Within the parameters of the Sales21 project, you would like to discontinue the current customer magazine SensMag over the medium-term, but continue to use its contents and expand to form a dynamic sales information system.

In the future, the company would like to supply all articles about the successes attained with the prominent customers both for the desktop as well as mobile. The project wishes to enable the seamless alternation of the screen: Beginning in the office at the desk, once again checking the latest news on the smartphone and making presentations on the tablet to the end customer.

The contents are supposed to continuously increase. The last eight issues of SensMag from the past 2 years are supposed to be integrated as an initial offering. In order to keep the users more up-to-date, you can register for the service with their complete contact data; they are supposed to then be informed of news via SMS.

In addition, the information content is supposed to increase for the user: In addition to each individual story, the current business news for the companies mentioned in the article from the filtered RSS feeds from a business newspaper are supposed to be displayed as supplemental information (with condensed inform and a link to the original article).

The offering is supposed to be used by your own and external sales employees both on the desktop as well as on mobile devices and it is also supposed to be displayed as sales information as well as the names and contact data of the current contact persons of the aforementioned customers from the customer relationship management system (CRM).

The mobile application is supposed to be developed as an app which is made available with identical information both on the smartphone as well as on the tablet. For the sales employees, it is important to not be dependent on network coverage; thus, after a screening process, the displayed articles and sales information can be downloaded for presentation purposes in the offline mode on the devices. An automatic deletion has not been prescribed; the user himself is supposed to decide if he would like to delete something.

In order to network the sales employees more strongly with one another and to keep them more up-to-date in the future, functions are supposed to be integrated for the data collection for new sales stories with the option of photo uploads for photos which are taken on-site on the customers' premises.

In order to determine the key indicators for the subsequent international rollout, a comprehensive system for tracking user behavior is supposed to be set up. It is planned to use a tracking service from Germany. For the supplying and storage of the data, a cloud service from the USA is supposed to be used due to the worldwide availability.

The project which does not look really spectacular is brushing against many legal minefields. We will try to discover them—for the informed layperson.

Copyright and purpose

The contents of the aforementioned customer magazine have been in part produced by its own employees, in part by freelance copywriters, in part by photographers—for the purpose of publication in the customer magazine printed at that time. In each case, it must be examined whether and in what scope usage rights for the corresponding contents have been explicitly granted. Otherwise, they must still be obtained. An unauthorized use of these copyright-protected work products may lead to cease-and-desist orders and damage compensation claims.

Reproduction right

An additional problem can be the planned offline use of the information. Thus, even if we have assumed that the required usage rights for the work products of our authors and photographers have indeed been granted for digital use on the web, then this in no way means that we are entitled to reproduce these data. Because the data for our project are supposed to be stored not just temporarily, but rather permanently on the device, a reproduction is taking place that is not permitted by copyright law—many small pirated copies are being created.

Ancillary copyrights

And then there was still the idea of the mashup: News from an RSS feed with contents from the business press. This is the latest of our antipersonnel mines—the ancillary copyright for press publishing houses. It already forbids the free use of this brief article with an image and link to the source with the complete article. We must already conclude a licensing agreement with the publishing house for this usage.

Right to your own image

Through our user-generated content components, new images of our successful customers are supposed to be created upon an on-going basis: Sensor in the machine, machine with the happy operator in front of the company logo. That would be a great story if there were no problems with the contents: The happy operator namely knows nothing about the fact that he is supposed to be published on the Internet, as well as his employer has not been asked whether it is allowed to make a photo inside his private property.

Trademarks

In addition, we have another problem with the user-generated content of our sales employee: The Company, whose logo our happy operator poses in front of, calls something like this the illegal use of its trademarks. It has namely neither approved its naming as a reference nor the depiction of its trademarks for the purpose of our own advertising. Thus, we should absolutely contemplate briefing our sales employees on their function as specialized authors.

Considering national legal rights when acting global (excurse to EU/ German laws)

Whenever you plan to act global you will have to consider national laws as well. As the author of this book is German it is natural to give you a short introduction into German law.

Data protection

In Germany, the Bundesdatenschutzgesetz [German Data Protection Act] (BDSG) is valid which serves to protect the private sphere. It regulates the collection, storage, processing, and dissemination of personal data. The exception to this shall be only private usage. Stated simply: First of all, everything is forbidden which has not been explicitly permitted by the approval of the affected person or a legal directive. On our project, we thus immediately have a whole bevy of problems which the commissioned data protection expert lists after reviewing the project outline.

Required scope of collected data

If we begin with the collection of the complete contact data for the use of the SMS notification function. In order to send a notification per SMS, only the disclosure of the cell phone number is required. Additional data are not required to render the service. Thus, it is also not permitted to ask the interested user for more data.

Data processing by third parties and passing on data

The BDSG also regulates the dissemination of personal data to third parties as this is required for the use of a tracking service. In order for the dissemination of tracking information (it contains personal data like the e-mail or the IP address) to be permissible at all, a commissioned data processing agreement must be concluded in advance with the service provider. The dissemination of personal data to third parties (in this case, sales partners)—as it is prescribed by notification from the customer's contact person from the CRM—is naturally likewise not permitted in the prescribed manner.

Scope of storage of transaction data

With regards to contents, we must also be more precise. As requested, after a comprehensive logging of the user transactions, we are confronted by the problem of the identifiable users. The storage of the transaction data may be undertaken only in a purposeful manner and for a fixed period of time; thus, a concept must still be designed in this case precisely as to which data are needed and for what reason. This must be elaborated on in the data protection declaration which must be drafted which the users of our offerings should approve.

No more Safe Harbor

If you offer a service to customers within the EU it is important to know that transferring user data outside the EU has to be considered. To clarify more precisely, the designated storage in a country which is not a member of the EU—in our case, the use of a cloud service from the USA—is a data export: With regards to data protection issues, a differentiation is made between the countries of the EU (classified as being secure) and non-EU countries (classified as being secure and non-secure). The USA is classified as being a non-secure country because of the widespread surveillance powers by the NSA lacking an adequate level of protection for the (non-US) individual that has no chance of effective judicial protection. In October 2015 the European Court of Justice declared the Safe Harbor data-transfer agreement—that had been governed by EU data flows across the Atlantic for the last years—invalid. In fact every organization has to make sure that it is in compliance with European data protection law. So every business which offers services, for instance, German and French users may find themselves under the jurisdiction of German or French Date Protection Agencies.

Conclusion

Don't worry! Multiscreen projects create no problems; they only make them visible! The issues regarding the rights to your own image, copyright, competition law, and the German Data Protection Act are not new. Even the issues regarding the operation of a mobile infrastructure did not only then appear during the implementation of the first multiscreen project. A "head-in-the-sand" policy does not help. If we pull our head out of the sand, then we recognize the following: Employees have personal data on their smartphones, store information in the cloud, and post photos with company contacts in social networks. That is already the reality and the responsibility lies with the companies. See also Section 5.15 "Privacy as User Experience Factor."

TIP

At the latest when the first project drawing has been completed, it is beneficial to actively seek out dialog with the Data Protection Manager. Many risks can be jointly recognized promptly and avoided. The implementation of a well-planned multiscreen project must be regarded as being an opportunity: It can result in generally valid principles for the professional handling of new information technologies at the company; principles which can then also be successfully applied to other tasks and projects.

5.20 CONCLUSION AND TIPS

1. **Choose the right one for you.**
   We list relevant ideas in this compendium. The patterns, principles, and suggestions shall not and cannot be applied and combined all at once. Not all tips make sense for every project or every project phase.

2. **Know the options.**
   It is important that you know the options that are available to you in given situations and/or at least know that they exist. If they appear to be relevant, you can then examine and apply them in a targeted manner.

3. **Recommendations and examples.**
   For the purposes of clarity, the tips listed are intentionally kept concise. Those interested in working with a pattern or a principle in detail can obtain information via more extensive sources. They are stated in the respective sections and listed in the references. There are also examples on the website.

4. **Begin with one area.**
   Multiscreen experience design is complex. It is challenging to reconcile various screens, user types, and contexts of use. If you cannot see the wood for the trees, it can be helpful to pick out a detail and (simply) start with it. Additional knowledge is obtained during the course of the project. And then the thicket is also thinned out.

5. **Ability to respond and adapt.**
   Design for breakpoints and use layout patterns. Design, layout, and contents must be dynamically and flexibly adapted to the respective device features (and other context related circumstances) and must be able to respond to changes.

6. **Start with the content.**
   How do you optimally begin a project? Josh Clark (2011b) recommends, "If you're going to deliver rich, complex experiences to all these contexts, you have to start with your content." Content strategy, structured content, and information management are central tasks in a multiscreen experience strategy. A detailed explanation of that approach is described in Chapters 6 and 7.

7. **Multiscreen means multiple screens.**
   Know the possibilities how screens can complement and control each other, and how information is synchronized and exchanged between devices. Apply and expand these possibilites in a sensible and user- and use case-oriented manner.

8. **Support multiscreen users.**
   Consider that users are constantly changing and switching between screens, and support a device fragmented daily routine.

9. **Users are humans.**

Understand the users and support their (potential and implicit) needs and goals by applying user-centered and emotionally appealing principles. Try to implement goal-oriented stories and game mechanics into your services.

10. **Be agile.**

Project plans that are inflexible and concretely designed for the future do not often help you to attain your goal in this case. The device landscape changes as well as the needs and behavioral patterns of the users. You must (be able to) respond to them and modify strategy and concept as agilely as possible.

11. **Bring aboard important people.**

Due to the demanding technical challenges and the legal issues, multiscreen projects are complex. Thus, for implementation that is as seamless as possible, it is advisable to correspondingly design projects to be big and involve important decision-makers.

12. **Use the templates.**

In the previous chapters, some work materials were introduced—for example, the touchpoint matrix, multiscreen day flow, and the emotion maps. We provide them as both blank forms and designed specifically for the individual user prototypes on the website (http://www.msxbook.com/en/templates).

13. **Be creative and ideate new approaches.**

Think beyond and combine established patterns and thoughts to potentially new ones.

14. **Ask Us. Or discuss with us.**

If you have any questions, suggestions, or tips, we look forward to receiving a message and discuss them with you.

The focus of this book is the methodical, conceptual, and strategic approaches for multiscreen projects. The previously described patterns and principles help to face that challenge. Another question is what multiscreen especially means for content flows, processes, and workflows now and in the future.

There are two more challenges and potentially recommendable solutions that you should take into consideration in all cases when realizing corresponding projects. These approaches have been discussed and applied recently with obviously helpful results. They should and will be discussed further and adjusted or optimized to specific needs and upcoming trends. The outcome is still open.

First, you have to consider how content is created, managed, and published in a multiscreen world. How will we as creators, administrators, and users handle content, information, and knowledge in the future?

Beyond that, you should likely update your processes and tools. What methods and rules for the conception, design, and implementation of layout, contents, and workflows are helpful and future-oriented?

You can also have a look at compact summaries to these both following chapters via the following links:

Chapter 6: www.msxbook.com/en/ngix
Chapter 7: www.msxbook.com/en/cduia

Next-Generation Information Experience and the Future Of Content (Management)

6

Challenges and Trends of Tomorrow

As creators, administrators, and users, how will we handle contents, information, and knowledge in the future?

What does multiscreen especially mean for content flows, processes, and workflows? You have to consider how content is created, managed and published.

In the future, digital information and services must be able to be obtained from a wide array of sources on various devices, in a wide array of media, for multiple screens and output channels. This chapter addresses the future "content scenarios," the potential requirements of users, and the challenges for content creators and content providers, website operators, publishers, journalists, and media companies. Actually everyone communicating via internet to a certain target audience or offering (digital) content can be considered as a kind of "publisher." In this regard, knowledge and selected sources are presented, and the chapter outlines the way in which information and content management may be handled in the future.

For the first time in its 200-year history media publishers aren't in control of how and where news are distributed. Publishers with their tradition-rich brands are now part of a much larger information-ecosystem. Sure, a "New York Times" still produces for the own print edition and the own website. But more and more contents are directly prepared for Facebook, Twitter, or YouTube.

The platform for breaking news are the push-notifications on the screen of the smartwatch or smartphone. Daily updated news are – coverage-optimized – published in the Facebook-News Feed. And yes, they still have an own website, but that's actually still just a big archive.

Emily Bell about journalism of the future (in Marti, 2015)

6.1 JUMPING-OFF POINT

The number of people who are using the Internet on various devices is constantly increasing. Digital information and services must be made available for retrieval on a wide array of media, for multiple screens and output channels. The standard of "create once, publish everywhere" (COPE; Jacobson, 2009)—generally how information and contents will be created, managed, disseminated, and consumed in the future—is one of the central challenges in the digital information society. A disruptive change is happening concerning journalism and news distribution. The (future) information needs of the users and the needs of the content creators must be taken into consideration as best as possible.

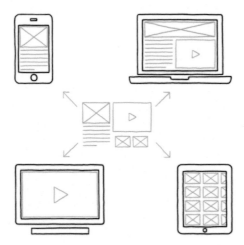

Smart content (see Chapter 5, Section 5.10): A wide array of content types must be able to be published on various media.

Information and contents can be regarded as being a product (information product). Regardless of whether it concerns product data, file formats, or contents of the most different kinds, in principle, it involves managing, combining, and standardizing this information, which is often provided in a wide array of sources and formats.

Can patterns and recommendations for a generally valid interface for content management systems (CMSs) be defined? Can a single CMS fulfill the various requirements? How do you ensure that contents are created with a wide array of systems and cannot be replaced by a standardized one in the short and medium term? Is content "management" (system) even the correct term, or is it more a matter of monitoring, aggregating, and channelizing various content *streams* and, in the context, also designing and optimizing the processes and workflows?

This chapter is based on the ideas that we described in Chapter 5 about "smart content" (see Section 5.10) and on a collection of statements about the future of CMS (Skjoldan, 2013a). It discusses possible future information scenarios and challenges and serves as food for thought, inspiration, and a contribution to a critical examination of the topic.

6.2 INNOVATIVE CONCEPTS AND TRENDS

The manner in which contents will be created and consumed in the future will change because the information needs of the users and thus their behavior and ultimately the processes affecting publications for the next generation will also change. The following examples show trends and provide approaches for future-oriented content management. The similar trait that they all share is that they need an interface for inputting and/or outputting content and a form of content and data management and content and data organization.

6.2.1 TRENDS AND CHALLENGES

Public journalist platforms (e.g., the Huffington Post) rely on user-generated content. The content comes from a wide array of sources and from various authors. A media-neutral, structured, and consistent management of the contents helps to offer a coherent, content-based service. With *crowdfunding journalism* (e.g., Krautreporter), the work of the authors is financed through the users' online subscriptions.

Independent (freelance) journalists, bloggers, and experts who discuss certain themes (e.g., Tim Pool and Richard Gutjahr) represent another trend of publishing individual news items without large media companies.

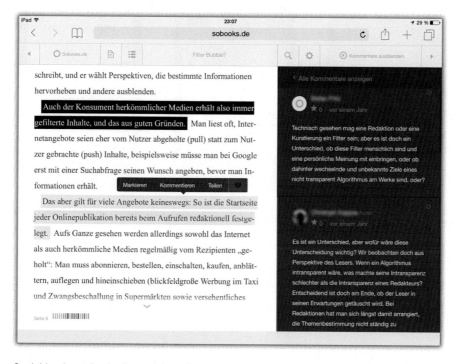

Social books: sobooks for social reading.

With *social books* (sobooks, see image on previous page), principles and approaches such as *communification* (the integration of community functionality and the networking of the readers with each other; see Chapter 5, Section 5.13) and user-generated content are integrated into (digital) books. The readers become quasi-coauthors of supplemental content. Text passages can be directly commented on and discussed or shared via the social networks.

Various providers (e.g., Circa News) produce contents exclusively for mobile channels and offer targeted, compact news snippets for short time frames. This approach requires structured contents that can be supplied in a suitable scope. This is similar to how, for example, NowThis functions, which uses solely social media as the exclusive channel and produces and/or aggregates original content for social media channels (its own app, Vine, and Instagram). Viral experts and content aggregators (e.g., Upworthy or Reddit) sort relevant news items and present them in an outlined form. Editors and users (through voting) select the contents and thus curate them directly or indirectly.

Mobile only: Circa News offers compact and stripped-down information for short time frames.

Some news concepts have turned against the increasing information overflow. For example, Yahoo! News Digest intentionally supplies a limited number of messages per day in order to not overwhelm the user. Journalists select the contents and curate them. For bundling purposes, algorithms are used.

Against information overflow: Yahoo! News Digest.

News filters monitor news worldwide, recognize correlations, and determine their relevance. Dataminr for News, for example, is a software for journalists that daily automatically filters current and relevant news from more than 500 million tweets.

News filter: Dataminr.

Content aggregators such as Flipboard or Paper collect contents from social media and other websites. The user can adjust his settings to decide from which channels or from which providers and users he would like to aggregate contents. They are then provided to him in the form of an individual, customized magazine.

Content aggregator: Flipboard.

If the contents are collected in a media-neutral manner, they can simply be processed with corresponding systems to create magazines. pag.es offers the possibility for enterprise publishers or publishing houses to publish contents across platforms and devices in the form of a magazine on various devices and channels.

Digital magazine publishing: pag.es (see http://www.pag.es).

In 10–15 years, the business model of regional newspapers will no longer function. Konrad Lischka (2013) envisions three new business models for local journalism and local newspapers. First, hard facts will be in demand for the decision-makers on-site. Another option is the financing of a local community by the local businesses. The third business model is a weekly newspaper financed by advertisements and a high-end Sunday newspaper.

The (local) newspaper of the future will not be just a classical "newspaper," just as the TV of the future will offer not just classical "TV" (moving images). The information of the future must always be retrievable in the form and the format that suit the device, the context, the user's needs, and the available time. Based on the statement of Conrad Fritzsch, cofounder of tape.tv, "I watch TV and it is awesome. I always get what I want to see. Although I really never knew at all what I even want" (as quoted in Cohrs and Rützel, 2012), you could also just ask for content or information that is just always awesome.

6.3 THE FUTURE OF CONTENT MANAGEMENT (SYSTEMS)

6.3.1 THE NEED FOR SMART CONTENT

In the future, contents will be supplied and displayed in increasingly more and diverse media (e.g., website, app, book, e-book, magazine, newspaper, TV, or via [application programming] interfaces). Thus, you should avoid redundant, inconsistent data and additional expenditures during the data maintenance. In order to do this, you need a system that you can use to create, manage, and process future-oriented contents.

In this regard, it must be differentiated between pure web publishing tools, by means of which contents can be maintained in a page-based manner, and a CMS, by means of which contents can be centrally maintained. If you must manage contents that are located in various sources and databases and must be created with various tools, it will become particularly tricky. The challenge then consists of standardizing contents and keeping those created via various input interfaces and content-creation tools coherent. In addition to people as the recipients of the information, you must also take into consideration the automated processing of the contents (e.g., through mashups). Mashups are (media) contents that are created through the (re)combination of already existing contents (see Chapter 5, Section 5.11). Content aggregators (described in Chapter 5) likewise require correspondingly flexible content that has been enriched with sufficiently helpful and coherent meta-information.

If content is flexibly adapted to a layout and to a context of use, the content is smart (see Chapter 5, Section 5.10)—comparable to water, which conforms to any container into which it is poured ("content like water"; Clark, 2011c).

6.3.2 SMART CONTENT MANAGEMENT

Today, almost everyone is both a creator and a recipient of information at the same time. Websites are not isolated and detached information sites but, rather, dynamic web applications. Via open interfaces, contents can be dynamically compiled like with a construction kit.

Media companies, website operators, publishers, journalists, editorial staffs, and publishing houses need a future-oriented application concept for media-neutral data management and multichannel publishing. They must be able to manage contents from a wide array of sources in a flexible, media-neutral, structured, redundancy-free, and comprehensible manner—that is, in a future-oriented manner in order to then be able to publish them in a device-independent, cross-media, and cross-platform manner. Processes and workflows must be adapted to the looming challenges and complemented, supported, and supplemented by corresponding systems.

An information system should offer the possibilities of networking pieces of information among themselves. In addition to the structure of information and suitable operating concepts, the focus in this regard is on complex data constructs that can be set up by creators and providers in a maximally granular and flexible manner.

COPE is a work- and time-saving system for future-oriented content that functions with various content suppliers and applications (Jacobson, 2009). If it does not matter whether the contents are created in an editorial system such as Medium, in an enterprise CMS (e.g., TYPO3 or Drupal), via Twitter or Facebook, or by any number of users in the form of comments (see Chapter 5, Section 5.12) and the information is then aggregated or managed at a central location, the flexibility increases during the "selection" of software for the content creation. The content creators are unaffiliated and can use their individually preferred tools for creating contents. Such a system is supposed to supply all communication channels, markets, and technical platforms with consistent information (applicable for example, by editorial staffs, publishing houses, TV companies, and media companies). This processing system does not necessarily have to be the content-collecting system but, rather, can also be "fed" via (application programming) interfaces by the content-creation systems.

6.3.3 SYSTEM, METHODS, AND PROCESSES

Centralized hub and content channeling

If the CMS or generally a system serves as the centralized content hub for the management of the various information and information sources, information and contents can be managed in a future-oriented manner according to the COPE principle.

"Content management system" is possibly no longer the correct term because not so much is being managed anymore. Accordingly, perhaps terms such as "content channeling system" or "content workflow system" are more suitable.

The system serves as a connective link for any type of digital communication and as a cross-media tool for all types of devices, media, and content types. Optimally, different and regularly recurring work steps can be automated. However, the responsible parties should at least always have a good overview and be kept informed of the current condition and status.

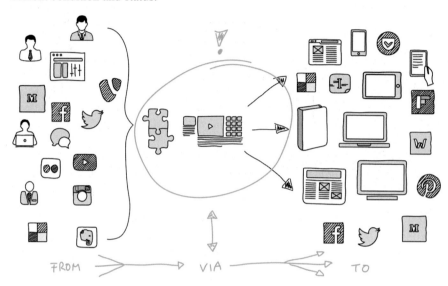

Schematization: A (central) system as the content hub with easy access for all editors and flexible content input from and output to various media and channels. There is a three-step content and information flow: (1) capturing, creating, and collecting; (2) managing, editing, and curating; and (3) using content (then, as required, commenting, modifying, supplementing = repeated collection).

Collaborating, curating, and combining

A system of the future supports the examination, filtering, and moderation of contents from a wide array of sources. Accordingly, it needs reliable processes for the management and dissemination of contents. You must endeavor to establish efficient processes and workflows that support the collaborative creation of contents by a wide array of authors. Editorially combined contents from "professional" authors and/or users, user-generated contents, comments, links, dynamically complemented information based on meta-data, integration and linking of other channels, social media and social media functionality, and open (application programming) interfaces to other networks and platforms together produce an individual information package or an information product.

Innovative concepts enable the collection or creation of contents in various source systems, structured data (delivery) and context-appropriate outputting of information in various target systems, and grant direct access via apps and operate corresponding interfaces for the use of information—regardless of when, where, and how.

Semantic labeling of contents

Processing contents according to the principle of "what you see is what you get" (WYSIWYG) is losing importance because the semantic meaning and expression are becoming and will become substantially more important—in view of the increasing number of output media—than what you "see." Semantic meta-data and meta-tags are more important than the purely typographical and/or visual text formatting. Thus, the principle should rather be "what you see is what you mean" (WYSIWYM) (Skjoldan, 2013a).

Authors must be able to create or edit contents on the basis of the semantic meaning as well as be able to maintain and manage content relationships and usage types.

> We're gonna have to break content creators out of the mindset that their job is creating web pages and instead give them tools that help them envision how their content will be published in new ways.
>
> Karen McGrane (as quoted in Skjoldan, 2013c)

6.3.4 CONTENT MANAGEMENT, CMS INTERFACE, AND USER EXPERIENCE

Many CMSs are largely unsuitable for platform-independent content maintenance. Back-end interfaces (the interfaces of databases, database software, or content management systems) are often unattractive, and the user experiences for the author and editor (discussed later) leave something to be desired: Usage is no fun. However, usability and user experience are exceedingly important to motivate those persons who create and maintain the information (see Chapter 3, Section 3.3).

Content creation tools

Various tools for creating content support authors during their daily work and guide their focus to what is essential. For example, Scrivener makes it possible for the author to concentrate on the creation and structuring of long and complicated documents. By so doing, you get complete control of the formatting.

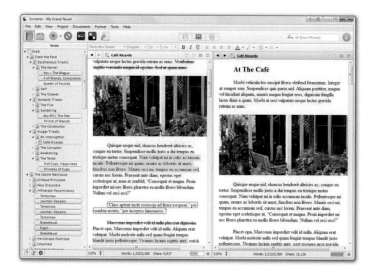

Scrivener: Creating and structuring long and complex documents.

iA Writer is a minimalistic text editor for Mac OS X and iOS. The idea behind this is that you can focus only on the writing.

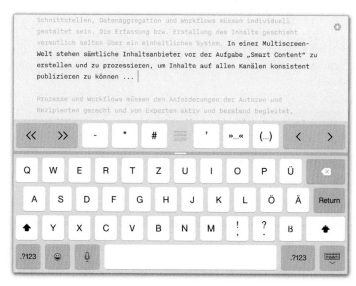

iA Writer is a minimalistic text editor that focuses only on writing.

Notion (www.notion.so) is a lightweight collaborative document editor for the browser, which enables focused writing and text structuring. There is a navigation column that shows the structure of the document and a column that offers different elements where you can choose from to structure your text (e.g., title, images, videos, data files, code, quotes, persons, and voting). The tool is comparable to Scrivener and iA Writer.

The Raw Content Mode in Neos CMS shows all content elements without any layout and typographical formatting in the "raw" state.

Raw Content Mode in Neos shows content elements without styling. We designed, developed and used a modified customized form according to the output independent bricklike building block principle (see Chapter 7). You can see the website's front-end at www.architektur-peterfischer.de

Medium is a magazine with an extremely minimalistic editing system. Even the web version of the articles is very tidy and minimalistic. Thus, it is also very well suited for reading contents.

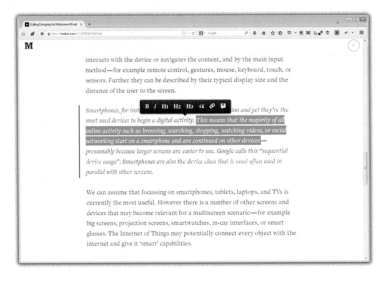

Medium offers an easy and minimalistic user interface for editors and writers.

It would be conceivable to combine the best features and approaches of the best tools in one user interface or to combine the tools and their functions in such a manner that the users are provided with advantages from each individual software overall. It would be excellent if information already structured in the background would be generated, for example, in XML format.

User experience for creating, managing, and curating

Good usability and a good user experience are important so that editors can concentrate on the creation of content. Content editors (curators) must be able to rely on the fact that the content is provided at the right time and for the right channel.

The graphical user interface must be comprehensible, clear, and fast. It is important that the so-called "author experience" (thus, the user experience of the content creator) is improved (Skjoldan, 2013d), regardless of the user experience on the front-end for the recipient of the information. Perhaps a large portion of the information can be collected via existing and simplified independent (graphical user) interfaces (e.g., *Medium*, iA Writer, and Neos), aggregated and curated via an (application programming) interface, and then prepared in an automated or manual way for media-neutral publication.

For the author, it is helpful if he gets a feeling during the creation and management of the contents of how the contents could be displayed. A kind of preview feature is conceivable that simulates scenarios in order to determine how the content could potentially look. However, it is only a simulation because the framework conditions can be extremely different and the context of use, with its wide array of parameters, can hardly be anticipated.

> *The preview button is a lie. It's time to invent a better preview button.*
>
> Karen McGrane (2013)

As an alternative, an approach could be employed in which the contents can in the future only be created and viewed without templates in order to take the illusion away from the author that he could predict and precisely set how and where his contents will be displayed. Such a generic preview of the contents without a web template is restricted to the raw view of the contents (Neos CMS has introduced such a feature with "Raw Content Mode").

6.3.5 INFORMATION EXPERIENCE: MAKING INFORMATION INTO AN EXPERIENCE

Various content creators require various tools in order to be able to publish high-quality content on various channels. The challenges for the systems—to support the new processes and workflows—are similar in this regard.

Customized content

Semantic information prevails over visual formatting. In a future-oriented CMS, you must be able to manage structured and unstructured content. Content must be relevant, personalizable, and customized for the potential users (customized content).

In order to confront the exponentially increasing information overflow, a (manual or an automated) relevance assessment of content must be upstreamed. This can be done by an editor who knows his target group. Meta- or profile information of the contents and recipients can likewise serve as the basis for a relevance assessment.

Chunks versus blobs

Data should be provided as structured and granular as possible as "chunks" instead of single content blobs. In blobs (I first heard this term in a presentation by Karen McGrane (2011)), the title, subtitle, images, and running text are collected as one single unit. This means that the contents cannot be further separated. If the contents are collected in chunks, all pieces of information are linked with each other but can be used in individual content elements in a separate and individual manner.

It is best if you create alternative titles for a piece of content—for example, a long and a short version that can be used differently and flexibly based on the usage purpose. The short title can, for example, be posted on Twitter together with the link without being cut off. Perhaps short URLs can also be generated for all contents that can be accessed via a URL whereby these short URLs can then at least provide an indicator for the potential link destination via the short domain.

Authors no longer have the authority to determine how and where contents are outputted. Thus, they must be sufficiently restrained so that the contents are suitable for displaying on various media and in various constellations. The displaying of content has been transformed in the direction that we see today with Flipboard and similar applications. Contents are aggregated, curated, and organized either automatically via corresponding settings or profile information or manually from the users themselves.

The fundamental requirement is that a positive, meaningful user experience is created during the reception of information (information experience) in the front-end output by the user. This can be fulfilled only if information can be maintained and provided in a clean, structured, and logical manner.

The term *information experience* refers to the user experience during the capture of information. It builds on the emotional and motivation psychological as well as action-theoretical fundamentals of the concept of the user experience. It entails using data and information to create experienceable knowledge with meaning or, in other words, utilizing emotion to support the conveyance of information.

6.4 NEW REQUIREMENTS FROM AUTHORS AND EDITORS

The processes and tools for the creators and managers of contents must be improved and adapted to new challenges.

6.4.1 AUTHOR EXPERIENCE VERSUS EDITOR EXPERIENCE

According to the visions of Rasmus Skjoldan and his discussants, you should separate between authoring (author experience [AX]) and editing, curating, and managing (editor experience [EX]) (Skjoldan, 2013d). For the "managing editor," a normal CMS may be sufficient, for editors ("actual writers"), it is probably not. Editors and authors who work on, and produce the actual content, need a tidy, clear, and focused user interface that does not detract from the actual task and offers the possibility of quickly and easily collecting and gathering contents (e.g., shortcuts in a type of "power user mode"). It helps if authors can see (or at least get a representative impression of) how the text will (or at least may) be displayed at the end.

For authoring, rich text/markup editors à la WYSIWYG or, better still, WYSIWYM (as discussed previously) are helpful. When editing, curating, and managing, workflow management tools are more in the forefront.

For smaller and medium-sized projects, separate budgets are recommended for AX and user experience (UX). This means that you will deploy UX designers in a targeted manner that will be particularly responsible for the author experience—regardless of the front-end UX (and thus regardless of the experience that is created for the recipient of the contents—for example, the website visitor). In order to differentiate between the classical front-end UX designers, "AX designers" attend to the user experience and the usability of the authors during the work with the back end.

6.4.2 CUSTOMIZED TOOLS AND EDITING MODES

If possible, you should provide the authors with a customized CMS or at least adapt the back end to their needs. The expenditure will have a positive effect on the efficiency of the authors and the quality of the contents.

Perhaps, you should allow the authors to use a system of their choice or offer them an interface to all available systems. Each author can then create his contents with his preferred tool. Meta-data can be automatically or manually complemented by, for example, analyzing contents semantically and setting the already-existing meta-information in relation to each other and to the content (e.g., as *Medium* does on the basis of user profiles, user behavior, and reconciled information from Twitter).

6.4.3 CONTENT MANAGER EXPERIENCE DESIGN PROCESS

The content manager experience (CMX) will generally be the key to the successful future of content management and also a relevant approach in the multiscreen context in the sense of "smart content." For content management projects, it can make sense to generally set up a separate explicit CMXD (content manager experience design) process that concentrates on the experience and usability of the users during the creating, curating, and processing of the contents (Skjoldan, 2013b).

First, you should know and define the various modes for the collection of contents. This depends on the respective projects and the target channels. What information, content elements, and content types are necessary in what scopes and what meta-data? What type of content is generally created (text, photo, moving-image, audio, combinations of these content types, etc.)? Based on these questions, you prioritize three to five channels for which you define representative "previews" for a rough impression. What are the five most important touchpoints (e.g., start page, smartphone, third-party website, another channel, Google search results, social web, Twitter, Facebook, WhatsApp News Channel, Flipboard, Instapaper, RSS)? For Facebook, there are, for example, special HTML snippets that are used for postings. In them, it is stated which image and which short text will be displayed with a link recommendation in Facebook.

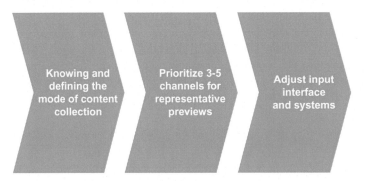

Content manager experience design (CMXD) process (inspired by Skjoldan, 2013b).

Through such a process, editors and authors learn to think more generically and more abstractly (learning effect). If the essential parameters are known, you can adjust the CMS input interface and create the most important preview templates. Iterative prototyping and testing lead step-by-step to a customized graphical user interface.

6.5 EDITOR- AND CONTENT-CENTERED PROCESS

The art and manner in which information is created and received in the digital information society is changing. In order to meet the needs of all parties, some exciting challenges and issues must be dealt with in the medium term:

Focus on content and editor

On the side of the creation of the content, the author and curator of the content is the focus. A CMS or an information management system and/or information management concept must look and function in such a manner that it supports the work of the content creators as best as possible.

Create once, publish (or "process") everywhere: A content management or content channeling system (generally each information management system) should be able to serve as a hub for all contents. Interfaces, data aggregation, and workflows must be individually designed.

The collection and/or creation of the content occurs presumably seldom via a standardized system. In a multiscreen world, all content providers have the task of creating and processing "smart content" in order to be able to publish contents on all channels consistently.

Processes and workflows

Processes and workflows must meet the requirements of the authors and recipients and must be supported, designed, and improved by experts actively and in a consulting capacity. The affected and acting persons must be enlightened and advised on requirements and challenges. It is necessary to propagate the "mental shift" and to provide enlightenment about which advantages will be gained by creating and consuming smart content. The prerequisites are suitable procedures and technologies.

Editor-centered approach

In order to provide the authors and editors with user-centered tools, it must be clarified how custom interfaces can look and which custom interfaces will be used for which touchpoints. Standard interfaces and representative and generally valid previews can possibly be derived for certain touchpoints. It would be helpful if the CMXD process could be standardized to a certain degree and could be defined as a generally implementable process in order to facilitate its use and integration into the project processes.

It is important to deal with these and additional issues. Also, you should handle, examine, and supplement the challenges in order to develop systems and processes for future-oriented content management.

In any case, the user experience while creating and curating content is crucial for the future of content (management).

6.6 CONCLUSION AND TIPS

1. **A Multiscreen-World demands Smart Content!**
   In the future, digital information and services from a wide array of sources will be used and have to appear on various devices, in a wide array of media, multiple screens, and output channels. Thus content has to meet these demands.

2. **Consider author and content curator.**
   It's important how content is created to prepare the best possible quality of information that will be consumed by recipients on any imaginable touchpoint. The content editors lay the base for content that can and will appear everywhere. They must be able to concentrate on the creation of content. Optimize the UX for them and support their work as much as possible.

3. **Use a centralized content hub for content channeling and aggregation!**
   You need one single point where every content arrives, can be managed and be delivered from.

4. **Processes and workflows have to fulfill authors and recipients needs.**
   Think about the users that create content and that consume content. What kind of screens do they use, in which environment? What are their goals? How are they and can they be motivated? Optimize the content flow for these conditions.

5. **Try to offer and implement custom interfaces and/or gateways (API).**
   If it's possible allow editors to use their preferred system. Use interfaces to gather, aggregate, and manage content as well as to deliver content to each channel that is important for your (potential) target group.

Content Design and User Interface Architecture for Multiscreen Projects

Methods and Rules for the Conception, Design, and Implementation of Layout, Contents, and Workflows in the Building Block Principle

Digital contents can appear everywhere today. It is just a fact that we use digital services daily on a wide array of devices and media. Information flows into all channels. In order to create a uniform user experience, a continuous flow of information is required. The requirement for this is a central hub for contents (as described in Chapter 6), a system for the definition of user interface (UI) elements, and rules regarding when which contents are displayed in which combination where and how. So that this can be solved technically, it is necessary to plan and develop the contents, user interfaces, and workflows based on a respectively similar model in a modular and structured manner—comparable with the building blocks in a building block system. Based on these requirements, there is a distinct need for design systems (Busse, 2015). This chapter describes how to combine well-known and established methods and patterns from content strategy, information architecture, content modeling, and UI design to create relationships in order to develop new added-value approaches.

> Information distribution is changing disruptively. Media publishers and content owners (which is nearly everyone that offers any kind of information on the web) are no longer in control of how and where their contents are distributed and retrieved (see Chapter 6, Section 6.1). But they can prepare their content (structure, flow and appearance) for such a scenario.

7.1 A CRUCIAL SHIFT FOR CONTENT (STRIKING NEW PATHS)

Many content offerings (e.g., individual articles from *The New York Times* or *Der Spiegel*) are today more frequently available in other channels (e.g., on Twitter, Facebook, WhatsApp, in an e-mail, in Flipboard or any other third party apps) than the original website. A content interface (content application programming interface, content API) supplies all information, and the recipient or the displaying channel decides which content elements to use. The visual design is then prescribed by the styling definitions of the target and third-party platforms.

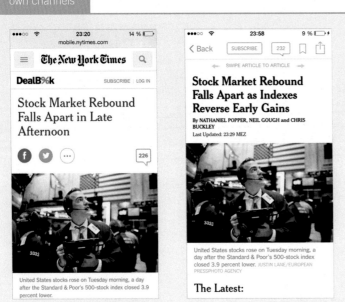

website, smartphone

iPhone app

Instapaper

2nd row: Sharing content from the smartphone browser via e-mail, on Facebook (incl. timeline) and on Twitter (incl. detailed view with source summary)

Displaying content from the same source and origin on different devices, for example smartphone app, smartwatch (push notification), and the website on the laptop or desktop-PC.

The content of news companies (for example the New York Times) can appear in many different channels and devices. These can be (on) the own channels (respectively touchpoints) as the original website in the browser, on the tablet or in the smartphone app, but third party channels as well, that can't be controlled by New York Times editors and designers. The content and its structure has to be appropriate for the original website on desktop or smartphone, for own or third party apps (like Instapaper), E-Mail Sharing, Facebook, Twitter (with or without summary), WhatsApp news channels, smartwatch or smartphone notification, and many more. In some of the examples you see the marked headline of a news used in different use cases (e-mail sharing, smartwatch notification, twitter post). Some content owners also have to publish their content on TV as well (just one more device with different requirements for content structure, complexity, and presentation).

In order to be able to supply the right content building blocks for automated usage, the content must be correspondingly structured—in the best case, even "intelligently."

You can create good experiences without knowing the content. What you can't do is create good experiences without knowing your content structure. What is your content MADE from, not what your content IS.

Mark Boulton

7.1.1 MULTISCREEN-READY INFORMATION EXPERIENCE

The Internet is an integral part of daily life; digital information is used on a wide array of devices. We live in a multiscreen world. The art and manner of how information is created are changing. On the side of the creation of the content is the author or curator of the content; on the other side is the recipient and thus the user of the information.

An information management system must support the work of content creators and should be able to serve as a hub for all contents. Its interfaces (API), data aggregation, and workflows must be able to be designed individually.

The collection and/or creation of the content seldom occurs via a uniform system. It would be best if authors could use their customary creation system and the collected contents could be consolidated, merged, and brought to the defined structure via corresponding (application programming) interfaces and a kind of content structure mapping in the content hub based on the content model. By so doing, it would be possible to collect contents based on and according to the structure of the content model and the content type with any system and via any input-channel (e.g., via e-mail, Evernote, a Tweet, a Facebook post, or another system), to edit it in the content hub, and to flexibly transmit and publish it again to any desired channel.

Content structure mapping (in a centralized content hub/examplified)

	E-Mail	Evernote	Twitter	Facebook
Title	subject	title of the notice	–	–
Short text	–	–	tweet text	text of post
Long text*	mailtext	notice text	linked content	linked content
Image	attachment	integrated	attached	attached
Document	attachment	reference	linked file	linked file
Date	mailing date	last date of change	date of tweet	date of post
Author	sender	originator	account	account

Content elements can be generated via variable input channels (each channel quasi serves as CMS) and then be mapped according to the underlying structure of the content type (for example a news article, compare New York Times example).
Semantic structuring (e.g. H1, bold, quote, listing, etc.) is adopted.

Thus, it would be possible—via a "simple" e-mail—to collect the content elements (of a news article, for example) of author/creator, creation date, title, brief description (short text), main text contents (long text), photos or media elements (as attachment), and other meta-information, for example via hashtags or other defined characters in the e-mail text as the Todo app Todoist does (www.todoist.com). The gathered contents could then be edited, optimized, and supplemented in the central hub.

Content providers are confronted with the problem that they should be able to consistently publish contents in many channels. Information should be able to be displayed everywhere. The requirements for this are a central and, insofar as this is possible, user-friendly hub for contents (e.g., content management system [CMS]), a central system for the definition of UI elements (e.g., style guide or UI pattern library), and corresponding rules (workflows) regarding when which contents will be displayed in which combination on which device and how.

In an upstreamed or at least a content manager experience design (CMXD) process initiated at the beginning of the project, the most important parameters for this can be defined (Nagel, 2014b) (see Chapter 6, Section 6.4.3). This includes recognizing the modes of content collection, defining the three to five most important target channels, and correspondingly adjusting or synchronizing the input interface and the systems (see Chapter 6, Section 6.3.3).

7.1.2 AN INDEPENDENT METHOD FOR AN UNCERTAIN FUTURE

It concerns, among other things, the fundamental principle and a uniform generally understandable language and interdisciplinary terms that are understood by all stakeholders (project managers, customers, developers, conceptualists, and designers). The core idea is to break down everything (similarly) atomically and/or in accordance with the building block principle and/or compile it and generically conceive it. Most important, we cannot anticipate for which future channels we will be designing contents and user interfaces at the current point in time (Frost, 2015b).

> *I have no idea what the hell I am doing. And neither do you. And that's ok.*
>
> Brad Frost

I think that if you create contents, user interfaces, and processes based on atomic, modular building block patterns, you will be largely independent of future developments.

Semantically similar contents should be variably utilizable in various media, channels, and devices. This applies to the smartphone, tablet, desktop, TV, and smartwatch as well as for contents on your own website, in Google search results, in the RSS feed, on Instagram or Facebook, or any other content presentation.

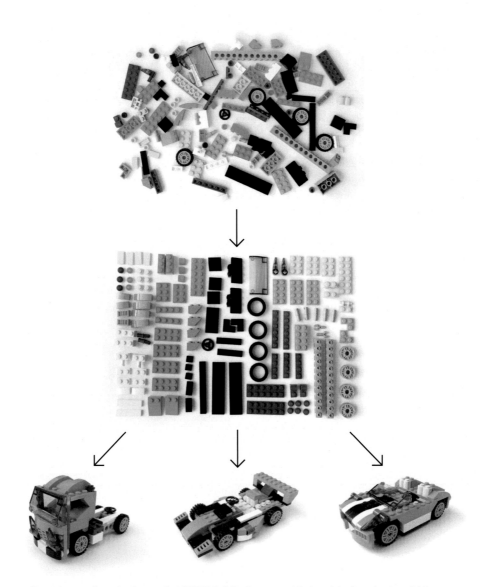

If you have a bunch of unsorted LEGO bricks (comparable to a lot of content and UI elements on a website, for example) you can (and should) first sort them to get an overview. **Make an inventory** of all the bricks that are available and shall be used to build any LEGO model. You can build different cars out of the same elements, if you combine them in a different manner. That's the same what you can do and must think about with your content (and your user interface). Different elements can and will be shown and differently used and combined on various channels and touchpoints (compare example with New York Times in Section 7.1). A systematic and structured approach helps to tackle that challenge.

7.1.3 FOUR CORE AREAS

In order to plan and implement services and processes in a flexible, structured, and modular manner, four core areas must be fundamentally observed during the course of the project: contents, user interfaces (UI), workflows, and application programming interfaces (API).

The content and its users, of course (they are both the authors and the editors as well as the recipients of the information), should be the focus of the analysis and the starting point for further steps.

Design from the content out.

Stephen Hay (as quoted in Frost, 2012f)

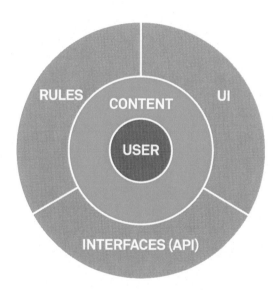

Four core areas. Start with the content. Initially you must know and understand all involved users. That can be described as *user- and content-centered design.*

Information (data/content)

Based on the thematic tendency (taxonomy, "unit," or domain), there are content elements for various content types. In addition, there are the corresponding form elements for the "front end of the back end" in order to build the input mask for the content objects (assumed that the contents are collected in your own CMS). A content type consists of various content elements. The semantic meaning influences the structure of the content type, its classification, corresponding categories, and labeling of the form fields.

UI (graphical user interface)

In this case, the UI (or graphical user interface) also includes visual design and interaction design. The UI elements are structured according to the atomic design principle (see Chapter 5, Section 5.8.1). They are relevant for the front end output, for the form elements in the back end, and for the (preview) display of the contents in the back end. Visual design and individual styling are described via a "living style guide" (as described in Chapter 5, Section 5.8.1) that is constantly being updated. The UI and the UI elements for the back end are generically prepared. The UI elements and libraries can be successively supplemented.

Processes and workflows (rules)

They define—according to the "if this then that" principle—how contents relate to each other or can change if an event occurs or a change takes place. In this regard, it concerns the definition of rule-based interaction between two objects.

API (application programming interface)

The concept of the original app with its independent content is dissolved by the concept of the app as a content supplier. It provides contents (broken down into small units) via an (application programming) interface to other services (Schätzle, 2015a)—within the content building blocks in the content hub and from and to other applications in order to exchange and/or synchronize the contents and data.

7.2 BUILDING BLOCK PRINCIPLE

7.2.1 MODULAR APPROACH: ATOMIC DESIGN AND CONTENT MODELING

Structure and modularity

Apps and websites will be less autonomous entities in the future; rather, they will be systems consisting of a wide array of modules. This aspect will become even more important if smartwatches are disseminated more widely in the shadow of the Apple Watch.

An information is composed structurally of individual elements. The corresponding elements are displayed based on the platform, target channel, and context. This structure is described by Brad Frost in the user interface design context with atomic design (Frost, 2013a). Based on the same principle, content can also be structured atomically whereby one could speak of "atomic content." (Other popular terms are structured content, future-friendly content, intelligent content, adaptive content, or smart content [see Section 5.10]).

With atomic design (see Chapter 5, Section 5.8.1), similar to chemistry (thus the atom metaphor), web projects are broken down into the smallest building blocks possible. These building blocks are subsequently combined to form larger entities (compare to molecules or organisms in chemistry) that extend to complete pages (see Chapter 5, Section 5.8.1).

With content modeling (Gibbon, 2015; Lovinger, 2012), based on the content concept, content models are created that describe structured content in the form of content types, individual attributes, and data types and their relationship to each other. In order to structure content, you must be familiar with the content types and also the thematic area it concerns because it decisively influences the structure and the semantics.

Content modeling gives you systematic knowledge; it allows you to see what types of content you have, which elements they include, and how they operate in a standardized way.

Sara Wachter-Boettcher (2012b)

Well-structured modular content can also be utilized as rich snippets for the search engine optimization. These elements are displayed in the search results. For example, quality assessments or—for recipes—photos, calorie data, cooking times, and ingredients.

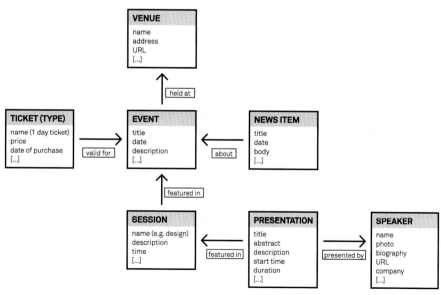

The **content model** (for example of a conference with location, tickets, presentations and speakers) describes the content structure with different content types, individual attributes and their relationship to each other. The figure is based on and adapted from Jonathan Kahn (2010).

Atomic design and content modeling are comparable with the LEGO system or similar principles. Common to both of them is the modularity and the structured development of the individual "parts."

We're not designing pages, we're designing systems of components.

Stephen Hay

A principle inspired by atomic design and LEGO

The goal of the presented building block ideas is to structure all elements similarly and to find collective comprehensible and generally valid wording for all project participants.

With atomic design (or UI modeling) and content modeling, individual elements (or building blocks) are assembled according to the building block principles similarly to LEGO. See also Section 6.3.4 and the example of the document editor Notion, which allows to structure content elements and components in a way that is described here. Because workflows and other areas can also be conceived and realized according to this principle, I utilize standard wording based on the content modeling.

Content and UI can be built brick-based comparable to LEGO models. Explained with the image example: First you have bricks (smallest possible units). If you combine them you get a bumper bar. That bumper bar is part of the driving cab, that again is part of the truck. And that truck is always built with nearly the same bricks and elements, no matter if it's a fire truck, police truck, or a wood truck (i.e., just the visual design, mainly color and some minor variations).

7.2.2 UI AND CONTENT INVENTORY (AND AUDIT)

In order to know with what visual and content building blocks you are working on a project, it is recommended that during an early project phase, you conduct an analysis of the existing elements and those that are to be used in the future. Via a *content inventory* (or *audit*), it is examined which sorts of content from which thematic area are being used and how these contents and content models are structured (Baldwin, 2010). It is also determined which content elements are required in order to supply all currently known channels with the content to be published and, as required, to supply the channels that are relevant in the future with adequate content. In a similar manner, via an (user) *interface inventory*, you will examine and define which UI elements are currently and will (or are supposed to) be used on a project (Frost, 2013b). After the inventory, the modeling of the individual elements and components will follow.

7.2.3 MODELING ACCORDING TO THE BUILDING BLOCK PRINCIPLE

If the contents and their potential structural and visual shape are known, you can commence the modeling of the content types and UI types. These types are developed in stages, beginning with the smallest possible unit (respectively element).

Generic five-stage building block principle

The individual (atomic) elements and/or building blocks build on one another and can be flexibly assembled to form a type (a conrete instance of a type is an object). Each type or object can be developed with five stages—from the smallest possible element to the generic template and the real, unique object (individual unicum).

	1 ELEMENT	2 COMPONENT	3 SEGMENT	4 TYPE	5 INSTANCE / OBJECT
	smallest possible unit / brick	*combination of smallest possible elements*		*generic / strukture (MADE from)*	*concrete / specific (IS)*
CONTENT	title, subtitle, description, reference, date, image, caption, metainfo, author	content module image + caption quote + author teaser with headline, image and description	module group text section, paragraph, chapter, rubric	content wireframe article, recipe, application for leave, product specification (semantic structure)	real content information object incl. tone of voice
USER INTERFACE	label, input field, button	search form (consisting of label, input field and button)	layout area (e.g. header with search form, logo, navigation)	UI template (+IxD) touchpoint-dependent and preview-relevant	real page instance of the template incl. visual design
Atomic Design	atom	molecule	organism	template	page

correlation

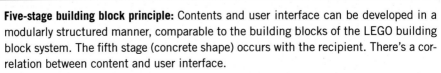

Five-stage building block principle: Contents and user interface can be developed in a modularly structured manner, comparable to the building blocks of the LEGO building block system. The fifth stage (concrete shape) occurs with the recipient. There's a correlation between content and user interface.

The terms from the chemistry metaphor can be replaced by generally valid generic terms:

- atom = element
- molecule = component or module
- organism = segment or area
- template or type (generic)
- instance or object (concrete)

There are also modular building block principles in other areas. Regardless of whether I am now assembling a LEGO product, planning my next new car purchase with the aid of a configurator, or would like to combine the available ingredients in the refrigerator to form a tasty dish—everything can be broken down, configured, and combined.

There's an interesting methodology (comparable to the described "building block principle") introduced by Sophia Voychehovski (2015) which she calls "object-oriented UX." First you analyze the project brief. By highlighting and extracting the concrete and relevant nouns you get the important objects first. Add core content and metadata (two different sorts of elements or components) to these objects. Discuss and experiment with structure, connection, and order (by importance). Objects, core content, and meta data can be nested and cross-linked. The result of that process is a structured object-, goal-, and priority-oriented content model. Prioritizing depends on what is important for your users, and therefore your order and structure may change based on the most important sorting or filtering mechanisms. That approach also helps to think of and work with a system of reusable building block-like content that can flexibly be assembled and combined for various outputs.

7.2.4 CORRELATION BETWEEN CONTENT AND UI

A correlation exists between the elements in atomic design and content modeling, i.e. between the individual content elements and their presentation in the target channel or medium being used by the recipient (see table in Section 7.2.3). Whenever I model content, I am thus quasi-indirectly also defining the related UI elements in a generic form at the same time (wireframe-like/without visual design). Whenever you define the content type, you are also indirectly automatically determining the corresponding form field types for the input interface (UI). Via the input interface the contents are collected. In the best case (for the content gatherer), this can be any kind of systems that he likes and/or prefers. For different systems the collected content elements must fit the structure of the content type so that they can be mapped on it.

It is known that content and UI—and thus the formatting of the content at the recipient—should be kept strictly separated from each other. However, the elements are in direct correlation to each other. The UI types and content types correlate. At the recipient and/or in the respective medium, the UI and the content are merged again. Through the strict separation, this merging can occur flexibly.

An argmuent for a modular UI: For Sunrise it was a big challenge to adapt the popular calendar app to the small screen of the Apple Watch (Sunrise, 2015). "We had to challenge our entire interface to make it fit on such a tiny screen, cropping out text and icons with every design iteration." (and they did it quite well).

The more atomic and more independent the UI elements are conceptualized, the easier it is to bring the contents to other viewports and adapt the UI elements.

7.2.5 THE CONTENT MODEL DEFINES THE (BACK END) UI (MODEL)

Chicken–egg: first the contents, then the UI (iterative)

The content models are assembled according to the building block principle. They consist of smallest possible (atomic) elements that can be assembled to form complete generic content types, based on which the concrete forms are built.

I call a concrete individual form of a content type a *content object*. A building block for form elements and/or content elements is the basis for all of this. The primary task for editors, authors, content maintainers, and content creators is to create and/or edit the content objects (information products).

Via the content model and the content type, the content elements and thus also indirectly the corresponding form elements of the back end are automatically defined (conceptual correlation). The content-collecting system requires a corresponding form-UI element for each content element. This form-UI element may differ based on the system or the type of collection or exist in variants (e.g., collection of date or location). For text, it would be a simple text input field or an RTE (rich text editor); for images, it would be a corresponding image upload form including caption text and supplemental meta-information about the image or just the option to use the built-in camera on a smartphone, for example. To input location information you can either offer a simple text input field or a geo-location functionality.

For each element, there is in turn a UI element in the front end (viewport and/or target channel) so that the content can be displayed.

Content elements, form elements on the back end in order to collect the contents, and front end UI elements in order to display the contents on the front end are thus in a direct correlation and are dependent on each other.

When you create and work on design and content, you should always have both in mind. It is important to know what kind of content you have to build an appropriate user interface. However, it is also important to test and check the user interface (patterns) in the back end and the front end with real content. Only then can you determine if it accurately reflects the real content. There is a close relationship between content and UI, and you should always consider both.

7.2.6 UNIVERSALITY AND COMPREHENSIBILITY

I want to establish a correlation between the various strategic and conceptual disciplines in the areas of content and UI. All aspects are built on the building block principle and are connected to each other. At the latest, when the information is received, the UI and content are in a direct relationship. The user consumes content and UI namely in a combined form. Moreover, the correlation also exists between UI, content, and workflows. Interfaces (API) form the bridge, for example, in order to synchronize the contents or exchange them between systems.

It should always be possible to use the principle (regardless of whether it concerns atoms, UI, layout, content, etc.). By means of the correlation matrix (in Section 7.2.3) that is being presented, I want to explain these generic and generally comprehensible models and want to ensure that they are applicable to all areas. The five stages and the atomic design approach are no dogma. On a customer project, we developed a living style guide according to the atomic design principle and introduced beforehand another level for the definition of basic elements such as grid, colors, typography, and interactive states. The smallest possible elements that cannot be broken down further should be defined at the lowest level.

7.3 PROCESSES AND TOOLS

If you select the atomic approach and gradually begin with the smallest elements that build on one another—the atoms—you will receive presentable pages only late during the course of the project. The requirement for this is that mood boards, scribbles, or Photoshop (mood) screens that indicate the visual design direction and, in my opinion, still have legitimacy, are sufficient for coordination purposes at the beginning. The more the project progresses, the more the initially higher expenditures at the project start pay off (Schätzle, 2015b).

A project from a user experience perspective is broken down basically into the disciplines of user research, content/information architecture, user interface, interaction design, visual design, and development/implementation.

During the course of a project, various methods should be employed that can be allocated across these disciplines. Due to budget, competence, time constraints, or other reasons, never all relevant methods can be applied to a project. However, you should at least focus on them and be clear about their relevance and benefit for the overall results. With the right method at the right time, unnecessary resource consumption during the course of the project can be avoided because you have to "stumble around" less and decisions can be made and justified based on solid findings.

7.3.1 METHODICAL APPROACH

The disciplines of UI modeling and content modeling, visual design, and multiscreen conception will overlap even more in the future. Projects will become more complex, and all disciplines and thematic areas will have to be considered and handled at the right time.

During the course of the project, you should (compactly formulated)—sequentially and iterated—recognize the theme, prioritize output channels, and define the content models. Based on the content, additional details can be defined and handled (structure, content wireframes, process of content collection, and application programming interfaces). When these parameters are known, while taking the building block principle into consideration, workflows can be modeled and output interfaces identified, designed, and developed. Such a process is seldom linear. Project phases can overlap, change and swap. Because content is most important, a central content (management) hub could address the previously mentioned plan. A more detailed example of a multiscreen project workflow with further information and recommended methods can be found at http://www.msxbook.com/en/pjwflw.

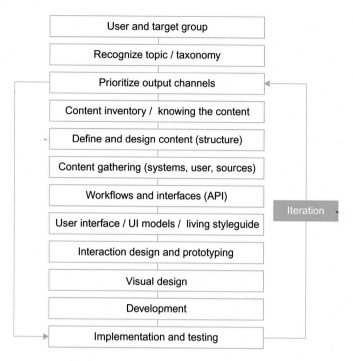

Project workflow: Start with the users and the topic. When you know these initial points you can successively get to know and work on the content. The user is always important, that means that authors, editors and recipients should always be taken into consideration. Don't forget to consider the potential context of use. Content modeling, UI modeling, visual design and development are iterative and **overlapping project phases. Such a process is seldom linear, phases can parallel, change and swap**. When you think you're done, think again (if possible). Define, create, refine, repeat....

This is just a rough overview. There are a lot of helpful methods, that have to be considered and applied (a few are mentioned in the previous chapters).

7.3.2 CENTRAL CONTENT (MANAGEMENT) HUB

The idea and the concept of the hub are based on the aforementioned breakdown of the four project parts of content, user interfaces (UI), workflows, and application programming interfaces (API). The content editor (thus, the user of the software) is in the foreground. The data structure for the back end is defined based on the structure of the content models and/or types. The editor interface consists of a form based on the data structure. In the central content hub, the contents can be filed and managed in a consolidated manner.

The content model defines the UI model

Even the back end has a front end. If a content audit is conducted at the beginning of a project and then the content models are created, the suitable UI form elements can be derived for the back end (and the UI elements for the front end). Through the correlation of content and UI, the content model fundamentally structurally also already defines the back end and the output in the front end.

Thematic relevance

The (project) theme is relevant with regard to the terminology for the content element and the labeling on the back end and/or the user interface for the collection and management of contents (unit, domain, and taxonomy). It makes a difference whether it is about cooking recipes, technical products, restaurants, business address data, or a request for vacation leave. The language and accordingly also the name of the labels for the content elements in the content collection system (classically a CMS back end) will be different.

Based on the respective unit- or theme-specific content models, a kind of specialized content manager will be derived that is suitable for the defined use case. For each defined content type, the user will receive the correlating UI form elements. A content model for a cookbook with recipes is substantially different from the content models for a product catalog with an e-shop functionality, a calendar application, or a classical news publication.

Via a form generator, the form elements can be generically combined according to the building block principle for the input interface. Through the content type, the predefined structure of the form type is fixed (atomic correlation of content, back end UI, and front end UI) but could nonetheless be expanded as required with own modules and templates.

Independent input interface

The data migration into the content hub can in principle occur independently of the input interface. The content objects must merely be correspondingly converted and its atomized elements be allocated to the particular content elements (content mapping).

The fundamental (structure of the) UI for the input interface is defined through the structural definition of the content types. But in contrast the exact styling is not yet defined (that is flexible and structure-independent). In addition, own UI elements can be supplemented at any time. The output is likewise independent of this and can take place in an own channel or in a third-party channel. The styling of the content elements in the front end is independent from the back end. Merely the structure (chunks of the content objects, not their order) is prescribed. The view mode in the back end is "only" a "content structure preview." The order, arrangement, and display of the content elements occur in the client and/or output medium.

Through the clear structuring and classification of the content types (concretely filled content types are content objects), the data are basically platform- and touchpoint-independent and can be displayed in as many output media and channels as desired. The output is configured on the back end (via rules regarding the respective contexts of use that again contain standards regarding channels, the layout and the medium, and also the interaction). For each content element, one or more UI forms must be available for your own channels.

Content flow

There are three parts in a content's (work) flow. It has to be created (written and structured). It has to be managed (by adding meta data, defining workflows and rules, and setting it up). And it has to be delivered to any kind of target channel or viewport where it is viewed and received by the (end) user. It could also be a preview check how it may roughly look anywhere.

The challenge for a content management software is to deal with these three steps equally well. If one solution cannot fulfill these requirements sufficiently, perhaps you can solve that challenge by using and combining different solutions via (application programming) interfaces (Boulton, 2013).

Three-step content hub

The content hub is structured in three steps (see figure in Chapter 6, Section 6.3.3 and the following figure). You can create, collect, and output contents—wherever and with whatever you would like.

For the output, a corresponding interface (API) is required. Thus, for example, you can input and collect content via the input form and/or in the CMS user interface of the content hub and then output it in WordPress, Flipboard, or any other channel). It is also conceivable to collect contents in any system as desired (step 1, flexible input interface), and after the mapping of the content in the content hub (step 2), they are once again flexibly outputted (step 3).

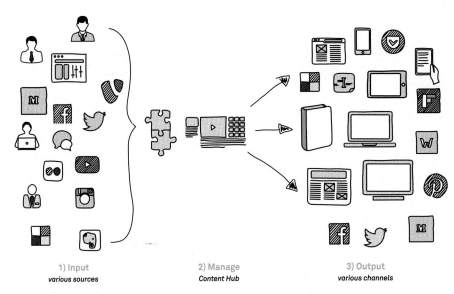

1) Input
various sources

2) Manage
Content Hub

3) Output
various channels

The **Three-Step Content Hub** (principle): 1) Collecting and authoring 2) combining and managing 3) outputting and distributing to various channels. The content hub in the middle plays a central and important role in the content flow. Content will be aggregated, mapped to a predefined structure (if there are different input channels), organized and prepared for flexible output in the content hub (see also the content mapping example at the beginning of this chapter).

Combining theory and practice

It is hoped that a tool will be developed that can be used to combine processes and methods from content modeling and UI architecture because it then serves as an interface (or link) between these both disciplines. It would unite the theory and the methods with the practice and provide concrete benefits for the project.

Whenever I can implement content modeling directly in or with the content (management) hub, I quasi automatically receive (generic, automated, but individualizable) work results that I can use for the interface and depiction for the recipient. One has to do everything only once, and directly gets a concrete result.

7.3.3 A MODELING SOFTWARE THAT IS SUITABLE FOR THE BUILDING BLOCK PRINCIPLE

SETU as the tool for future-oriented content

Based on the aforementioned ideas, we at SETU GmbH (www.setusoft.de) have developed a concept for such a "content management hub" that is integrated into our SETU 3.0 release. With it content management apps can be realized for various thematic focuses (units).

The content architect has predominantly free rein with the structuring of the data bodies. The software offers a large library of predefined (and extendable) form and output elements and supports iterating elements within a data model (including more complex structures such as text with an image) as well as relationships and kinds of relationships to other elements. It offers functions for the creation and management of language- and market-specific contents such as heredity and workflow support. Existing platforms can be supplemented with freely definable workflows in customer communication.

Moreover, rule-based and connected and related and individually personalizable context-based contents can be supplied. Context relevance can be recognized and utilized via rules and meta-information. Personalized contents dependent on, among others, the log-in, user profile and user type, Internet speed, device, output medium, channel, etc. (see Chapter 4 for more details in this regard). The structured information that has been supplied can be integrated into as many platforms and channels as desired.

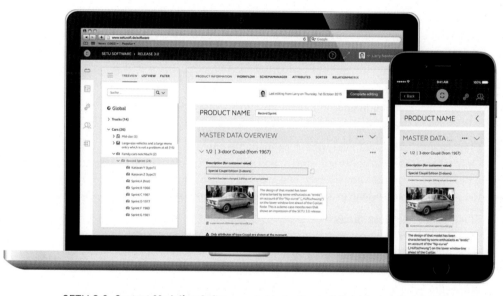

SETU 3.0: **Content Modeling Software** suitable for the building block principle. The mood-screen shows an impression of the user interface of a demo use case of the SETU 3.0 release (www.setusoft.de).

7.3.4 QUO VADIS CONTENT AND USER INTERFACE?

For the future, it is recommended to plan and collect information in any shape according to the building block principle in order to publish information in all conceivable channels with the right tools and without large additional expenditures insofar as this is possible. The suitable principles, methods, and processes should be described, established, and applied in a comprehensible manner. Out of this conviction, insofar as this is possible, I recommend that you break down all project parts into generic individual parts that can later be easily assembled once again—quite similar to how you can do this with LEGO.

We live in a multiscreen world. The number of screens and objects that have to receive, process, depict, and display content in any imaginable form is growing. Thus, it is highly recommended to have one single point of truth (for content and UI)—a centralized content hub with a user-friendly interface and an appealing editor-centered user experience (see Chapter 6, Section 6.4) and a living style guide and/or a UI pattern library (see Chapter 5, Section 5.8.1) to manage that challenge now and in the future.

7.4 CONCLUSION AND TIPS

1. **The (digital) content appears everywhere!**
   We live in a multiscreen world and use digital services daily on a wide array of screens. Information flows into all channels. Content offerings have to be available on own and foreign third party touchpoints.

2. **Know your content.**
   Conduct a content audit and/or content inventory. Analyze your content (structure) to start designing based on these findings.

3. **Prepare consistent and everywhere publishable content.**
   Only when content is collected, stored, and edited in one place, you can avoid redundancy, guarantee consistency and are able to structure and prepare it for the publication to and the usage in every imaginable context.

4. **Think about four core areas.**
   (Beside the user, context, and screens) Content, user interfaces, workflows, and APIs are the basic requirement to be able to publish content on a huge variety of screens and diverse channels. Start with the content.

5. **Flexibility by using the (generic five-stage) building block principle.**
   Strip content and user interfaces down to the smallest possible elements. Built content and UI in a modular and structured manner based on these elements. Define and built larger components and concrete objects as you would do this with LEGO® bricks.

6. **The content model defines the UI (model).**
   Start with the content and use the correlation between content elements and UI elements (in the back end and the front end) to design your user interfaces and plan (for the uncertain) appearance of your content in different channels and touchpoints.

Conclusion and Outlook

8

8.1 SUMMARY

These days, each project is a project for multiple screens. Multiscreen has become digital reality, and it is part of the core of a professional communications strategy. Media creators may no longer create stand-alone solutions but, rather, must develop holistic concepts for multiple screens in order to realize the goal as best as possible of offering a fluid multiscreen experience. Customers or project participants should and can be enlightened with good examples.

> *The good news is you only need one web design: a multidevice design. The bad news is it's not how you've designed things in the past.*
>
> Luke Wroblewski

Adapted standard (fluid) experience

In order to find an elegant solution and make possible a consistent and user-appropriate user experience, you should take into consideration device classes and device features, the device experience, all other previously discussed parameters, restrictions, and options, and, for mobile devices, the typical behavioral patterns (see Chapter 4, Section 4.4.1). The classification into layout categories, parameter classes, and device classes can vary from project to project, but it is very helpful to categorize relevant device classes or screen types. An interesting approach would be to utilize reusable layout patterns.

Challenges

Device fragmentation and the various screens are one of the central challenges for future digital projects. You must identify the relevant devices or screens and their combination possibilities. You must also know, take into consideration, and support the users (target group) and their needs, their user journeys, and their changing user behavior.

Flexible and dynamic layouts and contents, generally multiscreen-capable data, and suitable content management workflows are prerequisites for good concepts and (digital) services. When you start designing, begin with the content. Data security and connectivity are additional fundamental tasks. It is important to always focus on the people who use the various devices and corresponding information offerings. Although it is a multiscreen approach, we have to design for the users (or "the people" as Josh Clark points out in his talks) who use these screens—not just for the screens.

When beginning a multiscreen project, start by asking questions about the users' needs, their goals, and their motives. Think about the potential context of use and user journeys. Then try to answer questions concerning relevant devices, principles, conceptual approaches, and technical issues. And of course think beyond.

8.2 MULTISCREEN AND BEYOND

This book is an introduction. In the future, we will have to take into consideration not only the aforementioned screens but also many interfaces and other Internet-compatible devices that will make the multiscreen world more fragmented but even more exciting.

> *A part of multi-device strategy is simply embracing the uncertainty.*
>
> **Josh Clark**

Technological evolution

With technologies that respond to movements (e.g., Microsoft's Kinect), a new type of TV experience can be realized in your living room. The way in which the TV is operated will change. For example, a software for facial recognition (CNN, 2010) can identify persons and channel-hop through their preferred channels when they tap with two fingers in the air or move one of their hands back and forth (Pagán, 2012). With the aid of voice control, even more complex actions can be carried out (Punchcut, 2012b).

Regardless of whether it involves laptops, MP3 players, mobile telephones, smart TVs, hi-fi systems, or fully electronically controlled heating, each small device will soon have a chip. Also, the user will be more powerful. He will consciously opt for an application or a service and only then will he decide which device he will buy. The device is useful for him only if it can also process and display the information that is important to him.

Information and information overflow

For users in the future, the features of a product will not be as important as whether and how access to information will optimally function (access is more important than ownership, and the service is more important than the product). Jeff Bezos (founder and CEO of Amazon) opines, "People don't want gadgets anymore. They want services. They want services that improve over time" (as quoted in Frommer, 2012). The information itself is of prevailing importance as well as the objects with which the user would like to interact. The service is in the forefront.

It will also be a major challenge to filter out relevant information from the immense flood of information or receive it in an already filtered-out form (Evsan, 2013c). For example, Jeff Bezos states, "We don't think of the Kindle Fire as a tablet. We think of it as a service" (as quoted in Potter, 2011).

Providers of contents must guarantee a high quality and stand out from the competition. For them, once again, the creation and the ownership and/or the controlling of the dissemination of the information will be of critical importance in the future.

Big data

In the future, we will be confronted with an immense flood of data. Everyday devices such as smartphones, cameras, electrical power meters, or cars produce data—sometimes without any human involvement. On the other hand, humans produce an enormous quantity of data via social networks, in job portals, during online auctions, through the use of search engines, or through recreational activities (Fischermann and Hamann, 2013). Sometimes, humans are presumably not even fully aware of how, where, when, and which data they produce and what can happen with these data.

All these data can be valuable and useful. They can be processed and sensibly combined. From them, additional new challenge are always arising (e.g., data protection issues).

Clearly visualized complex data and information constructs can be collected better and faster than pure tables or series of numbers. The responsible handling of data must be learned and taught. Dealing with media and data will be a core competence in the digital information society. The technology will continue to develop. Many problems will disappear and new ones will appear.

Internet of Things

On the Internet of Things, everything (that can be) will be cross-linked: homes and cars with clothes and consumer goods. Even ice makers will be connected to the Internet. Everyday objects become digital objects. Information will always be exchanged. The single hurdle is that there is still no uniform standard for the exchange, transfer, and networking of data (Fitchard, 2012).

People, systems, and products are combined directly with each other and interact. The web conquers the road and only then unfurls its true potential here.

Nils Müller (founder and CEO of TrendONE)

It is difficult or easy (it depends) to imagine what kind of new and exciting experiences with new technologies can be created. It is challenging enough to get all the information and services combined and synchronized across all different platforms and devices, especially tasks that are executed and continued and services that are used on more than one screen (Thurston, 2014). The way we shift tasks across devices can be made even better and should be much more continuous—on visible screens and on invisible objects.

There will be different sensors and inputs and physical digital objects, and everything will be connected. Potentially there will be interactions without screens or with invisible devices (note that sensors are already in some of the devices discussed in this book).

Some kind of development will happen, always with the following mission and challenge in mind: assisting people as well as possible to get their tasks accomplished. Refer to Josh Clark's (2014) inspiring thoughts about how to "design for the space between devices"—the gap between phone, tablet, desktop or laptop, and television.

At the moment it is not that difficult to identify the core or main devices in a multiscreen-world. In the future, the number of connected screens and devices will increase dramatically. There won't be just new screen sizes or screen classes. There will be completely novel interaction possibilities.

Smartwatches are just one kind of wearables. There will be voice-controlled devices as Amazon Echo, for example. Devices and services for and to control your (smart) home, like Nest or Tado. And there will be a lot more connected devices that are hardly imaginable at present. New interaction patterns will evolve; the possibilities of input and output will change or at least expand and will affect the way we use devices and services and interact with, modify, and consume information and content in the future.

The existing screens won't disappear but there will be new kinds of (invisible) devices and things that will complement these screens and that should be considered in a completely connected and holistic information experience scenario.

Industry 4.0 and the digitalization of the economy

Driven through the Internet real and virtual world will merge more and more (see Internet of Things). The economy is on the cusp of the fourth industrial revolution. Components will and do already independently communicate with production plants, service units and cause a repair of themselves, if necessary. Humans, machines, devices, and industrial processes will cross-link intelligently. The close networking of technologies will cause an intensive exchange of data. Therefore the importance of IT-security will increase. The ongoing growth of data will lead to the need of a higher level of automation. Workflow modeling tools such as BPMN (Business Process Model and Notation) will become a necessity to cover changes fast in this interdependent world.

New device classes

Interfaces, screens, and devices (classes), as we know them today, will change, become more invisible and nonetheless more omnipresent, or disappear completely. Data glasses may become the next important screen (Evsan, 2013a,b), and do not forget smartwatches, which were already mentioned and discussed in this book, as well. Of course, these interfaces must also be conceived and designed. Design remains important, but the design task will be a different from what we know and understand it to be today. Instead of visual interfaces, perhaps increasingly connections will be designed. Or meta-data will be aggregated automatically to form new information packages. Sensors will also play an important role.

Automotive and connected cars

Cars will be a part of the Internet (of Things). Automotive interfaces and infotainment systems will increasingly be integrated into various ecosystems and networked with other information and services. The interface must be adapted to the interaction capability of the user. If you are traveling by car, you have a reduced ability to pay attention to operate a touch interface. Where applicable, original text contents are translated into audio output, and the touch interface is correspondingly reduced based on the cognitive abilities and options of the user. Ultimately, it is a matter of making a service as smart as possible for the users.

Voice recognition and voice control is a challenge (not only, but especially) for automotive interfaces. During the voice dialog the information that is shown on the car's infotainment system in the center console has to be synchronized with the driver's audio commands and manual (or haptic) interaction options. A coherent overall voice control and UI concept is needed (Hofmann, 2015). Audio, visual, and manual input and output have to be coherent. The visual interface of the infotainment system must be controllable via (touch) interaction on the screen and voice at once. All graphical user interfaces (and/or services) will potentially have to be controlled by voice as well. And that information generated by audio input has to be potentially processed to be editable, manageable, and reusable by any kind of content hub or information management system.

In the future, we will presumably use mobile devices in self-driving cars (as "drivers" while driving). The devices will be connected to the driving system, and the driver will be alerted automatically if a dangerous traffic situation occurs and he should take over the steering wheel. Thus, traffic information, information from surrounding objects, driving system information, information from the car's sensors, and the user interface on the (mobile) device have to be synchronized immediately and permanently. All this will affect the way we consider "mobile user experience" and is another interesting challenge in our prospective multiscreen world.

Future-oriented contents

Information and content must increasingly be adapted to various devices and be suitably conformed to the context and user. You will ponder whether and how moving-image contents are being read. Purely text contents could be displayed audiovisually, and contents in general are aggregated perhaps automatically on the basis of metadata with corresponding content types to form new content with other information.

Rise of context-based information

It is quite possible that we move from an era of multiscreen to the age of context, in which smart data (e.g., personal data, data generated from social media usage and behavior, publicly available data, app-level data, and data collected by devices and sensors) will be analyzed and combined to intelligently drive us toward an action or offer us information that is presumably helpful and relevant for us in that particular situation and thus will enhance the subjectively perceived user experience (Hernandez, 2015).

It is becoming increasingly important to make sense of all the collected and accumulated information and use it careful and responsibly. The combination and utilization of rising technology trends, considering context relevance, and using smart content at once could support the accomplishment of an even more personalized experience than ever before.

Siri, for example, Apple's intelligent personal assistant and knowledge navigator tries to answer questions before they are asked (available with the feature "Proactive," since iOS 9). That feature will suggest a playlist or audio book when you plugin your earphones or connect the iPhone to the car. In the morning, the iPhone welcomes you with exactly the apps that you use each morning (Johannsen, 2015).

> *Collecting information about people allows you to make significantly better products.*
>
> Dustin Curtis (2014)

Privacy versus user experience

But what about privacy? When many companies are able to (and do) collect and store much information about our behavior, our communication activities, and our personal information to enhance user experience (across devices) in order to make better and fluently behaving products, we risk losing the sovereignty of our private information. I think positive and have the same opinion as Dustin Curtis (2014) that the improvements in user experience that can be made based on collected information outweigh the potential security risk. The precondition is that everyone in a multiscreen world using digital connected products is aware of these risks and that companies (as well as user experience designers and developers) treat private content and information very sensitively and responsibly.

8.3 THE FUTURE OF CONTENT CREATION AND USER INTERFACES

The world is changing: adapt to it

The way in which information is created is changing. Focus on content and those who are responsible for the content because it is crucial how smart, easily, and smoothly the content can be created and curated to deliver and offer the best possible content (thus information) to potential recipients. Processes and content flows should meet the requirements of the authors and recipients.

Use a central content hub to collect, store, manage, and deliver information in and from one single point of truth. Also use a single point of reference for your UI styling definitions.

Plan and try to collect information in any form according to the building block principle in order to be able to publish it in all conceivable channels. Suitable principles, methods, and processes have been recommended and explained in this book. Keep them in mind and choose the right ones depending of your project setting. I recommend breaking down all project components into general individual parts that can later be easily assembled.

Text messages as the future UI?

This thought is not as absurd as it may seem at first glance. Texting is easy, familiar, and an interactional medium in which people are already fluent (VanHemert, 2015). Thus, it is often easier to text a message than to learn various usage and interaction patterns from different operating systems, apps, and services.

Nearly everybody is capable of sending a text message, and it is the most widely used smartphone feature (Smith, 2015). Thus, everyone would generally be able to control an interface by text input (with the precondition that text input is available, either directly on the device or by a complementary interaction).

The idea is not too futuristic and not proven at all, but it is worth considering because in many cases texting is easier for many people than "naturally" interacting with voice and gestures (i.e., natural user interface). If natural user interfaces will spread and become widely accepted and adopted will depend on if they evolve with interaction patterns that are understandable and easy to learn for all kinds of users.

And what's next?

In any case, it remains exciting. Now and in the future information will be displayed on screens and we will interact with them. For now, we concern ourselves during the short term with the four expatiated screens—or probably five screens, if the smart-watch will play as important a role in multiscreen scenarios as it is expected to do. Nothing stays the same. Be open for change. The future will show us how to proceed.

I look forward to it!

Wolfram

Appendix

9.1 PERSONS IN THIS BOOK

Many thanks to everyone who inspired us with their presentations, articles, reports, comments, books or in personal conversations.

Barbara Ballard is a UI Designer, UX Architect, and Author of "Designing the Mobile User Experience." http://www.linkedin.com/in/barbaraballard

Cennydd Bowles is an independent Digital Product Designer and Leader with many years of experience helping companies see the benefits of a good design. He regularly gives presentations and is the Author of the book "Undercover User Experience Design." http://www.cennydd.co.uk

Josh Clark is a Designer specializing in multi-device design, strategy, and user experience. He is the Author of four books inter alia "Tapworthy: Designing Great iPhone Apps" and "Designing for Touch." He keynoted more than 100 events in 16 countries. In 2002 he founded his agency as Global Moxie and changed the name to Big Medium in 2015. https://bigmedium.com/

Sebastian Deterding is a Designer and Researcher working on playful, gameful, and motivational design for human flourishing and co-editor of the book "The Gameful World." http://codingconduct.cc

Darryl Feldman is a Speaker, Author, and Designer. He has worked for more than 20 years in the segments of the Internet, mobile, and interactive media. http://darrylfeldman.com

Valentin Fischer drew most of the illustrations in this book. He is Co-author of the German book "Multiscreen Experience Design." He completed his study program at the University of Design in Schwäbisch Gmünd, earning the Master of Arts in Communication Planning and Design. He is currently working at the Intuity Media Lab in Stuttgart. http://www.valentinfischer.com

Brad Frost is a passionate Web Designer and Consultant and likewise a passionate Speaker on this theme. He is constantly tweeting, writing, and speaking about the web and other topics. And he is Author of "Atomic Design." http://bradfrostweb.com

Bertram Gugel is an Independent Consultant in the segments of Internet TV and online video and, since 2005, has written in his blog "Digital Film" about the interface of TV, film, and the Internet. http://www.gugelproductions.de

Marc Hassenzahl is Professor for "Experience and Interaction" at the Folkwang University of Arts in Essen. He is interested in designing meaningful moments through interactive technologies, in short, Experience Design. https://hassenzahl.wordpress.com/

Stephen Hay is an Art Director, Designer, Developer, Strategist, and Speaker on the themes of CSS, (web) design, development, and web accessibility. He is Author of the book "Responsive Design Workflow." http://the-haystack.com

Rachel Hinman is a Designer and Researcher who focuses on the "mobile user experience," and is the Author of the book "The Mobile Frontier: A Guide for Designing Mobile Experiences." http://rachelhinman.com

Avi Itzkovitch is a Web Designer and Author of "Design-It-Yourself: Websites: A Step-by-Step Guide." http://www.xgmedia.com

Scott Jenson wrote the foreword for this book. He is a UI Designer, Creative Director, and Consultant. He has been doing user interface design and strategic planning for over 20 years. In the late 1980s, he was a member of the UI Division at Apple. He worked at Apple on System 7, Newton, and the Apple Human Interface guidelines. He was the Director of Symbian's DesignLab, VP of product design for Cognima, a Manager of mobile UX for Google for 5 years, and a Creative Director at Frog Design in San Francisco. In November 2013 Scott returned to Google working on the Chrome team. http://jenson.org

Serge Jespers is an Adobe Evangelist and longtime Web enthusiast and has been working for many years with the latest web technologies. http://sjespers.com

Michal Levin is a User Experience Designer and Expert in the segments of desktop, mobile, and TV. She is Author of the book "Designing Multi-Device Experiences" and studied psychology, communication, and business management at the university. https://twitter.com/michall79

Ethan Marcotte is a Web Designer and prominent Speaker (among others, at An Event Apart and South by Southwest). He is the Author of "Responsive Web Design" and "Responsive Design: Patterns & Principles." http://ethanmarcotte.com

Karen McGrane is a User Experience Designer who focuses on content strategy for web and mobile. She teaches design management and is the Author of "Content Strategy for Mobile" and "Going Responsive." http://karenmcgrane.com

Stephanie Rieger is an Experience Designer, Researcher, Strategist, and Closet Anthropologist working on Internet of Things (IoT) and connected products at Yiibu. She holds workshops, speaks at design and technology focused conferences around the world, and regularly publishes her thinking in presentations and on Medium. https://stephanierieger.com/

Dan Saffer is a Creative Director, Interaction Designer, Speaker, and Author of four books inter alia "Designing for Interaction" and "Microinteractions." http://www.odannyboy.com/

Christoph Stoll and Johannes Schardt are the Owners of the design studio *precious* in Hamburg, develop interfaces and applications for various screens and introduced the "Patterns for Multiscreen Strategies" in 2010. Both teach interface design at the *Good School* in Hamburg and have already carried out teaching mandates at various design schools. http://www.precious-forever.com

Rasmus Skjoldan is a Content Strategist and (former) UX lead of the open source CMS "Neos." His main topics are concept development, user experience planning, information architecture, interaction design, and brand management. http://rasmusskjoldan.com

Gabriel White is a Designer and Owner of *Small Surfaces*. His focus is on the "mobile user experience" theme. http://smallsurfaces.com

Luke Wroblewski is the Founder of LukeW Ideation & Design, Digital Product Leader, Speaker, and Author of "Web Form Design" and "Mobile First." He writes a lot of articles about digital product design and strategy. He is a Co-Founder of IxDA (Interaction Design Association) and made the mobile first approach popular. http://www.lukew.com

9.2 ABOUT THE AUTHOR

Wolfram Nagel is a UX Designer, UI Architect, and Concept Developer. As the Head of UX at SETU GmbH (a German software engineering company) he is responsible for conception and design and supervises internal and external web and software projects in the areas of content design, UI architecture, and visual design in close interaction with front end and back end developers.

Wolfram is very engaged and has worked for many years with the themes of multiscreen, UX, and the future of information and content (management). In 2013 he published the German book "Multiscreen Experience Design." He speaks regularly about these topics at various conferences, such as Usability Professionals, IA Konferenz (the German IA Summit), or regional World Usability Days.

He worked as a Media Designer for Digital and Print Media and studied at the Hochschule für Gestaltung Schwäbisch Gmünd, Germany (University of Applied Sciences). He holds degrees in Information Design and Design Management (Master of Arts).

He is the Co-Initiator of the award-winning *Design Methoden Finder* (www. designmethodenfinder.de), a web-based collection of design methods, and he holds main management duties for the *Multiscreen Experience Projekt*. These initial ideas and approaches were already created during his first studies around 2005.

He is always searching for new ideas, approaches, methods, and processes that support the strategic development, conceptual design, and implementation of projects. He endeavors to continue to expand, adapt, combine, and sensibly integrate them into his work in order to find new added-value approaches and to obtain additional benefits and efficient synergistic effects.

Besides all that multiscreen and UX design stuff, Wolfram loves his family, spending time with his wife, playing LEGO with his son, and hiking in the nature around his hometown. He likes barbecuing with friends, playing football (soccer), football culture in general, and travelling to football games.

You can contact Wolfram inter alia via the following channels:
→ E-Mail (private): hello@wolframnagel.com
E-Mail (SETU GmbH): wn@setusoft.de
Web: www.wolframnagel.com
Twitter: @wolframnagel

9.3 REFERENCES AND SOURCES

Anderson, C., 2006. *The Long Tail*. New York: Hyperion.

Andjelic, A., 2012. Twitter (andjelicaaa): Graphic design = organization of information. Experience design = organization of behavior. (09/11/2012).

Anhalt, N., 2012. Mobile Go Home! Welcome Multi-Context! <http://www.slideshare.net/nielsa/mobile-go-home-welcome-multicontext> (07/12/2012).

Appleseed, J., 2011a. Responsive Web Design and Mobile Devices. <http://baymard.com/blog/responsive-web-design> (05/23/2011).

Appleseed, J., 2011b. Spoiled Milk Blog: Responsive Design. <http://spoiledmilk.dk/blog/responsive-design> (06/24/2011).

Arcade Fire, 2013. Just a Reflektor. <https://www.chromeexperiments.com/experiment/just-a-reflektor> (07/28/2015).

ARD/ZDF, 1997–2010. ARD/ZDF-Onlinestudien. (01/12/2011).

ARD/ZDF, 2010a. MedienNutzerTypologie 2.0. <http://www.ard-zdf-onlinestudie.de/index.php?id=238> (01/12/2011).

ARD/ZDF, 2010b. ARD/ZDF-Onlinestudie 2010. <http://www.ard-zdf-onlinestudie.de/index.php?id=265> (02/15/2011).

Arnold, R., Wieckenberg, U., 1999. Herausforderungen an die Erwachsenenbildung.

Baekdal, T., 2014. Stop Thinking about Devices. <https://www.baekdal.com/insights/stop-thinking-about-devices> (06/15/2015).

Baldwin, S., 2010. Doing a content audit or inventory. <http://nform.com/blog/2010/01/doing-a-content-audit-or-inventory> (04/14/2015).

Ballard, B., 2011. Barbara Ballard's Posterous: Mobile Context. <http://barbaraballard.posterous.com/mobile-context> (06/17/2011).

Barden, P., 2013. IPA Eff Fest: Phil Barden, Decode Marketing. <http://de.slideshare.net/The_IPA/ipa-eff-fest-phil-barden-deco> (09/19/2015).

Bartel, H., 2012. Wie viel kostet Responsive Webdesign? <http://welearned.net/2012/07/wie-viel-kostet-responsive-webdesign> (01/11/2013).

Bauer, E., 2011. Elmastudio: Responsive Webdesign mit CSS3 Media Queries: So funktioniert's. <http://www.elmastudio.de/webdesign/responsive-webdesign-mit-css3-media-queries-so-funktionierts> (06/24/2011).

Berners-Lee, T., 1989. CERN: Information Management: A Proposal. <http://www.w3.org/History/1989/proposal.html> (03/06/2011).

Bernett, C., 2010. Method. 10 × 10. Place, Space, and the Mobile Interface. <http://method.com/uploads/files/pdf/Method_10x10_Place_Space_Mobile_Interface.pdf> (02/19/2011).

Bilton, N., 2012. New York Times (Blog): Designing for Multiple Screen Sizes Is about Consistency. <http://bits.blogs.nytimes.com/2012/09/20/designing-for-multiple-screens-is-about-consistency> (10/25/2012).

Bitkom, F., 2010. PresseInformation vom 14.10.2010. Jeder fünfte Handynutzer besitzt ein Smartphone. <http://www.bitkom.org/de/themen/54894_65506.aspx> (06/25/2011).

Bodeit, S., 2015. Microinteractions. Task Force Micro UX. In: PAGE Ausgabe 01.15. S. 46–50.

Böhm, F., Nölgen, T. (deloitte), 2008. Web-to-go. Wachstumsmarkt Mobile Internet—auch für Deutschland? Studie zur Zukunft des mobilen Internets in Deutschland.

Bohn, R. (Hrsg), Wilharm, H. (Hrsg.), 2009. Inszenierung und Ereignis: Beiträge zur Theorie und Praxis der Szenografie. Transcript Verlag.

Boulton, M., 2013. WYSIWTFFTWOMG! <http://www.markboulton.co.uk/journal/wysiwtfftwomg> (10/31/2015).

Boven, L. V., Gilovich, T., 2003. To do or to have? That is the question. *J. Pers. Soc. Psychol.*, 85(6), 1193–1202.

Bran, T., 2011. UX Magazine: Defining the Interactions. <http://uxmag.com/design/defining-the-interactions> (06/26/2011).

Brand, M., Ion, F.K., 2008. 30 Minuten für mehr Work-Life-Balance durch die 16 Lebensmotive (fourth ed.). GABAL. Offenbach, Germany.

Bundesverband Informationswirtschaft, Telekommunikation und neue Medien e.V., 2010. Internet per Handy erobert den Massenmarkt (Studie).

Bunk, A., 2013. The Internet of Things—New Inforgraphics. <http://blog.bosch-si.com/the-internet-of-things-new-infographics> (01/22/2013).

Burmester, M., Sproll, S., 2010. World Usability Day (Vortrag). UX Design: Erlebnisse mit Technologie verstehen und gestalten.

Busse, J., 2015. The Revolution Will Be Designed Responsively. <http://blog.bussedesign.com/2015/02/the-revolution-will-be-designed-responsively> (07/23/2015).

Carlsson, N., 2012. SAS—Couple Up to Buckle Up. <https://vimeo.com/36829185> (01/30/2013).

Carse, J.P., 2003. Finite and Infinite Games. Notes by Generative Leadership Group. <http://www.glg.net/pdf/Finite_Infinite_Games.pdf> (06/24/2011).

Carter, T. J., Gilovich, T. D., 2010. The relative relativity of material and experiential purchases. *J. Pers. Soc. Psychol.*, 98, 146–159.

CeBIT, 2011a. Website: Das Internet als riesige Daten-Wolke. <http://www.cebit.de/de/ueber-die-messe/themen-und-trends/top-themen/cloud-computing_1> (05/03/2011).

Cebit, 2011b. Cloud Computing Inforgrahpic Overload. <http://blog.cebit.de/2011/01/30/cloud-computing-infographic-overload> (06/14/2011).

Celko, M., 2009. The Outernet. Say Hello to the Wild World Web! TrendOne, Proximity.

Cerda, M., 2015. Music Stories: A Better Way to Discover and Share Music. <http://media.fb.com/2015/11/05/music-stories-a-better-way-to-discover-and-share-music/> (11/06/2015).

Cerejo, L., 2012. Smashing Magazine: The Elements of the Mobile User Experience. <http://mobile.smashingmagazine.com/2012/07/12/elements-mobile-user-experience> (09/09/2012).

Cho, B., 2011. Brand New Thinking. Forget about Mobile. <http://www.brandnewthinking.de/2011/05/forget-about-mobile> (06/01/2011).

Cipriani, J., 2013. Play Google's Chrome Racer Game across Multiple Screens. <http://www.cnet.com/how-to/play-googles-chrome-racer-game-across-multiple-screens> (07/24/2015).

Clark, J., 2010. *Tapworthy: Designing Great iPhone-Apps* (<http://shop.oreilly.com/product/0636920001133.do>). Sebastapol, CA: O'Reilly Media. <http://shop.oreilly.com/product/0636920001133.do>

Clark, J.,, 2011a. Responsive Web Design or Separate Mobile Site? Eh. It Depends. <http://globalmoxie.com/blog/mobile-web-responsive-design.shtml> (07/24/2012).

Clark, J., 2011b. MobX Conference 2011: Mobile Context Is a Myth. (11/18/2011).

Clark, J., 2011c. Twitter (@globalmoxie): Content like water: Design flexible content to flow anywhere. 'Put water into a cup, it becomes the cup'—Content strategist Bruce Lee #fowd. <https://twitter.com/globalmoxie/status/133587842654937088> (03/14/2012).

Clark, J., 2011d. Swipe Conference 011. Teaching Touch. <http://swipeconference.eventer.com/swipe-conference-2011-1002/teaching-touch-by-josh-clark-1012> (04/05/2012).

Clark, J., 2012a. Desknots. <http://globalmoxie.com/blog/desknots.shtml> (07/18/2012).

Clark, J., 2012b. Twitter (@globalmoxie): Techniques deprecate, but principles and values do not.'—@scottjehl channeling <http://futurefriend.ly/come-aboard.html … #reflx>. <https://twitter.com/globalmoxie/status/249147742813839360> (09/22/2012).

Clark, J., 2012c. Twitter (@globalmoxie): It's not a newspaper; it's a platform. APIs: Guardian <http://j.mp/tU7Hf5>, USA Today <http://j.mp/sbuRVj>, NYT <http://j.mp/sN9BDe #fowd>. <https://twitter.com/globalmoxie/status/133589037603762176> (12/15/2012).

Clark, J., 2014. Designing for the space between devices. <http://blog.invisionapp.com/designing-space-between-devices> (07/22/2015).

CNN, 2010. YouTube Video: Facial Recognition Ads in Use. <http://youtu.be/VZ2VGstxcKI> (09/03/2012).

Cognitive Media, 2012. YouTube: Coca-Cola Content 2012 Part Two. <http://www.youtube.com/watch?v=fiwIq-8GWA8> (12/13/2012).

Cohrs, C., Rützel, A., 2012. Der smarte Kanal. Business Punk Ausgabe 03/2012. S. 78ff.

Colborne, G., 2012. cxpartners: Mobile app or mobile web? <http://www.cxpartners.co.uk/cxblog/mobile-app-or-mobile-web> (06/16/2012).

Cooper, A., 2004. *The Inmates Are Running the Asylum: Why High Tech Products Drive Us Crazy and How to Restore the Sanity.* Upper Saddle River, NJ: Sams – Pearson Education.

Cooper, A., Reimann, R., Cronin, D., 2007. *About Face 3: The Essentials of Interaction Design.* Indianapolis, IN: Wiley.

Cousins, C., 2015. Why micro-interactions are the secret to great design. <http://thenextweb.com/dd/2015/08/17/why-micro-interactions-are-the-secret-to-great-design/> (09/17/2015).

Crane, A., 2011. UX Magazine. A Gamification Framework for Interaction Designers. <http://uxmag.com/design/a-gamification-framework-for-interaction-designers> (06/07/2011).

Cultured Code, 2010. State of Sync, Part 1. <http://culturedcode.com/things/blog/2010/12/state-of-sync-part-1.html> (12/27/2010).

Cultured Code, 2011. State of Sync, Part II. <http://culturedcode.com/things/blog/2011/01/state-of-sync-part-ii.html> (02/15/2011).

Curtis, D., 2014. Privacy vs. User Experience. <http://dcurt.is/privacy-vs-user-experience> (07/27/2015).

Desmet, P. M. A., 2012. Faces of product pleasure: 25 positive emotions in human-product interactions. *Int. J. Design*, 6(2), 1–29.

Design Methods Finder, n.d.-a. Personas. <http://www.designmethodenfinder.de/Personas> (10/11/2012).

Design Methods Finder, n.d.-b. Sinus Milieus (Methodenbeschreibung). <http://www.designmethodenfinder.de/sinus-milieus> (10/11/2012).

Deterding, S., 2011. Vortrag auf der re:publica 2011: Spiel das Leben. Gamification zwischen Hoffnung und Hype. <http://www.youtube.com/watch?v=_WnE5PC8Nks> (06/19/2011).

Dictionary.com, 2012. Context. <http://dictionary.reference.com/browse/context> (07/25/2012).

DIVSI, 2012. DIVSI Milieu-Studie zu Vertrauen und Sicherheit im Internet. Deutsches Institut für Vertrauen und Sicherheit im Internet (DIVSI).

Dole, A., 2010. Method: 4 Things Video Games Teach Us About Motivating People. <http://www.fastcodesign.com/1662460/method-4-things-video-games-teach-us-about-motivating-people?ref=nf> (01/12/2011).

Doody, S., 2011. UX Magazine: Why We Need Storytellers at the Heart of Product Development. <http://uxmag.com/strategy/why-we-need-storytellers-at-the-heart-of-product-development> (05/23/2011).

dschlacht1, 2012. YouTube-Video: PrimeSense Movie Gesture CES 2012. <http://youtu.be/qmpec1RkV5g> (09/03/2012).

Duden, n.d. Gerät. <http://www.duden.de/rechtschreibung/Geraet> (06/25/2011).

Dueck, G., 2011. re:publica 2011 Gunter Dueck—Das Internet als Gesellschaftsbetriebssystem (Video/Vortrag). <http://www.youtube.com/watch?v=MS9554ZoGu8> (04/14/2011).

DWDL.de, 2011. Interview mit UFA Lab-Producer Costa-Zahn: Dina Foxx im ZDF: Dem Worst Case entkommen. <http://www.dwdl.de/interviews/31054/dina_foxx_im_zdf_dem_worst_case_entkommen/page_0.html> (06/24/2011).

Eichstädt, B., Kuch, K., 2012. t3n Magazin: Social Media: So kommunizieren Marken mit Instagram, Pinterest und Co. <http://t3n.de/magazin/markenkommunikation-instagram-pinterest-co-lasst-bilder-230330>.

Erdmann, D., 2013. Der Unterschied zwischen Responsive & Adaptive Webdesign. <http://denniserdmann.de/der-unterschied-zwischen-responsive-adaptive-webdesign/> (06/15/2015).

Erle, M., 2012. Accessible Content Strategy—Inhalte für die Zukunft fit machen. In: Brau, H., Lehmann, A., Petrovic, K., Schroeder, M.C. (Eds.), German UPA. Usability Professionals 2012. Tagungsband, 2012, pp. 264–267. <http://issuu.com/germanupa/docs/usability-professionals-2012?mode=window&pageNumber=264> (11/29/2012).

Etronika, 2012. YouTube ETRONIKA Kinect App Using NUI for Online Banking. <http://www.youtube.com/watch?v=zs-jJhY4ZK4> (06/26/2012).

Evans, B., 2015. Forget about the mobile internet. <http://ben-evans.com/benedictevans/2015/9/1/forget-about-mobile-internet> (10/24/2015).

Evsan, I., 2013a. Die Revolution der Google Glasses. <http://www.ibrahimevsan.de/2013/01/30/die-revolution-der-google-glasses> (02/01/2013).

Evsan, I., 2013b. Die Google Brille—Vernetzung biologischer Systeme. <http://de.slideshare.net/ibrahim.evsan/die-google-brille-vernetzung-biologischer-systeme> (02/04/2013).

Evsan, I., 2013c. Wer hat da an meinem Gehirn herumgebastelt? <http://www.ibrahimevsan.de/2013/04/05/wer-hat-da-an-meinem-gehirn-herumgebastelt> (04/06/2013).

Faletski, I., 2013. Make the Mobile Web Better: Don't Make These 4 Responsive-Design Mistakes. <http://venturebeat.com/2013/04/01/make-the-mobile-web-better-by-not-making-these-4-responsive-design-mistakes> (04/06/2013).

Farmer, R., 2011a. UX Australia. Creating Multi-Channel Design Frameworks—Mobile Experience. <http://de.slideshare.net/rodfarmer/creating-multichannel-design-frameworks-mobile-experience-9016224> (12/09/2011).

Farmer, R., 2011b. MobX Conference, Berlin. Multi-Device Experience Strategy. Live (Vortragsnotizen) und via Slideshare. <http://de.slideshare.net/rodfarmer/mob-x-con-keynote-20120402-reduced> (08/05/2012).

Farmer, R., 2012. Melbourne Spring Fashion Week. Keynote: Mobile and the Changing Face of Retail. <http://de.slideshare.net/rodfarmer/mobile-and-the-changing-face-of-retail> (11/29/2012).

Fedorov, A., 2013. Mastering Real-World Constraints (A Case Study). <http://uxdesign.smashingmagazine.com/2013/03/28/mastering-real-world-constraints> (04/06/2013).

Feige, S., 2010. *Taktile Symbole für Notifikationen in hochmobilen Szenarien. Disertation.* Universität Bremen.

Feldman, D., 2011. MobX Conference 2011: Designing for Microexperiences. <http://darrylfeldman.com/wp-content/Microexperience.pdf> (12/15/2011).

Ferrara, J., 2011. UX Magazine: The Elements of Player Experience. <http://uxmag.com/design/the-elements-of-player-experience> (05/30/2011).

Fischbein, V., 2010. User Experience. <http://www.info-design.net/laborbuch/2010/10/user-experience> (11/30/2012).

Fischermann, T., Hamann, G., 2013. Handelsblatt: Die digitale Revolution der Wirtschaft. Big Data. Wer hebt das Datengold? <http://www.handelsblatt.com/unternehmen/digitale-revolution-der-wirtschaft/big-data-wer-hebt-das-datengold/7613108.html> (02/06/2013).

Fitchard, K., 2012. GigaOM: Why We Need a Standard for the Internet of Things. <http://gigaom.com/2012/07/12/internet-of-things-standard> (09/03/2012).

Fling, B., 2011. Twitter: Anyone That Claims Responsive Design… <https://twitter.com/fling/status/50205432458915841>, <https://twitter.com/fling/status/50206474382741504>, and <https://twitter.com/fling/status/50207477844819968> (07/26/2012).

Forlizzi, J., Battarbee, K., 2004 Understanding Experience in Interactive Systems. In: Proceedings of DIS04: Designing Interactive Systems: Processes, Practices, Methods, & Techniques 2004. S. 261–268. <http://portal.acm.org/citation.cfm?doid=1013115.1013152> (06/14/2011).

Fraunhofer I.A.O., Hermann, F., et al., 2010. Augmented Identity. Fraunhofer Challenge Projekt (Vortrag). <http://www.aid.iao.fraunhofer.de/Images/augmented-identity-projektfolien_tcm505-40558.pdf>.

Freimark, S., 2015. Desiningng Multi-Device Experiences [book review]. <http://de.slideshare.net/sfreimark/designing-multidevice-experiences-book-review> (07/27/2015).

Frommer, D., 2012. readwrite.com: What the Kindle Fire Says about Amazon's Whispered Phone. <http://www.readwriteweb.com/archives/what-the-kindle-fire-says-about-amazons-whispered-phone.php> (09/25/2012).

Frommer, D., Goldman, L., 2010. Business Insider: iPAD Survey Results: Everything You Need to Know about How People Use the iPad. <http://www.businessinsider.com/ipad-survey-results-2010-11> (11/15/2010).

Frost, B., 2012a. BDConf: Josh Clark Presents the Seven Deadly Myths of Mobile. <http://bradfrostweb.com/blog/mobile/bdconf-josh-clark-presents-the-seven-deadly-myths-of-mobile> (07/11/2012).

Frost, B., 2012b. Twitter: Design for Breakpoints, Not Devices. <https://twitter.com/brad_frost/status/225674041804066816> (10/11/2013).

Frost, B., 2012c. How Much Does a Responsive Web Design Cost? <http://bradfrostweb.com/blog/web/how-much-does-a-responsive-web-design-cost> (01/11/2013).

Frost, B., 2012d. Responsive Navigation Patterns. <http://bradfrost.com/blog/web/responsive-nav-patterns> (07/12/2015).

Frost, B., 2012e. Complex Navigation Patterns for Responsive Design. <http://bradfrost.com/blog/web/complex-navigation-patterns-for-responsive-design> (07/12/2015).

Frost, B., 2012f. BDConf: Stephen Hay Presents Responsive Design Workflow. <http://bradfrost.com/blog/mobile/bdconf-stephen-hay-presents-responsive-design-workflow> (02/03/2015).

Frost, B., 2013a. Brad Frost Blog: Atomic Design. <http://bradfrost.com/blog/post/atomic-web-design> (03/06/2015).

Frost, B., 2013b. Interface Inventory. <http://bradfrost.com/blog/post/interface-inventory> (01/07/2015).

Frost, B., 2015a. Book: Atomic Design. <http://atomicdesign.bradfrost.com> (07/12/2015).

Frost, B., 2015b. I Have No Idea What the Hell I Am Doing. <http://bradfrost.com/blog/post/i-have-no-idea-what-the-hell-i-am-doing> (06/03/2015).

Future Friendly, 2011. Future Friendly. <http://futurefriend.ly> (11/14/2011).

Gabler Verlag (Herausgeber), 2011. Gabler Wirtschaftslexikon: Stichwort: Daten, online im Internet. <http://wirtschaftslexikon.gabler.de/Archiv/54483/daten-v5.html> (05/02/2011).

Gamification Wiki, n.d. Gamification. <http://gamification.org/wiki/Encyclopedia> (01/26/2012).

Gartenberg, M., 2011. Macworld.com: Apple Cuts Cord, Brings Post-PC World Closer. <http://www.macworld.com/article/160575/2011/06/post_pc_world_cuts_cord.html> (06/26/2011).

Gartner, Inc., 2009. Gartner Research Press Release: Gartner Says Context-Aware Computing Will Provide Significant Competitive Advantage. <http://www.gartner.com/it/page.jsp?id=1190313> (07/25/2012).

Gartner, Inc., 2010. Gartner Research Press Release: Gartner Highlights Key Predictions for IT Organizations and Users in 2010 and Beyond. <http://www.gartner.com/it/page.jsp?id=1278413> (03/13/2011).

George, S., 2014. Multi-Screen Experience : Websites That Sync with Mobile. <https://medium.com/@saijogeorge/multi-screen-experience-websites-that-sync-with-mobile-b82f0a90d9aa> (07/28/2015).

Geser, 2008. Vom Brockhaus zum Worldwide Wiki. In: Willems, H. (Hrsg.): Weltweite Welten: Internet-Figurationen aus wissenssoziologischer Perspektive. VS Verlag für Sozialwissenschaften, Wiesbaden 2008. pp. 119–142.

Gibbon, C., 2015. Cleve Gibbon Website: Content Modeling. <http://www.clevegibbon.com/content-modeling> (02/04/2015).

Giesler, M., 2013. Sieben Internet-Seiten, Personen und Startups, die die Grenzen des Journalismus neu verhandeln. <http://martingiesler.de/2013/10/journalismus-neu-definieren> (11/07/2013).

Goldhammer, W., Becker, S., 2008. Goldmedia Mobile Life Report 2012: Mobile Life in the 21st Century, Status Quo and Outlook. Goldmedia GmbH. <http://www.bitkom.org/files/documents/081009_BITKOM_Goldmedia_Mobile_Life_2012.pdf> (12/05/2010).

Goldmann, M., 2010. Videomarketing-News.de: Was ist Lean Forward und Lean Back? <http://videomarketing-news.de/was-ist-lean-forward-und-lean-back> (01/18/2011).

Goldmedia, 2012. Social TV Monitor 2012. TV & Facebook. Social TV im deutschen Fernsehen. <http://www.goldmedia.com/presse/newsroom/social-tv-monitor-2012-tv-facebook.html> (01/30/2013).

Google Chrome, 2010. How to remain calm, despite what's about to happen to your Chrome notebook. <https://www.youtube.com/watch?v=lm-Vnx58UYo#t=127> (09/05/2015).

Google Chrome, 2013. Racer: A Chrome Experiment. <https://youtu.be/KOCM9_qGccY> (07/28/2015).

Google, iab, Ipsos, and Mobile Marketing Association, 2011. Our Mobile Planet. <http://www.thinkwithgoogle.com/mobileplanet/en. (04/15/2011).

Google, PSOS OTX MediaCT U.S., 2011. Think Mobile with Google. The Mobile Movement. Unterstanding Smartphone Users. <http://www.gstatic.com/ads/research/en/2011_TheMobileMovement.pdf> (06/23/2011).

Google, Sterling Brands, and Ipsos, 2012. The New Multi-Screen World: Understanding Cross-Platform Consumer Behavior. <http://services.google.com/fh/files/misc/multi-screenworld_final.pdf> (08/30/2012).

Google, n.d. Material Design. Animation. Delightful Details. <http://www.google.com/design/spec/animation/delightful-details.html> (07/20/2015).

Gordon, P., 2011. Adaptive or Responsive Design? <http://pgdev.posterous.com/adaptive-or-responsive-design> (03/17/2011).

Gove, J., 2015. MobX Conference 2015: Apps and the Mobile Web: Building UX Bridges. (09/11/2015).

Gray, T., 2012. Mobile Website vs. Native App vs. Mobile Web App. <http://www.bluefountainmedia.com/blog/mobile-app> (04/07/2013).

Greif, S., 2013. Flat Pixels. The Battle between Flat Design & Skeuomorphism. <http://sachagreif.com/flat-pixels> (02/15/2013).

Grosch, A., 2008. Wie uns Bier belohnen kann? <https://neuromarket.wordpress.com/2008/06/22/wie-uns-bier-belohnen-kann/> (09/15/2015).

Gugel, B., 2012. Digitaler Film (Blog). Social TV: Die fünf Stufen der Interaktion. <http://www.gugelproductions.de/blog/2012/social-tv-die-funf-stufen-der-interaktion.html> (12/20/2012).

Gutjahr, R., 2013. Der Apple-Fernseher, der keiner ist. <http://gutjahr.biz/2013/01/apple-tv> (03/09/2013).

Hannemann, U., 2012. Wir langweilen uns zu Tode. WIRED Nr. 02/2012, 80ff.

Harper, R., Rodden, T., et al., 2008. *Being Human: Human–Computer Interaction in the Year 2020*. Cambridge, UK: Microsoft. <http://research.microsoft.com/en-us/um/cambridge/projects/hci2020/downloads/BeingHuman_A3.pdf> (06/25/2011).

Hassenzahl, M., 2010. *Experience Design: Technology for All the Right Reasons*. San Francisco: Morgan & Claypool.

Hassenzahl, M., 2011. User experience and experience design. In M. Soegaard & R. F. Dam (Eds.), *Encyclopedia of Human–Computer Interaction*. Aarhus, Denmark: The Interaction Design Foundation. Available online at <http://www.interaction-design.org/encyclopedia/user_experience_and_experience_design.html> (03/02/2011).

Hassenzahl, M., 2013. Experience Design Tools. Need Cards. 7 needs as a starting point for designing interactive technology. <https://hassenzahl.wordpress.com/experience-design-tools/> (10/02/2015).

Hassenzahl, M., Diefenbach, S., Göritz, A., 2010. Needs, affect, and interactive products—facets of user experience. *Interact. Comput.*, *22*(5), 353–362.

Hassenzahl, M., Eckoldt, K., Diefenbach, S., Laschke, M., Lenz, E., Kim, J., 2013. Designing moments of meaning and pleasure. Experience design and happiness. *Int. J. Design*, *7*(3), 21–31.

Hassenzahl, M., Eckoldt, K., Thielsch, M., 2009. User Experience und Experience Design—Konzepte und Herausforderungen. In Brau, H., Diefenbach, S., Hassenzahl, M., et al., (Eds.), German UPA. Usability Professionals 2009. Tagungsband, 2009, pp. 233–237.

Häusel, H.-G., 2007. Innovation Management: Neuromarketing mit Limbic: Emotions- und Motivwelten im Gehirn des Kunden treffen. <http://www.markenlexikon.com/texte/im_haeusel_neuromarketing_mit_limbic_3_2007.pdf> (09/14/2010).

Häusel, H.-G., 2011. Gruppe Nymphenburg Consult AG. Limbic: Das Innovative und Einzigartige Neuromarketing-Instrumentarium. <http://www.nymphenburg.de/limbic.html> (10/17/2011).

Hay, S., 2011. There Is No Mobile Web. <http://www.the-haystack.com/2011/01/07/there-is-no-mobile-web> (07/26/2012).

Hay, S., 2012. Great Works of Fiction Presents: The Mobile Context. <http://www.the-haystack.com/2012/07/09/great-works-of-fiction-presents-the-mobile-context> (07/26/2012).

Hellweg, J., 2015. Adaptive Website vs. Responsive Website. <http://blog.kulturbanause.de/2012/11/adaptive-website-vs-responsive-website/> (06/15/2015).

Hernandez, C., 2015. Into the Age of Context. <https://medium.com/crossing-the-pond/into-the-age-of-context-f0aed15171d7> (07/27/2015).

Hinman, R., 2011. UX Magazine: Peanut Butter in Denver: De-mystifying the Elusive Mobile Context. <http://uxmag.com/design/peanut-butter-in-denver> (06/17/2011).

Hofmann, H., 2015. Linguatronic 2.0: der persönliche Assistent fürs Auto. <http://blog.daimler.de/2015/10/30/sprachsteuerung-linguatronic-2-0-assistent-auto/> (10/30/2015).

Hohenauer, F., 2012. Hotwire-Blog: Shazam Goes TV: Von Second Screens und Social Watching. <http://interactive.hotwirepr.de/opinion/shazam-goes-tv-von-second-screens-und-social-watching.html> (12/15/2012).

Hollister, S., 2010. engadget. Exclusive: VW's Terminal Mode Prototype with a Nokia N97 at the Helm, We Go Hands-On. <http://www.engadget.com/2010/09/29/exclusive-vws-terminal-mode-prototype-has-a-nokia-n97-at-the-h> (02/13/2012).

Holthuis, J., 2011. TEDx Hamburg: Invest in customer insights. <http://de.slideshare.net/edenspiekermann/invest-in-customer-insights> (07/15/2012).

Horvath, S., 2012. Aktueller Begriff. Internet der Dinge. Deutscher Bundestag, wissenschaftliche Dienste. Fachbereich WD 10, Kultur, Medien und Sport. <http://www.bundestag.de/dokumente/analysen/2012/Internet_der_Dinge.pdf> (02/18/2013).

Hulick, S., 2015. MobX Conference 2015: Growing Your Userbase with Better Onboarding. (09/11/2015).

Hulick, S., n.d. UserOnboard (Website). <https://www.useronboard.com>. (10/24/2015).

Hutter, T., 2010. Hutter Consult GmbH. Facebook: Infografik und demographische Daten Deutschland, Österreich und Schweiz per Oktober 2010. <http://www.thomashutter.com/index.php/2010/10/facebook-infografik-und-demographische-daten-deutschland-osterreich-und-schweiz-per-oktober-2010> (01/05/2011).

Inchauste, Francisco, 2011. Finch (Blog): Design Is Not the Goal. <http://www.getfinch.com/finch/entry/design-is-not-the-goal> (05/02/2011).

Initiative D21, 2010a. Die digitale Gesellschaft in Deutschland—Sechs Nutzertypen im Vergleich. Eine Sonderstudie im Rahmen des (N)Onliner Atlas. Initiative D21 e.V. (Hrsg.), TNS Infratest (December 2010).

Initiative D21, 2010b. (N)Onliner Atlas 2010—Initiative D21. Eine Topographie des digitalen Grabens durch Deutschland. Nutzung und Nichtnutzung des Internets, Strukturen und regionale Verteilung. <http://www.initiatived21.de/wp-content/uploads/2010/06/NONLINER2010.pdf> (01/22/2011).

Initiative D21, 2011. Digitale Gesellschaft 2011. Die digitale Gesellschaft in Deutschland—Sechs Nutzertypen im Vergleich. Eine Sonderstudie im Rahmen des (N)Onliner Atlas. Initiative D21 e.V. (Hrsg.), TNS Infratest (December 2011). <http://www.initiatived21.de/wp-content/uploads/2011/11/Digitale-Gesellschaft_2011.pdf> (02/16/2012).

ING-DiBa, 2015. ING-DiBa Fotoüberweisung. <https://www.ing-diba.de/kundenservice/mobile-apps/banking-und-brokerage/> and <https://youtu.be/F6kVzV4OOX0> (07/28/2015).

Internet Live Stats, n.d. Internet users in the world. <http://www.internetlivestats.com/internet-users> (06/27/2014).

Itzkovitch, Avi, 2012. UX Magazine: Designing for Context: The Multiscreen Ecosystem. <http://uxmag.com/articles/designing-for-context-the-Multiscreen-ecosystem> (07/19/2012).

Jacobson, D., 2009. programmableweb: COPE: Create Once, Publish Everywhere. <http://blog.programmableweb.com/2009/10/13/cope-create-once-publish-everywhere> (03/16/2012).

Jenkins, H., 2007. Confessions of an Aca-Fan (Blog): Transmedia Storytelling 101. <http://www.henryjenkins.org/2007/03/transmedia_storytelling_101.html> (04/29/2011).

Jensen, L., 2000. Zeit Online. Hab ich schon. <http://www.zeit.de/2000/36/200036_early_adapters.xml> (aus Die Zeit, 36/2000).

Jenson, S., 2010. UX Magazine: The Coming Zombie Apocalypse: Small, Cheap Devices Will Disrupt Our Old-School UX Assumptions. <http://uxmag.com/technology/the-coming-zombie-apocalypse> (12/20/2010).

Jenson, S., 2011. UX Magazine: The UX of Data. <http://uxmag.com/articles/the-ux-of-data> (05/02/2011).

Jespers, S., 2010. Think Multi-Screen. <http://www.webkitchen.be/2010/12/15/think-multi-screen> (01/28/2011).

Johannsen, J., 2015. iOS 9 ist fertig: Das kann die finale Version. <https://curved.de/news/ios-9-ist-fertig-das-kann-die-finale-version-297871> (09/15/2015).

Jordan, P. W., 2000. *Designing Pleasurable Products: An Introduction to the New Human Factors*. New York: Taylor & Francis.

Jordan, P.W., 2012. This Looks Like Fun: The Walking Dead: Walkers Kill Count for iPad—UK Only for Now Though. <http://ipadinsight.com/ipad-apps/this-looks-like-fun-the-walking-dead-walkers-kill-count-for-ipad-uk-only-for-now-though> (04/08/2013).

Kadlec, T., 2014. Performance Budget Metrics. <http://timkadlec.com/2014/11/performance-budget-metrics/> (10/31/2015).

Kafka, P., 2011. Music Everywhere: Spotify's New Direction. <http://allthingsd.com/20111128/music-everywhere-spotifys-new-direction> (08/15/2012).

Kagan, M., 2010a. Espresso. Präsentation: What the F**k Is Social Media NOW? <http://www.slideshare.net/mzkagan/what-the-fk-is-social-media-now-4747637> (12/09/2010).

Kagan, M., 2010b. Espresso. Präsentation: What the F**k Is Social Media: One Year Later. <http://www.slideshare.net/mzkagan/what-the-fk-is-social-media-one-year-later> (12/09/2010).

Kahn, J., 2010. A List Apart: Strategic Content Management. <http://alistapart.com/article/strategic-content-management> (08/05/2015).

Kahneman, D., 2003. Objective happiness. In D. Kahneman, E. Diener & N. Schwarz (Eds.), *Well-Being: The Foundations of Hedonic Psychology* (pp. 3–25). New York: Russell Sage Foundation.

Kalbach, J., 2011. Boxes and Arrows: Alignment Diagrams. <http://www.boxesandarrows.com/view/alignment-diagrams> (10/11/2012).

Kaltner, O., 2012. Audiovisual Media Days 2012: Multiscreen Strategy: Das Entertainment der Zukunft—Keynote. <http://www.youtube.com/watch?v=kaI3ZJpp4vw> (05/26/2012).

Kaptelinin, V., Nardi, B., 2006. *Acting with Technology: Activity Theory and Interaction Design*. Cambridge, MA: MIT Press.

Kim, J.-H., 2010. engadget German: Wie die Zeit vergeht. iMac'00 und iPhone 4 im Faktenvergleich. <http://de.engadget.com/2010/06/23/wie-die-zeit-vergeht-imac00-und-iphone-4-im-faktenvergleich> (10/15/2010).

Kirst, 2010. Verbraucher Analyse 2010: Mobiles Web wächst so stark wie einst das Internet. Haymarket Media GmbH - kress. <http://kress.de/mail/tagesdienst/detail/beitrag/106221-verbraucheranalyse-2010-mobiles-web-waechst-so-stark-wie-einst-das-internet.htm>.

Knecht, S., 2011. edenspiekermann_welcome, wonder weapon! <http://www.edenspiekermann.com/blog/welcome-wonder-weapon> (10/12/2011).

Knight, K., 2011. Smashing Magazine. Responsive Web Design: What It Is and How to Use It. <http://coding.smashingmagazine.com/2011/01/12/guidelines-for-responsive-web-design> (03/03/2012).

Knorr, E., 2003. CIO: Fast Forward 2010—The Fate of I.T.; 2004—The Year of Web Services. <http://books.google.com/books?id=1QwAAAAMBAJ&printsec=frontcover&source=gbs_summary_r&cad=0_0#v=onepage&q&f=false> (06/26/2011).

Knüwer, T., 2012. Indiskretion Ehrensache. Coca-Cola's Content-Strategie: der nächste Schritt. <http://www.indiskretionehrensache.de/2012/11/coca-cola-content-strategie> (12/11/2012).

Krökel, M. Limbach, T. Brau, H., 2012. Milieubeschreibungen als Meta-Personas. Eine neue Ebene der User Experience Evaluation? In: Brau, H., Lehmann, A., Petrovic, K., Schroeder, M.C., (Eds.), German UPA. Usability Professionals 2012. Tagungsband, 2012, pp. 132–136. <http://issuu.com/germanupa/docs/usability-professionals-2012?mode=window&pageNumber=132> (11/29/2012).

Krug, S., 2005. *Don't Make Me Think! A Common Sense Approach to Web Usability* (second ed.). Indianapolis, IN: New Riders.

Kuehlhaus, 2011. autoMOBILE: Vortrag von Dr. Marcus Trapp (Fraunhofer IESE). <http://youtu.be/4jYU2xcO1pY?t=14m28s> (11/16/2011).

Lardinois, F., 2013. Google's Chrome Super Sync Sports Turns Your Smartphone's Browser into a Game Controller. <http://techcrunch.com/2013/02/27/googles-chrome-super-sync-sports-turns-your-smartphones-browser-into-a-game-contoller> (03/20/2013).

Laugero, G., 2011. Digital Product Strategy, Gamification, and the Evolution of UX. <http://johnnyholland.org/2011/11/digital-product-strategy-gamification-and-the-evolution-of-ux> (05/28/2012).

Leibtag, A., n.d. Creating Valuable Content. A Step-by-Step Checklist. <http://content-marketinginstitute.com/wp-content/uploads/2011/04/leibtag_content_checklist.pdf> (11/23/2012).

LfM Nova GmbH, 2011. Pressemitteilung: Medienforum. NRW: Multimedia Storytelling. Eine neue Art des Geschichtenerzählens. <http://www.medienforum.nrw.de/nc/de/presse/pressemitteilungen/volltext/article/medienforumfilm-multimedia-storytelling.html>.

LfM, Landesanstalt für Medien Nordrhein-Westfalen, 2013. Digital kompakt #06: Kleine Daten, große Wirkung. Big Data einfach auf den Punkt gebracht. <https://www.lfm-nrw.de/fileadmin/lfm-nrw/nrw_digital/Publikationen/DK_Big_Data.pdf> (02/13/2013).

Li, Y., 2011. What You Capture Is What You Get: A New Way for Task Migration across Devices. <http://googleresearch.blogspot.de/2011/07/what-you-capture-is-what-you-get-new.html> (07/28/2015).

Lindahl, E., 2015. Designing the best experiences across platforms means being responsive to the user, not the device. <http://uxmag.com/articles/let-users-drive-cross-platform-design> (07/20/2015).

Lipsman, A., 2015. Comscore Blog: Why Mobile-Only Audiences Are Key to Digital Publishers' Monetization. <http://www.comscore.com/Insights/Blog/Why-MobileOnly-Audiences-Are-Key-to-Digital-Publishers-Monetization> (07/16/2015).

Lischka, K., 2010a. Spiegel Online: Dreidimensionales Fotomodell. Google legt den Bilderteppich über die Welt. <http://www.spiegel.de/netzwelt/web/0,1518,680879,00.html> (05/15/2010).

Lischka, K., 2010b. Nutzungs-Statistik: Web-Erfinder warnt vor Facebooks Datenmonopol. <http://www.spiegel.de/netzwelt/web/0,1518,730259,00.html> (12/12/2010).

Lischka, K., 2011. Ein Jahr iPad: So sähe die ideale Tablet-Zeitung aus. <http://www.spiegel.de/netzwelt/web/0,1518,748324,00.html> (04/15/2011).

Lischka, K., 2013. Spiegel Online: Was kommt, wenn die Regionalzeitung geht <http://www.spiegel.de/netzwelt/web/mediendebatte-was-kommt-wenn-die-regionalzeitung-geht-a-915746.html> (04/13/2014).

Lobo, S., 2011. re:publica XI. Vortrag: Jüngste Erkenntnisse der Trollforschung. <http://www.youtube.com/watch?v=smKKsVGL3Ig> (09/28/2011).

Lobo, S., 2012. Spiegel Online. Die Mensch-Maschine: Der wahre Alptraum der Medien. <http://www.spiegel.de/netzwelt/web/sascha-lobo-social-media-brennt-die-werbung-nieder-a-869481.html> (12/19/2012).

Loo, Y.P., 2012. The Walking Dead "Kill Count" App. <https://vimeo.com/37516900> (01/30/2013).

Lovinger, R., 2012. A List Apart. Content Modelling: A Master Skill. <http://alistapart.com/article/content-modelling-a-master-skill> (02/11/2015).

Lunden, I., 2012. TechCrunch: If Content Is King, Multiscreen Is the Queen, Says New Google Study. <http://techcrunch.com/2012/08/29/if-content-is-king-Multiscreen-is-the-queen-says-new-google-study> (08/30/2012).

Lustig, C., 2012. net magazine: The Case for Responsive Web Content: It's All about the Users. <http://www.netmagazine.com/features/case-responsive-web-content-its-all-about-users> (07/01/2012).

Maguire, M., 2001. Context of use within usability activities. Int. J. Hum. Comput. Stud. 55, 453–483. <http://citeseerx.ist.psu.edu/viewdoc/download?doi=10.1.1.107.7143&rep=rep1&type=pdf> via <http://citeseerx.ist.psu.edu/viewdoc/summary?doi=10.1.1.107.7143> (07/25/2012).

Marcotte, E., 2010. Responsive Web Design. A List Apart, 306. <http://www.alistapart.com/articles/responsive-web-design> (01/12/2011).

Marcotte, E., 2011. *Responsive Web Design*. New York: A Book Apart. <http://www.abooka-part.com/products/responsive-web-design>

Marsden, P., 2014. Decoded – The Science Behind Why We Buy [Speed Summary]. <http://brandgenetics.com/decoded-the-science-behind-why-we-buy-speed-summary/> (09/15/2015).

Marti, M., 2015. Zeitungen sind zäh. Sie sterben langsam. <http://desktop.12app.ch/articles/22368360> (11/01/2015).

Marx, R., 2010. Multiscreen Development Means Multiple Screens, Not All-in-One. <http://radleymarx.com/blog/Multiscreen-development> (02/10/2011).

Mass Relevance, 2012. How the X Factor Became the Most Talked about TV Show of the Year. <http://www.massrelevance.com/how-the-x-factor-became-the-most-talked-about-tv-show-of-the-year> (01/30/2013).

McCrory, A., 2000. Computerworld: Ubiquitous? Pervasive? Sorry, They Don't Compute. <http://www.computerworld.com/s/article/41901/Ubiquitous_Pervasive_Sorry_they_don_t_compute> (06/15/2011).

McGrane, K., 2011. MobX Conference: Adapting Ourselves to Adaptive Content. <http://de.slideshare.net/KMcGrane/adapting-ourselves-to-adaptive-content-10566605> (12/12/2011).

McGrane, K., 2012a. Mobile> Local. <http://karenmcgrane.com/2012/07/10/mobile-local> (07/26/2012).

McGrane, K., 2012. *Content Strategy for Mobile*. New York: A Book Apart. <http://www.abookapart.com/products/content-strategy-for-mobile>.

McGrane, K., 2013. A List Apart: WYSIWTF. <http://alistapart.com/column/wysiwtf> (12/19/2013).

Mediascope Europe, 2010. EIAA Multi-Screeners Summary Report November 2010. <http://www.eiaa.net/Ftp/casestudiesppt/EIAA_Multi-screeners_Summary_Report.pdf> (12/02/2010).

Meeker, M., 2010. Internet Trends. Präsentation am 12. April 2010). <http://www.morganstanley.com/institutional/techresearch/pdfs/Internet_Trends_041210.pdf> (06/23/2011).

Menzl, M., 2012. mathiasmenzl.ch: Social TV: Stand und weitere Entwicklung. <http://www.mathiasmenzl.ch/2012/09/11/social-tv-stand-und-weitere-entwicklung> (11/01/2012).

Microsoft Advertising, 2010a. EMEA Multi-Screen Whitepaper: What's on Their Screens. What's on Their Minds: Reaching & Engaging the Multi-Screen Consumer. <http://advertising.microsoft.com/europe/wwdocs/user/europe/researchlibrary/researchreport/EMEA%20Multi-screen%20Whitepaper.pdf> (02/08/2011).

Microsoft Advertising, 2010b. Microsoft Advertising Reveals Power of Multi-Screen Campaigns. <http://www.microsoft.com/presspass/emea/presscentre/pressreleases/MSA_MultiscreenCampaigns.mspx>.

Middelhoff, E., 2012. Newcast macht's möglich: Der erste deutsche Toyota TV-Spot mit Shazam. <http://www.newcast.net/blog/toyota-tv-spot-mit-shazam> (01/30/2013).

Miller, B., 2013. Apple überarbeitet iCloud-Webseite—neue Funktionen. <http://www.giga.de/webapps/icloud/news/apple-uberarbeitet-icloud-webseite-neue-funktionen> (01/31/2013).

Mischel, J., 2011. SmartBear-Blog. Re-Thinking User Interface Design for the TV Platform. <http://blog.smartbear.com/software-quality/bid/167284> (07/15/2012).

mobileartlab, 2010. YouTube: iPhone Phonebook. <http://www.youtube.com/watch?v=AQ-oQihxBws>. (07/15/2011).

Mod, C., 2011. A List Apart: A Simpler Page. <http://alistapart.com/article/a-simpler-page> (07/27/2015).

Mücke, Sturm, & Company GmbH, 2011. Presseecho.de: Multiscreen auf mobilen Endgeräten - Erfolgsbringer für TV- und VoD-Anbieter. <http://www.presseecho.de/vermischtes/PE13040693323226.htm> (06/15/2011).

Mulholland, A., 2010. CTO Blog: The Information Experience. <http://www.capgemini.com/ctoblog/2010/12/the_information_experience.php> (01/19/2011).

Myers, C.B., 2011. The Next Web (TNW): Josh Clark Debunks the 7 Myths of Mobile Web Design. <http://thenextweb.com/dd/2011/11/07/josh-clark-debunks-the-7-myths-of-mobile-web-design> (07/12/2012).

mytaxi, 2015. mytaxi auf der Apple Watch. <https://www.youtube.com/watch?v=ZljWB4BNUY8> (09/23/15).

Nagel, W., 2006. Tactic to Go—Mobiles Interface für Taktikanalyse und Visualisierung von Spielsystemen im Fußball. Unveröffentlichte Diplomarbeit, Hochschule für Gestaltung Schwäbisch Gmünd.

Nagel, W., 2012a. brainsight (Blog): Keynote: Multiscreen Strategy. <http://wolframnagel.wordpress.com/2012/05/26/keynote-Multiscreen-strategy> (05/26/2012).

Nagel, W., 2012b. brainsight (Blog): Multiscreen Definition (Wikipedia Entwurf). <http://wolframnagel.wordpress.com/2012/06/20/Multiscreen-definition-wikipedia-entwurf> (08/16/2012).

Nagel, W., 2012c. brainsight (Blog): (User) Experience (Design). <http://wolframnagel.word-press.com/2012/08/29/user-experience-design> (09/26/2012).

Nagel, W., 2012d. digiparden-Blog. Mensch & Computer und Usability Professionals 2012—vier Tage im Paradies. <http://blog.die-digiparden.de/mensch-computer-und-usability-professionals-2-7280> (09/14/2012).

Nagel, W., 2012e. Multiscreen Experience Design. Prinzipien, Muster und relevante Faktoren für die Konzeption und Strategieentwicklung von Multiscreen Projekten. In: Brau, H., Lehmann, A., Petrovic, K., Schroeder, M.C., (Eds.), German UPA. Usability Professionals 2012. Tagungsband, 2012, pp. 222–229. <http://issuu.com/germanupa/docs/usability-professionals-2012?mode=window&pageNumber=222> (11/29/2012).

Nagel, W., 2012. *Usability Professionals 2012*. Konstanz: Multiscreen Experience Design. <http://de.slideshare.net/wolframnagel/multiscreen-experience-design-september-2012-muc-up12> (09/12/2012).

Nagel, W., 2014a. Next Generation Information Experience: Trends und Herausforderungen von morgen. <https://wolframnagel.wordpress.com/2014/12/09/next-generation-information-experience-trends-und-herausforderungen-von-morgen>.

Nagel, W., 2014b. Next Generation Information Experience: Trends und Herausforderungen von morgen. EXD Prozess. <https://wolframnagel.wordpress.com/2014/12/09/next-generation-information-experience-trends-und-herausforderungen-von-morgen/#EXD_Prozess> (04/13/2015).

Nagel, W., Fischer, V., 2011. *Multiscreen Experience—Medien und plattformübergreifendes Informationsmanagement für die Digitalen Gesellschaft. Unveröffentlichte Master Thesis.* Hochschule für Gestaltung Schwäbisch Gmünd.

Nagel, W., Fischer, V., 2013. *Multiscreen Experience Design: Prinzipien und Muster für die Strategieenwticklung und Konzeption digitaler Services für verschiedene Endgeräte.* Schwäbisch Gmünd. digiparden GmbH.

Nagel, W., Fischer, V., 2014. Multiscreen Experience Design (website). Communification. <http://www.multiscreen-experience-design.com/communification> (06/30/2014).

Neeb, C., 2011. Spiegel Online: Digitaltrend Gamification. Das ganze Leben wird zum Spiel. <http://www.spiegel.de/netzwelt/games/0,1518,735202,00.html> (04/15/2011).

Neubauer, N., 2015. Mit User-Onboarding-Design überzeugen: Neue Nutzer sollen es einfach haben. <http://t3n.de/magazin/user-onboarding-design-neue-nutzer-239013/> (10/24/2015).

New York Times (NYT), 2013. Developer Network BETA. API Documentation and Tools. <http://developer.nytimes.com> (03/20/2013).

Newsweek, 1993. AT&T-Werbespots: You Will. <http://www.youtube.com/watch?v=TZb0avfQme8>.

NFL, 2010. Get the NFL anywhere, anytime (Werbespot). <http://www.nfl.com/videos/nfl-videos/09000d5d81d25f15/Get-the-NFL-anywhere-anytime> (01/30/2013).

Nielsen, J., 1995. 10 Usability Heuristics for User Interface Design. <http://www.nngroup.com/articles/ten-usability-heuristics/> (09/04/2015).

Norman, D., 2004. Ad-Hoc Personas & Empathetic Focus. <http://www.jnd.org/dn.mss/personas_empath.html> (10/12/2015).

Notion, 2010. MetaMirror & the Future of TV. <http://www.designbynotion.com/metamirror-next-generation-tv> (06/15/2011).

nurun, 2013. Navigating and Expanding the Multi-Screen Ecosystem. <http://www.nurun.com/en/our-thinking/multi-screen-experiences/navigating-and-expanding-the-multi-screen-ecosystem> (07/26/2015).

Oehmichen, E., 2008. Die MedienNutzerTypologie 2.0—Konzepte, Befunde, offene Fragen. Symposium (am 11./12. September 2008): Medienrepertoires sozialer Milieus im medialen Wandel—Perspektiven einer medienübergreifenden Nutzungsforschung. Gefunden z. B. hier. <http://www.hans-bredow-institut.de/webfm_send/212> (06/17/2011).

Oehmichen, E., Schröter, C., 2009. Zur Differenzierung des Medienhandelns der jungen Gencration. <http://www.ard-zdf-onlinestudie.de/fileadmin/Onlinestudie_2009/Schroeter_Oehmichen.pdf> (03/11/2013).

Oltmanns, B., 2012. Cross-platform mobile application design. In: Brau, H., Lehmann, A., Petrovic, K., Schroeder, M.C., (Eds.), German UPA. Usability Professionals 2012. Tagungsband, 2012, pp. 212–221. <http://issuu.com/germanupa/docs/usability-professionals-2012?mode=window&pageNumber=212> (11/29/2012).

Oral, O., 2015. Medium: Mobile: 2015. UI/UX Trends. <https://medium.com/interactive-mind/mobile-2015-263ab694e60e> (09/05/2015).

Oschatz, A., 2010. Mobile Metrics: Mobile Web überholt Desktop Web in 5 Jahren. <http://mobilemetrics.de/2010/05/19/mobile-web-uberholt-desktop-web-in-5-jahren> (zitiert nach Meeker, 2010). (06/23/2011).

Pagán, B., 2012. UX Magazine: New Design Practices for Touch-Free Interactions. <http://uxmag.com/articles/new-design-practices-for-touch-free-interactions> (09/03/2012).

Palfrey, J., Gasser, U., 2008. *Born Digital: Understanding the First Generation of Digital Natives*. Philadelphia, PA: Basic Books.

Perez, S., 2011. Read Write Mobile: Mobile Phones Will Serve as Central Hub to Internet of Things. (06/15/2011).

Pohlmann, J., 2015. Smartwatch-UX: Wie man Apps für die Wearables am Handgelenk entwickelt. <http://www.eresult.de/ux-wissen/forschungsbeitraege/einzelansicht/news/smartwatch-ux-wie-man-apps-fuer-die-wearables-am-handgelenk-entwickelt/> (10/27/2015).

Potter, N., 2011. ABC News: Amazon Kindle Fire: Against iPad, Battle of the Tablets. <http://abcnews.go.com/Technology/amazon-kindle-fire-announced-jeff-bezos-beat-apple/story?id=14623497> (11/27/2012).

Prensky, M., 2001. Digital Natives, Digital Immigrants. On The Horizon 9(5).

Prüfer, 2009. Bis zum twitteren Ende. Lösen die Kurzmeldungen von Twitter den klassischen Journalismus ab? In Novo Argumente, Heft 99, 93f.

Punchcut, 2012a. Shrink to Fit: Designing Scalable User Interfaces (Andy Gilliland and Nate Cox). <http://punchcut.com/perspectives/scalable-user-interface> (07/09/2012).

Punchcut, 2012b. Speaking in Context: Designing Voice Interfaces (Mike Sparandara, Lonny Chu, and Jared Benson). <http://punchcut.com/perspectives/speaking-context-designing-voice-interfaces> (08/29/2012).

Punchcut, 2012c. Windows 8: The New Modernism. <http://punchcut.com/perspectives/posts/windows-8-new-modernism> (11/29/2012).

Punchcut, 2012d. Windows 8: Designing the Metro Experience. <http://punchcut.com/perspectives/posts/Windows-8-Designing-Metro-Experience> (11/29/2012).

Radish, C., 2012. Glen Mazzara and Robert Kirkman Talk THE WALKING DEAD Season Three, Changes from the Comic Book, Fan Reactions & Possibly Killing Off All the Characters. <http://collider.com/glen-mazzara-robert-kirkman-walking-dead-season-3-interview> (04/07/2013).

Ray, K., 2010. Web 3.0. <http://vimeo.com/11529540> (11/17/2010).

Reiberger, A., 2012. Nativ, Hybrid, Web App? Oder darf es eine mobile Website sein? <http://blog.fonda.at/2012/03/nativ-hybrid-web-app-oder-darf-es-eine-mobile-website-sein> (04/08/2013).

Reiss Profile Europe B.V., n.d. A new perspective on personality. <http://www.reissprofile.eu/basicdesire> (09/19/2015).

Ressmann, R., 2011. Information Architects. Die Zeitungsapplikationskomplikation—wer zahlt? <http://informationarchitects.ch/die-zeitungsapplikationskomplikation-wer-zahlt> (04/23/2011).

Riedel, C., 2009. Transmedia Storytelling—Eine Welt ist nicht genug! <http://creativeglasses.blogspot.com/2009/04/transmedia-storytelling-eine-welt-ist.html> (04/15/2011).

Rieger, S., 2011. Yiibu-Präsentation auf Slideshare zur IA Konferenz 2011: The Trouble with Context. <http://www.slideshare.net/yiibu/the-trouble-with-context> (06/21/2011).

Rieger, S., 2012. Twitter: "You Don't Know Where Your Content Is Going to Appear Next Year … You Probably Don't Know Where It's Going to Appear Next Week." #mobX <https://twitter.com/#!/stephanierieger/status/137557965996699648> (10/26/2012).

Roberts, H., 2011. CSS Wizardry: Forget Responsive Web Design … You Need Adaptive Web Design. <http://csswizardry.com/2011/01/forget-responsive-web-design> (03/17/2011).

Robertson, M., 2010. Can't Play, Won't Play. <http://hideandseek.net/2010/10/06/cant-play-wont-play> (03/12/2013).

Roth, M., Saiz, O., 2014. *Emotionen gestalten – Methodik und Strategie für Designer.* Basel: Birkäuser Verlag.

Sackl, P., 2011, February-March. Werbung, Design & Kunst: Storytelling ist wichtig. In: WEAVE Ausgabe 01.11, 24–28.

Saffer, D., 2010. A Taxonomy of Device Forms (auf designingdevices.com). <http://www.designingdevices.com/a-taxonomy-of-device-forms> (03/21/2011).

Saffer, D., 2013a. *Microinteractions: Designing with Details. Uncorrected Proof.* Sebastapol, CA 95472: O'Reilly Media, Inc. <http://microinteractions.com/downloads/microinteractions_chapter1_DRAFT.pdf> (04/06/2013).

Saffer, D., 2013b. *Microinteractions: Full Color Edition: Designing with Details. O'Reilly Media* (first ed.). Sebastapol, CA: O'Reilly Media, Inc.

Sattler, C., Gaida, K., 2011. Goldmedia-Vortrag. Kurzfassung-Auszug. Multiscreen: Nahtlose Einbindung mobiler Endgeräte in Hybrid-TV. <http://www.slideshare.net/goldmedia/vortrag-goldmedia-claus-sattler-hybridtv2011> (04/27/2011).

Schatter, G., 2010. Techniken der gemeinschaftlichen Medienrezeption. Hintergrund Anspruch und Tendenzen des Social TV. In 13. Buckower Mediengespräche: Die Bedeutung der Unterhaltungsmedien für die Konstruktiondes Politikbildes (pp. 67–77). München: Kopaed.

Schätzle, A., 2013, December–January. Gamification: Angriff aufs Belohnungszentrum. WEAVE 06.12, 106–110.

Schätzle, A., 2015a. Modulare Systeme. PAGE 02.15, 24f.

Schätzle, A., 2015b. Im Teilchenbeschleuniger. PAGE 06.15, 82ff.

Schätzle, A., 2015c. PAGE online: Das sagen Experten zur Apple Watch und neuem MacBook. <http://page-online.de/tools-technik/das-sagen-experten-zur-apple-watch-und-neuem-macbook/> (06/09/2015).

Scheier, C., & Held, D. 2007. Was marken erfolgreich macht: *Neuropsychologie in der Markenführung. Haufe-Lexware.* (first ed.). München.

Schmidt, H., 2010. Frankfurter Allgemeine Zeitung (FAZ.net): Das Internet ist Medium Nummer eins bei jungen Menschen. <http://faz-community.faz.net/blogs/netzkonom/archive/2010/09/14/das-internet-ist-medien-eins-bei-jugendlichen.aspx> (12/11/2010).

Schmidt, A., 2015. A List Apart. Privacy is UX. <http://alistapart.com/article/privacy-is-ux> (11/12/2015).

Schmid, M., 2013. Innovative Bedienkonzepte mit Gestensteuerung und Leap Motion. <http://blog.app-agentur-bw.de/innovative-bedienkonzepte-mit-gestensteuerung> (01/31/2013).

Schneider, J., & Stickdorn, M. 2011. *This is Service Design Thinking. Bis Publishers Bv,* (second ed.). Amsterdam. <http://thisisservicedesignthinking.com>.

Schönleben, D., 2015. Das Smartphone könnte bald vor Gefahren im Self-Driving Car warnen. <https://www.wired.de/collection/tech/das-system-mobifas-soll-vor-gefahren-im-self-driving-car-warnen> (07/27/2015).

Schräder, A., 2011. persoenlich.com: Interview mit Oliver Reichenstein: Die einzige Killerapp, die es bis jetzt gibt, ist der Browser. <http://www.persoenlich.com/news/show_news.cfm?newsid=93149> (02/15/2011).

Schräder, A., 2012. Integriert klickbare TV-Werbung im Programm. <http://www.persoenlich.com/news/show_news.cfm?newsid=103551> (01/30/2013).

Schubert, U., 2011. User Experience Blog. IAK11: The Trouble with Context. <http://www.user-experience-blog.de/archives/2011/05/iak11-the-trouble-with-context.html> (06/21/2011).

Schubert, U., 2012. User Experience Blog. Personas sind kein Allheilmittel. <http://www.user-experience-blog.de/archives/2012/10/Personas-sind-kein-allheilmitt.html> (12/14/2012).

Schuller, 2009. Fraunhofer-Institut für Arbeitswirtschaft und Organisation IAO. Augmented identity. Über die Herausforderungen der Integration digitaler Daten ins soziale Leben (Studie).

Schulte Strathaus, R., 2013, February–March. Neurodesign. Reptil-Hirn surft mit. WEAVE Ausgabe 01.13, 90–94.

Sheldon, K. M., Elliot, A. J., Kim, Y., Kasser, T., 2001. What is satisfying about satisfying events? Testing 10 candidate psychological needs. *J. Pers. Soc Psychol*, *80*, 325–339.

Siebert, J., 2013. Fundstücke von Jürgen Siebert. Visueller Aderlass. PAGE Ausgabe 03.13, 114.

Sinus Institut, n.d. SINUS Markt- und Sozialforschung GmbH. <http://www.sinus-institut.de/loesungen/sinus-milieus.html>.

Skjoldan, R., 2013a. 2017 WCM Forecast. Hi Future! How Will the Web Be Built in 2017? <http://de.slideshare.net/rasmusskjoldan/2017-wcm> (12/11/2013).

Skjoldan, R., 2013b. Editor Experience Design. <http://rasmusskjoldan.com/post/64666373967/editor-experience-design> (11/05/2013).

Skjoldan, R., 2013c. Karen McGrane about TYPO3 Neos. <http://www.youtube.com/watch?v=RhOQfnEQ7lc> (10/31/2013).

Skjoldan, R., 2013d. World-Wide Labeling Decision: Editor Experience or Author Experience? <http://rasmusskjoldan.com/post/68771788707/world-wide-labeling-decision-editor-experience-or> (02/04/2014).

Smith, A., 2015. Pew Research Center: U.S. Smartphone Use in 2015. <http://www.pewinternet.org/2015/04/01/us-smartphone-use-in-2015> (07/24/2015).

socialbakers, n.d. socialbakers.com: Heart of Social Media Statistics. (Facebook Statistik Portal). <http://www.socialbakers.com> (02/26/2011).

Solis, B., Thomas, J., 2008. The Conversation Prism—The Art of Listening, Learning and Sharing.

Spool, J., 2011. User Interface Engineering: Designing for Mice and Men: UI across Platforms Q&A with Bill Scott. <http://www.uie.com/BSAL/trans/Bill_Scott_WAMT_transcript.html> (06/17/2011).

Stickdorn, M., 2012. Service Design Thinking. <http://de.slideshare.net/MarcStickdorn1/presentation-stickdorn-englishfall2012web> (11/27/2012).

Stoll, C., Schardt, J., 2010. Precious Design Studio: Patterns for Multiscreen Strategies. <http://precious-forever.com/Multiscreen-patterns> (06/07/2011).

Sunrise, 2015. Sunrise Blog: Sunrise Is Taking over Your Apple Watch. <http://blog.sunrise.am/post/120436887179/sunrise-is-taking-over-your-apple-watch> (06/16/2015).

Svarytsevych, D., 2015. 7 Secrets for Enhancing UX with Micro-Interactions. <http://www.webdesignerdepot.com/2015/07/7-secrets-for-enhancing-ux-with-micro-interactions> (07/19/2015).

TAT Open Innovation, 2010. The Future of Screen Technology—Experience a Normal Day in 2014. <http://www.flixxy.com/future-of-screen-technology.htm> and <https://www.youtube.com/watch?v=g7_mOdi3O5E>.

Teinaki, V., 2015. The Facebook 'Like' Button Microinteraction Is So Important That It's Become Part of Their Brand. Dan Saffer on Microinteractions and Practical Creativity. <https://medium.com/ux-scotland/can-a-microinteraction-become-a-signature-moment-1c664787038e> (07/28/2015).

Telkmann, J., 2010. Create or Die: Max 2010—Adobe erobert die vier Screens. <http://create-ordie.de/cod/news/Max-2010-%26ndash%3B-Adobe-erobert-die-vier-Screens-057350.html> (01/12/2011).

The, Ronald, 2010. Hochschule für Gestaltung Schwäbisch Gmünd. Workshop 10. und 11.06.2010. Die Geschichte des Internets. <http://lecture.infotectures.com/content/e7/e317/index_ger.html> (11/15/2010).

Thielsch, M. T., Jaron, R., 2012. Das Zusammenspiel von Website-Inhalten, Usability und Ästhetik. In H. Reiterer & O. Deussen (Eds.), *Mensch & Computer 2012* (pp. 123–132). München: Oldenbourg. <http://www.thielsch.org/download/proceedings/Thielsch_Jaron_2012.pdf> (11/29/2012).

Thomas, J., 2010. Presentation Advisors. Präsentation: Social Media for Business. <http://www.slideshare.net/PresentationAdvisors/social-media-for-business-5456817> (12/14/2010).

Thurston, B., 2014. Mind the Gap—Designing in the Space between Devices: Josh Clark at an Event Apart Seattle. <http://brianthurston.com/2014/mind-the-gap-designing-in-the-space-between-devices-josh-clark-at-an-event-apart-seattle> (07/22/2015).

Tiedtke, N., 2012, October–Novemeber. Zeit für Content-Strategie! WEAVE Ausgabe 05.12, 98–102.

TNS Emnid, 2011. DigitalBarometer. Parallelnutzung: Interaktivität beim Fernsehen. Studie, Dezember 2011. <http://www.tns-emnid.com/presse/pdf/presseinformationen/Digitalbarometer_Herbst_2011.pdf> via <http://www.vprt.de/thema/marktentwicklung/marktdaten/mediennutzung/tv-nutzung/content/parallele-nutzung-von-tv-und-onli?c=2>.

TNS Infratest, Trendbüro, 2010. Go Smart. 2012: Always-In-Touch. Studie zur Smartphone-Nutzung 2012. Google, Otto Group, tnsinfratest, Trend Büro. <http://www.ottogroup.com/media/docs/de/studien/go_smart.pdf> (01/16/2011).

Tolksdorf, R., 2007. Der Tagesspiegel: Web 3.0—die Dimension der Zukunft. <http://www.tagesspiegel.de/zeitung/web-3-0-die-dimension-der-zukunft/1028324.html> (11/17/2010).

Tollmien, S., 2007. medianet. Feature: Mobile Intelligence. <http://www.4thgm.com/071031_Medianet_Feature_Mobile_Intelligence.pdf> (12/17/2010).

Tomorrow Focus Media, 2010a. Studie: iPad EFFECTS 2011—"inPad-Forschung" auf der Focus Online iPad-App. <http://www.tomorrow-focus-media.de/uploads/tx_mjstudien/iPad_Effects.pdf> (12/18/2010).

Tomorrow Focus Media, 2010b. Marktforschung Studie: The Digital Day—Mediennutzung 2011. <http://www.tomorrow-focus-media.de/uploads/tx_mjstudien/Digital_Day.pdf> (01/18/2011).

Tran, L., 2011. Designer Daily. Responsive Web Design and Adapting for Mobile Designs. <http://www.designer-daily.com/responsive-web-design-and-adapting-for-mobile-designs-15885> (06/07/2011).

Trapp, M., 2011. Vortrag World Usability Day Mannheim. Auto Mobile. (11/10/2011).

Treiß, F., 2010. Mobiles Web. Vortrag on Florian Treiß am 25.10.2010 auf der Tagung M2o—IdeeNetZukunft der Ostfalia Hochschule in Salzgitter. <http://www.slideshare.net/floriantreiss/trends-im-mobile-web?from=ss_embed> (01/05/2011).

Trends, 2010. Trends. Effektive Distribution. Interview mit Nils Müller: Das Internet explodiert aus dem Computer in die reale Welt. <http://blog.trendone.de/wp-content/uploads/2010/07/Interview_in_der_Trends_NM.pdf> (06/27/2011).

Treffenstädt, A., 2010. Axel Springer AG. Das Mobile-Web—auf dem Weg in den Massenmarkt? <http://www.verbraucheranalyse.de/publikationen/forschungsberichte> (11/22/2010).

Trendone, Nils Müller communications, 2007. Trendstudie Dezember 2007, Schlüsseltrend Mobile Intelligence.

Trendone, 2010. Trendone Nils Müller Communications: Media Evolution. <http://blog.trendone.de/wp-content/uploads/2010/02/TRE-01-10-Media-Evolution-5.0-01-VP.jpg> (12/03/2010).

Trust, A., 2013. Google stellt Chrome Super Sync Sports vor. <http://www.macnotes.de/2013/02/28/chrome-super-sync-sports-veroeffentlicht> (03/20/2013).

Tschersich, M., 2010. Was ist ein mobiles Endgerät? mobile-zeitgeist.com (Blog). <http://www.mobile-zeitgeist.com/2010/03/09/was-ist-ein-mobiles-endgeraet> (03/14/2011).

Turber, M., 2015. Beyond continuous: How new players broaden the connected car's horizon. <http://www.intuity.de/beyond-continuous-connected-car-revolution/> (10/30/2015).

Twitter, 2012. Case-Studies: MTV. <https://business.twitter.com/optimize/case-studies/mtv> (01/30/2013).

Uhrenbacher, S., 2010. Die wirkliche Bedeutung des iPad—Nutzungssituation Sofa. <http://stephan-uhrenbacher.com/die-wirkliche-bedeutung-des-ipad-nutzungssituation-sofa/421> (01/05/2011).

University of St. Gallen, 2012. Design Thinking Method. <http://dthsg.com/design-thinking-method> (04/17/2012).

UX Booth, 2014. Experiencing the Author Experience. <http://www.uxbooth.com/articles/experiencing-the-author-experience> (12/11/2014).

Vanhemert, K., 2012. A Modified Moleskine for Shooting Two-Way iPhone Video. <http://www.fastcodesign.com/1671387/a-modified-moleskine-for-shooting-two-way-iphone-video#1> (01/15/2013).

VanHemert, K., 2015. Wired: The Future of UI Design? Old-School Text Messages. <http://www.wired.com/2015/06/future-ui-design-old-school-text-messages> (07/24/2015).

Visnjic, F., 2010. Creative Applications Network. PhoneBook Ride! Ride! [iPhone]. <http://www.creativeapplications.net/iphone/phonebook-ride-ride-iphone> (11/15/2012).

Vogel, M., 2012. Kleines EDV-Lexikon. Skeuomorph. <http://lexikon.martinvogel.de/skeuomorph.html> (11/29/2012).

Voychehovski, S., 2015. A List Apart: Object-Oriented UX. <http://alistapart.com/article/object-oriented-ux> (11/08/2015).

Wachter-Boettcher, S., 2012a. We'll Tell You What You Really Want: Mobile Context, Top Tasks, and Organization-Centric Thinking. <http://sarawb.com/2012/07/11/mobile-context-top-tasks> (07/26/2012).

Wachter-Boettcher, S., 2012b. *Content Everywhere* (first ed.). Brooklyn, NY 11215 USA: Rosenfeld Media.

Walton, T., 2014 Device-Agnostic. <http://trentwalton.com/2014/03/10/device-agnostic/> (07/10/2015).

Watson, S., 2014. Why iOS 7 Didn't Kill Skeuomorphism—and Why That's a Good Thing. <http://www.digitalartsonline.co.uk/features/interactive-design/why-ios-7-didnt-kill-skeuomorphism-why-thats-good-thing> (07/19/2015).

Weiser, M., 1991. The Computer for the 21st Century. Scientific American, 265. <http://nano.xerox.com/hypertext/weiser/SciAmDraft3.html> (03/21/2011).

Welch, C., 2015. Your Windows 10 Phone Can Turn into a Full PC. <http://www.theverge.com/2015/4/29/8513519/microsoft-windows-10-continuum-for-phones> (07/29/2015).

Wellmann, S., 2007. InformationWeek Mobility: Google Lays out Its Mobile User Experience Strategy. <http://www.informationweek.com/mobility/business/google-lays-out-its-mobile-user-experien/229216268> (04/14/2012).

White, G., 2011. Mob X Conference 2011. Multi-Device User Experience. <http://www.slide-share.net/gabrielwhite/multidevice-user-experience> (11/18/2011).

Wigdor, D., Wixon, D., 2011. UX Magazine. Sample Chapter from Brave NUI World. <http://uxmag.com/design/sample-chapter-from-brave-nui-world> (05/27/2011).

Wikipedia, n.d. Benutzerfreundlichkeit. <http://de.wikipedia.org/wiki/Benutzerfreundlichkeit> (06/26/2011).

Wikipedia, n.d. Cloud Computing. <http://de.wikipedia.org/wiki/Cloud_Computing> (03/08/2011).

Wikipedia, n.d. Cross Media Publishing. <https://de.wikipedia.org/wiki/Cross_Media_Publishing>.

Wikipedia, n.d. Didaktik. <http://de.wikipedia.org/wiki/Didaktik> (01/19/2011).

Wikipedia, n.d. Die Geschichte des Internets. <http://de.wikipedia.org/wiki/Geschichte_des_Internets> (06/12/2011).

Wikipedia, n.d. Digital Native. <http://de.wikipedia.org/wiki/Digital_Native> (06/12/2011).

Wikipedia, n.d. Distribution. <http://de.wikipedia.org/wiki/Distribution> (04/09/2011).

Wikipedia, n.d. Early Adopter. <http://de.wikipedia.org/wiki/Early_Adopter> (06/12/2011).

Wikipedia, n.d. EN ISO 9241. <http://de.wikipedia.org/wiki/EN_ISO_9241> (12/10/2012).

Wikipedia, n.d. Erweiterte Realität. <http://de.wikipedia.org/wiki/Erweiterte_Realität> (03/17/2011).

Wikipedia, n.d. Everything as a Service. <http://de.wikipedia.org/wiki/Everything_as_a_Service> (06/16/2011).

Wikipedia, n.d. Filesharing. Wki <http://de.wikipedia.org/wiki/Filesharing> (06/16/2011).

Wikipedia, n.d. Gebrauchstauglichkeit. <http://de.wikipedia.org/wiki/Gebrauchstauglichkeit_%28Produkt%29> (06/26/2011).

Wikipedia, n.d. Google Project Glass. <http://de.wikipedia.org/wiki/Google_Project_Glass> (02/04/2013).

Wikipedia, n.d. Grafische Benutzeroberfläche. <http://de.wikipedia.org/wiki/Grafische_Benutzeroberfl%C3%A4che> (02/01/2013).

Wikipedia, n.d. Information. <http://de.wikipedia.org/wiki/Information> (02/17/2011).

Wikipedia, n.d. Informationsarchitektur. <http://de.wikipedia.org/wiki/Informationsarchitektur> (01/09/2011).

Wikipedia, n.d. Inhalt. <http://de.wikipedia.org/wiki/Inhalt> (02/17/2011).

Wikipedia, n.d. Instant on. <http://en.wikipedia.org/wiki/Instant_on> (06/26/2011).

Wikipedia, n.d. Interaktion. <http://de.wikipedia.org/wiki/Interaktion> (06/26/2011).

Wikipedia, n.d. Internet der Dinge. <http://de.wikipedia.org/wiki/Internet_der_Dinge> (02/18/2013).

Wikipedia, n.d. Interoperabilität. <http://de.wikipedia.org/wiki/Interoperabilit%C3%A4t> (09/22/2012).

Wikipedia, n.d. Kollaboration. <http://de.wikipedia.org/wiki/Kollaboration> (04/09/2011).

Wikipedia, n.d. Kommunikation. <http://de.wikipedia.org/wiki/Kommunikation> (04/09/2011).

Wikipedia, n.d. Koordination. <http://de.wikipedia.org/wiki/Koordination> (04/09/2011).

Wikipedia, n.d. Mashup (Internet). <http://de.wikipedia.org/wiki/Mashup_%28Internet%29> (03/08/2011).

Wikipedia, n.d. MedienNutzerTypologie. <http://de.wikipedia.org/wiki/MedienNutzer Typologie> (11/30/2012).

Wikipedia, n.d. Mediennutzung. <http://de.wikipedia.org/wiki/Mediennutzung> (04/09/2011).

Wikipedia, n.d. Mensch-Computer-Interaktion. <http://de.wikipedia.org/wiki/Mensch-Computer-Interaktion> (06/26/2011).

Wikipedia, n.d. Metadaten. <http://de.wikipedia.org/wiki/Metadaten> (10/26/2012).

Wikipedia, n.d. Mobile-Device-Management. <http://de.wikipedia.org/wiki/Mobile-Device-Management> (04/07/2013).

Wikipedia, n.d. Mobile Marketing. <http://de.wikipedia.org/wiki/Mobiltelefon> (03/25/2011).

Wikipedia, n.d. Mobiltelefon. <http://de.wikipedia.org/wiki/Mobiltelefon> (06/25/2011).

Wikipedia, n.d. Multi-Touch. <http://de.wikipedia.org/wiki/Multi-Touch> (06/25/2011).

Wikipedia, n.d. Natural User Interface. <http://de.wikipedia.org/wiki/Natural_User_Interface> (01/30/2013).

Wikipedia, n.d. Natural User Interface. <http://en.wikipedia.org/wiki/Natural_user_interface> (05/11/2012).

Wikipedia, n.d. Networking. <http://de.wikipedia.org/wiki/Networking> (04/09/2011).

Wikipedia, n.d. Nutzerorientierte Gestaltung. <http://de.wikipedia.org/wiki/User_Centered_Design> (06/26/2011).

Wikipedia, n.d. Personal Computer. <http://de.wikipedia.org/wiki/Personal_Computer> (06/25/2011).

Wikipedia, n.d. Pervasive Computing. <http://de.wikipedia.org/wiki/Pervasive_Computing> (03/14/2011).

Wikipedia, n.d. Planung. <http://de.wikipedia.org/wiki/Planung> (04/09/2011).

Wikipedia, n.d. Programmierschnittstelle. <http://de.wikipedia.org/wiki/Programmierschnittstelle> (03/14/2011).

Wikipedia, n.d. Prozess. <http://de.wikipedia.org/wiki/Prozess> (06/27/2011).

Wikipedia, n.d. Publikation. <http://de.wikipedia.org/wiki/Publikation> (04/09/2011).

Wikipedia, n.d. Rich Internet Application. <http://de.wikipedia.org/wiki/Rich_Internet_Application> (06/26/2011).

Wikipedia, n.d. Second screen. <http://en.wikipedia.org/wiki/Second_screen> (12/20/2012).

Wikipedia, n.d. Semantisches Web. <http://de.wikipedia.org/wiki/Semantisches_Web> (06/26/2011).

Wikipedia, n.d. Situation. <http://de.wikipedia.org/wiki/Situation> (10/12/2012).

Wikipedia, n.d. Smartdust. <http://en.wikipedia.org/wiki/Smartdust> (02/13/2011).

Wikipedia, n.d. Social Media. <http://de.wikipedia.org/wiki/Social_Media> (06/25/2011).

Wikipedia, n.d. Social Television. <http://en.wikipedia.org/wiki/Social_television> (04/15/2012).

Wikipedia, n.d. Software as a Service. <http://de.wikipedia.org/wiki/Software_as_a_Service> (06/25/2011).

Wikipedia, n.d. Synchronisation. <http://de.wikipedia.org/wiki/Synchronisation> (06/16/2011).

Wikipedia, n.d. Tablet-PC. <http://de.wikipedia.org/wiki/Tablet-PC> (06/26/2011).

Wikipedia, n.d. Ubiquitous Computing. <http://de.wikipedia.org/wiki/Ubiquitous_Computing> (03/14/2011).

Wikipedia, n.d. Uncanny Valley. <http://de.wikipedia.org/wiki/Uncanny_Valley> (01/14/2013).

Wikipedia, n.d. User Experience. <http://de.wikipedia.org/wiki/User_Experience> and <http://en.wikipedia.org/wiki/User_experience> (06/14/2011).

Wikipedia, n.d. User Generated Content. <http://de.wikipedia.org/wiki/User_Generated_Content> (06/26/2011).

Wikipedia, n.d. User Generated Content. <https://en.wikipedia.org/wiki/User-generated_content> (07/24/2015).

Wikipedia, n.d. Web 2.0. <http://de.wikipedia.org/wiki/Web_2.0> (06/26/2011).

Wikipedia, n.d. Web 3.0. <http://de.wikipedia.org/wiki/Semantisches_Web#Web_3.0> (06/12/2011).

Wikipedia, n.d. Widget. <http://de.wikipedia.org/wiki/Widget> (04/12/2011).

Wiktionary, n.d. Gerät. <http://de.wikipedia.org/wiki/Gerät> (06/25/2011).

Wiktionary, n.d. Inhalt. <http://de.wiktionary.org/wiki/Inhalt> (02/17/2011).

Wiktionary, n.d. Klasse. <http://de.wiktionary.org/wiki/Klasse> (06/25/2011).

Wiktionary, n.d. Prozess. <http://de.wiktionary.org/wiki/Prozess> (06/27/2011).

Wiktionary, n.d. Situation. <http://de.wiktionary.org/wiki/Situation> (10/12/2012).

Wiktionary, n.d. Umfeld. <http://de.wiktionary.org/wiki/Umfeld> (10/12/2012).

Wilson, M., 2013. Infographic: The Intricate Anatomy of UX Design. <http://www.fastcode-sign.com/1671735/infographic-the-intricate-anatomy-of-ux-design#1> (02/22/2013).

Wilson, M., 2011. UX Booth: When Is Learnability More Important Than Usability? <http://www.uxbooth.com/blog/when-is-learnability-more-important-than-usability> (04/15/2011).

Wolfermann, S., 2015. Responsive and fast. <http://maddesigns.de/responsive-fast/#/> (10/28/2015).

Workman, S., 2011. UX Magazine: App Equality: The Same Experience Whoever You Are. <http://uxmag.com/technology/app-equality> (05/23/2011).

Wroblewski, L., 2009. Networked Consumer Device Platforms. <http://www.lukew.com/ff/entry.asp?862> (03/12/2011).

Wroblewski, L., 2010a. Design for Mobile: Mobile Diversity. <http://www.lukew.com/ff/entry.asp?1195> (03/15/2011).

Wroblewski, L., 2010b. Mobile First. <http://www.lukew.com/presos/preso.asp?26> (05/23/2011).

Wroblewski, L., 2010c. Mobile Device Capabilities. <http://www.lukew.com/ff/entry.asp?1140> (02/13/2011).

Wroblewski, L., 2010d. Design for Mobile: What Gestures Do People Use? <http://www.lukew.com/ff/entry.asp?1197> (06/16/2011).

Wroblewski, L., 2011a. Device Classes & Responsive Design. <http://www.lukew.com/ff/entry.asp?1258> (01/20/2011).

Wroblewski, L., 2011b. What's a Smartphone? (for Web Designers). <http://www.lukew.com/ff/entry.asp?1267> (03/14/2011).

Wroblewski, L., 2011c. Web App Masters: Native or Web-Based Mobile Apps? <http://www.lukew.com/ff/entry.asp?1337> (05/15/2011).

Wroblewski, L., 2011d. Mobile First. New York: A Book Apart. <http://www.abookapart.com/products/mobile-first> (07/15/2012).

Wroblewski, L., 2011e. When People Use Different Devices. <http://www.lukew.com/ff/entry.asp?1451> (07/16/2012).

Wroblewski, L., 2012a. Multi-Device Layout Patterns. <http://www.lukew.com/ff/entry.asp?1514> (09/28/2012).

Wroblewski, L., 2012b. Twitter: This Good News Is You Only Need One Web Design: A Multi-Device Design. The Bad News Is It's Not How You've Designed Things in the Past. <https://twitter.com/lukew/status/262917285398863873> (10/30/2012).

Wroblewski, L., 2014a. Mobile & Multi-Device Design: Lessons Learned. <http://www.lukew.com/ff/entry.asp?1919> and <http://static.lukew.com/MobileMultiDevice_LukeWsm.pdf> (07/18/2015).

Wroblewski, L., 2014b. UI19: Screen Time: Multi-Device Design. <http://ui20.uie.com/videos/screen-time-multi-device-design> (07/26/2015).

Wroblewski, L., 2014c. Responsive Web Design: Relying Too Much on Screen Size. <http://www.lukew.com/ff/entry.asp?1816> (07/26/2015).

Wroblewski, L., 2015a. Google+: Never Been a Better Time to Make Software. Just Look at All the Inputs We Get to Play With. <https://plus.google.com/u/0/+LukeWroblewski/posts/BnRCz8usU68> and <https://plus.google.com/u/0/+LukeWroblewski/posts/BnRCz8usU68?pid=6129450300505139698&oid=100817211548713875249> (04/10/2015).

Wroblewski, L., 2015b. On the Wrist... <http://www.lukew.com/ff/entry.asp?1943> (05/19/2015).

Wroblewski, L., 2015c. On the Wrist: Android Wear vs. Apple Watch. <http://www.lukew.com/ff/entry.asp?1948> (06/11/2015).

Wroblewski, L., 2015d. Google+: Always Online: Screen-Switching in 2015. <https://plus.google.com/u/0/+LukeWroblewski/posts/SBqSzUassob> and <https://plus.google.com/u/0/+LukeWroblewski/posts/SBqSzUassob?pid=6111655905686514578&oid=100817211548713875249> (07/02/2015).

Wroblewski, L., 2015e. Google+: Design Is Never Done. We Got More Than Wrists to Worry About. <https://plus.google.com/u/0/+LukeWroblewski/posts/5hskXKs31gC> <https://plus.google.com/u/0/+LukeWroblewski/posts/5hskXKs31gC?pid=6124373613326887922&oid=100817211548713875249> (07/24/2015).

Yadav, S., 2011. UX Magazine: Framework for Designing for Multiple Devices. <http://uxmag.com/articles/framework-for-designing-for-multiple-devices> (05/18/2012).

Yiibu, 2010. Präsentation: Rethinking the Mobile Web. A Pragmatic Look at Creating an Accessible and Inclusive Mobile Experience. <http://www.slideshare.net/bryanrieger/rethinking-the-mobile-web-by-yiibu> (12/07/2010).

Yoon, J., Jeong, N., 2013. Positive Emotional Granularity Cards. <http://studiolab.ide.tudelft.nl/diopd/library/tools/embodied-typology-of-positive-emotions/> and <http://studiolab.ide.tudelft.nl/diopd/wp-content/uploads/2013/05/positive_emotional-granularity_card1.pdf> (10/02/2015).

Yoon, J., Desmet, P., Pohlmeyer, A., 2013. Embodied Typology of Positive Emotions; The Development of a Tool to Facilitate Emotional Granularity in Design. The Proceedings of the IASDR2013, the Fifth World Conference on Design Research.

Yoon, J., Pohlmeyer, A.E., Desmet, P.M.A., 2014. Nuances of emotions in product development: seven key opportunities identified by design professionals Presented at the International Design Conference-DESIGN, Dubrovnik, Croatia, pp. 643–652.

Young, I., 2008. *Mental Models: Aligning Design Strategy with Human Behavior*. New York: Rosenfeld Media.

Zeit Online, 2012. Stratosphäre: Extremsportler Baumgartner gelingt Rekordsprung. <http://www.zeit.de/sport/2012-10/felix-baumgartner-rekord> (03/13/2013).

Zichermann, G., 2011. O'Reilly Radar: Gamification Has Issues, But They Aren't the Ones Everyone Focuses On. Gamification expert Gabe Zichermann on three areas that deserve meaningful attention. <http://radar.oreilly.com/2011/06/gamification-criticism-overjustification-ownership-addiction.html> (06/24/2011).

Zillgens, C., 2012. Responsive Webdesign—Eine Herausforderung für Webdesigner. Beitrag im Design Tagebuch. <http://www.designtagebuch.de/responsive-webdesign-eine-herausforderung-fuer-webdesigner/2> (12/06/2012).

ZURB, 2010. ZURBsoapbox Podcast: Luke Wroblewski. Design for Mobile First! <http://www.zurb.com/soapbox/events/10/luke-wroblewski-design-for-mobile-first> (06/24/2011).

9.3.1 IMAGE CREDITS

All illustrations and drawings have been created by the author Wolfram Nagel and the illustrator Valentin Fischer or are based on screenshots. Valentin Fischer (co-author of the German book) has drawn nearly all illustrations, with the exception of the following illustrations. Most of the screenshots (of apps and websites) are made by Wolfram Nagel, © by respective rights holders. Screenshots and press images © by respective rights holders.

DEVICE ILLUSTRATIONS

The image composing's with the device illustrations of the smartphone, smartwatch, tablet, laptop, and TV are based on the following image materials:

Smartphone (iPhone): © Can Stock Photo Inc./mtkang
Tablet (iPad): © Can Stock Photo Inc./manaemedia
Laptop (MacBook): © Can Stock Photo Inc./MPFphotography
TV: © iStockphoto.com/bamlou
Tablet at an angle (upright/horizontal format combination): Can Stock Photo Inc./ adamr
Tablet held at an angle with two hands: © iStockphoto.com/TommL
Smart phone held diagonally in the hand: © iStockphoto.com/hocus-focus
Apple Watch: Source of the PSD file by Emske.com (http://emske.com/ apple-watch-sport-psd-mock-up/)

REMAINING ILLUSTRATIONS

Illustration of the screen sizes in relation in Chapter 2.3: own illustration, adapted from and inspired by Luke Wroblewksi (2015e)
Emotion Map: based on various sources (see Section 3.3)
TV screenshot of ARD Tagesschau courtesy of the current ARD Main Editorial Office
MetaMirror & The Future of TV. Photos courtesy of notion (thanks to Ian Walton) More at: http://www.designbynotion.com/metamirror-next-generation-tv
Images of "Deep Shot" courtesy of Yang Li (Google).
Auto Interface (Nokia Terminal Mode): Image (via Hollister, 2010) courtesy of engadget (thanks to Darren Murph)
Images of "Just a Reflektor": justareflektor.com, written and directed by Vincent Morisset, music by Arcade Fire, coproduced by Google Creative Lab, Unit9, and AATOAA, Images courtesy of Vincent Morisset

Index

Note: Page numbers followed by "*f*" and "*t*" refer to figures and tables, respectively.

Needs, 173
    motives and, 45–51, 49*f*, 204–205
Neos CMS, 240–241, 240*f*
Nest thermostat, 212
Netflix, 145
Network appliances, 181–182
Networked consumer device platforms, 17
Neuropsychology, 47–49, 205
New York Times, 161*f*, 181, 229, 247–249, 249*f*
News filters, 233
    Dataminr, 233*f*
Next-generation information experience, 229
    editor- and content-centered process, 245
    and future of content management, 235–243
        content management, CMS interface, and user
           experience, 238–241
        making information into an experience,
           241–243
        smart content, 235
        smart content management, 236
        system, methods, and processes, 236–238
    innovative concepts and trends, 231–235
        trends and challenges, 231–235
    jumping-off point, 230
    new requirements from authors and editors,
        243–245
        author experience versus editor experience,
          243
        content manager experience design (cmxd),
          244
        customized tools and editing modes, 243
Nike app, 212
Nike+ iPhone app, 189–190, 189*f*
Norm EN ISO 9241-11, 76
Notion, 239
NowThis, 232

O

Occasional users, 53, 56, 61–62
Off canvas, 151–153
On the go, 81, 94, 122, 138
Orientation aids, 9–10

P

Padracer, 125
pag.es, 234, 234*f*
Parallel users and second screen, 109–111
PayPal, 208
Performance, 152
Persona prototypes, 46–47, 54–57
Personas, 56
  device, 21

real, 54–55
realistic, 54–55
PhoneBook, 215
Photo transfer, 19
Photoshop, 125, 141
Physical environment, 79, 87
Pioneers as role models, 72
Pocket, 122*f*
Prius models, 192
Privacy as user experience factor, 206
Privacy versus user experience, 274
Private environment, 80
ProCamera, 132*f*
Professional users, 53, 63
Prototypes
    context, 99–100
    device, 13, 20, 24–33
    persona, 46–47, 54–57
    user, 41, 54–73
Prototypical users, 41
    digital society, 41
Public journalist platforms, 231
Public space, 81

Q

Qwiki iPad app, 182*f*

R

Racer, 142
Raw Content Mode, in Neos CMS, 240–241, 240*f*
Real personas, 54–55
Realistic personas, 54–55
Red Bull, 187
Reproduction right, 221
Responsive design, 108, 147–149, 152, 160–161,
    174, 216–217
Responsive navigation patterns, 152–153
Responsive or adaptive web design, 17, 147–149

S

Safe Harbor data-transfer agreement, 223
Samsung SmartTV, 184
Scandinavian Airlines, 143
Scrabble Tile Rack, 126*f*
Screen, 1, 3, 5, 12, 16–17, 30, 44, 72, 96, 106, 109–
    110, 144, 147–148, 152, 268–270, 272, 275
    versus information versus context of use, 91
    multiscreen. *See* Multiscreen
    second screen, 109–111
    sequential screening, 40
    sharing, 103*f*, 141–143
    size, 13, 33

Printed in the United States
By Bookmasters